CW01471661

The Encheiridion,

OR

DAILY HOURS OF PRIVATE DEVOTION,

ACCORDING TO SARUM *USE.*

TRANSLATED AND ARRANGED

BY A

Layman of the English Church.

WITH APPENDICES OF HYMNS AND THE COLLECTS FOR THE YEAR.

LONDON:
LUMLEY, 514, NEW OXFORD STREET.
1860.

J. ALFRED NOVELLO,
TYPOGRAPHICAL MUSIC AND GENERAL PRINTER,
DEAN STREET, SOHO, LONDON.

ADVERTISEMENT.

More than one hundred editions of the "Hours according to Sarum Use" were published in England previously to the Reformation, besides as many, under the title of "Primers," during the sixteenth century. The fullest and most complete of all is named "The Encheiridion," printed in 1528 and 1530; that title, therefore, has been adopted to designate this work. As every one of the abovementioned volumes differs more or less from the others in the contents, and the order, or rather disorder, in which they are placed,—and many of the devotions had become wholly antiquated, and were unsuited for general practical use,—a selection and re-arrangement became a necessity. In place of what has been omitted, a few Hymns, Psalms, and Antiphons, from the Sarum Breviary, have been introduced into the body of the work; but the main portion of it is wholly unaltered.

It will be found to consist of a series of several Offices, each complete in itself, and capable of being used separately. From each, however, certain portions may be taken and introduced into the other services, and used along with them; as, for instance, Psalms, Antiphons, and Collects may be selected from the "Hours of the Blessed Virgin," or at the corresponding seasons from the "Hours of The Name of

Jeſus," or of "The Croſs," and intercalated in their proper places into the ordinary order of private prayer, which ſtands firſt in the book; and of courſe the Collect for the day or week will always be added.

Whatever be the merits of this little book, which has coſt no little time and trouble to the tranſlator, it is at all events an effort to fill up a void which Catholics of the Engliſh Communion have long felt. The want of ſuch a Manual was perceived ſubſequently to the Reformation, and many adaptations of theſe "Horæ" were attempted; but ſince, in order to humour the puritaniſm of the day, they were deprived of point and fervour, of any realization of the Communion of Saints and of the continual Sacramental preſence of our Lord in His Church here upon earth, and were moreover devoid of that devout and paſſionate fellowſhip with Him and His Sufferings which is found in the earlier forms, it is no wonder that they ſoon fell into deſuetude. It is the prayer of the Compiler that this work may have a happier reſult, and may contribute as much to the ſpiritual help of others as he truſts it has to his own.

J. D. C.

London, March 1, 1860.

TABLE OF CONTENTS.

THE CALENDAR.

JANUARY *hath days* xxxi. *The Moon*, xxx. *and* vi. *hours*.

A	1	CIRCUMCISION OF THE LORD, Inferior Double. Principal Double. (York.)
b	2	Octave of S. Stephen Protomartyr.
c	3	Octave of S. John Evangeliſt.
d	4	Octave of the Holy Innocents.
e	5	Octave of S. Thomas Martyr. Depoſition of Edward, King and Confeſſor.
f	6	EPIPHANY OF THE LORD, Greater Double, Principal Feaſt.
g	7	*The Keys of Septuageſima.* TRANSLATION OF S. WILHELM. Double; on Firſt Sunday after Epiphany. (York.)
A	8	Lucian Preſbyter with his Companions; Memorial only.
b	9	
c	10	Paulinus Abbot; Memorial only.
d	11	The Sun in Aquarius.
e	12	
f	13	Octave of the Epiphany. Triple Invitatory. The middle Leſſon of S. Hilary. S. Hilary Biſhop and Confeſſor, and S. Remigius.
g	14	Felix Preſbyter and Martyr. Simple Invitatory.
A	15	Maurus Abbot. Simple Invitatory.
b	16	Marcellus Pope and Martyr. Simple Invitatory.
c	17	Sulpicius Biſhop and Confeſſor. S. Anthony Confeſſor. Simple Invitatory.
d	18	Priſca Virgin and Martyr. Simple Invitatory. *Firſt of* lxx.
e	19	WULSTAN Biſhop and Confeſſor. S. Germanicus Martyr.
f	20	SS. FABIAN and SEBASTIAN Martyrs.
g	21	AGNES Virgin and Martyr.
A	22	VINCENT Martyr.
b	23	Encreſcentiana Virgin and Martyr.
c	24	Babille Biſhop with Three Children Martyrs.
d	25	CONVERSION OF S. PAUL. Triple Invitatory. Memorial of Polycarp Biſhop and Martyr. S. Prejectus.
e	26	
f	27	Julianus Biſhop and Confeſſor. Double Invitatory.
g	28	S. Agnes in the ſecond place. Double Invitatory. *The Keys of Lent.*
A	29	
b	30	Batildis Queen Virgin non Martyr. Simple Invitatory.
c	31	

¶ *All the leſſer Feaſts which happen within Septuageſima have a Simple Invitatory. In* xl., *however, there is no Service of any ſuch Feaſt, except a Memorial at Veſpers and Matins of Mary before the Memorial of The Holy Ghoſt.*

THE CALENDAR.

February *hath days* xxviii. *The Moon*, xxix.

d	1	Brigida Virgin, Simple Invitatory.
e	2	Purification of B. Mary, Greater Double, not a Principal Feaſt. Double Invitatory.
f	3	Blaiſe Biſhop and Martyr. Double Invitatory.
g	4	Gilbert Confeſſor non Pontif.
A	5	Agatha Virgin and Martyr. Double Invitatory.
b	6	SS. Vedaſtus and Amandus Biſhops. Simple Invitatory.
c	7	¶ *Whenever ſhall be the firſt Moon after the Feaſt of S. Agatha, the firſt Sunday following will be a Sunday in* xl.
d	8	
e	9	Sun in Piſces.
f	10	Scholaſtica Virgin. Simple Invitatory.
g	11	Tranſlation of S. Frideſwide Virgin.
A	12	
b	13	
c	14	Valentine Biſhop and Martyr. Simple Invitatory.
d	15	
e	16	Juliana Virgin and Martyr. Simple Invitatory.
f	17	¶ *When you are able to divide the years from The Lord into four great even parts, then it is Biſſextile.*
g	18	
A	19	
b	20	
c	21	*The Laſt of Septuageſima.*
d	22	The Chair of S. Peter. Triple Invitatory. Inferior Double.
e	23	
f	24	S. Matthew Apoſtle. Double Invitatory. Inferior Double.
g	25	¶ *If it be a Biſſextile, on the fourth day from the Chair of S. Peter incluſive let there be the Feaſt of S. Matthew, and the letter* f *be reckoned twice.*
A	26	
b	27	
c	28	Depoſition of S. Oſwald. Double Invitatory.
	29	¶ *Whatever Feaſt of* ix. *Leſſons happen from the Head of the Faſt up to the Paſſion, although it be a Double Feaſt, let there ever be ſolemn Memorial made of the Faſt at both Veſpers and at Matins, for after Maſs of the Feaſt is ſaid Maſs of the Faſt, both at the principal Altar.*

THE CALENDAR.

MARCH *hath days* xxxi. *The Moon*, xxx.

d	1	DAVID Bishop and Confessor. Albinus Bishop and Confessor.
e	2	Ceadda Bishop and Confessor.
f	3	¶ *So often as any Feast of* ix. *Lessons happens within Easter-tide, let nothing be done of the Feast unless it be a Double, but in that case let the whole Service of the Feast be done, with Neumes to Gloria Patri and Jesus Christ.*
g	4	
A	5	
b	6	
c	7	Perpetua and Felicitas Virgins and Martyrs.
d	8	¶ *After the Nones* (*7th*) *of March, then look for the place of the New Moon. The third Lord's Day from this is Easter.*
e	9	
f	10	
g	11	*The Keys of Easter.* Sun in Aries. The Equinox.
A	12	GREGORY Pope and Confessor. Inferior Double.
b	13	
c	14	*The Last of Quadragesima.*
d	15	
e	16	Entry of Noah into the Ark.
f	17	PATRICK Bishop and Confessor.
g	18	EDWARD King and Martyr.
A	19	
b	20	CUTHBERT Bishop and Confessor. The Ancient Equinox.
c	21	BENEDICT Abbot.
d	22	*The First for Easter.*
e	23	Here Adam was created.
f	24	
g	25	THE ANNUNCIATION OF THE LORD. Inferior Double. Principal Double. (York.)
A	26	Vigil.
b	27	THE RESURRECTION OF THE LORD. Principal Greater Double.
c	28	
d	29	
e	30	
f	31	

April *hath days* xxx. *The Moon*, xxix.

g	1	
A	2	
b	3	Richard Biſhop and Confeſſor.
c	4	Ambrose Biſhop and Confeſſor. Inferior Double.
d	5	¶ *Note that if any Feaſt or Faſt happen the week of Eaſter, nothing is done of the Feaſt or Faſt either before or after, unleſs it be a Double, when the Feaſt is deferred till after the Octave of Eaſter; but of the Faſt nothing ſhall be done in that year.*
e	6	
f	7	
g	8	
A	9	
b	10	
c	11	
d	12	The Sun in Taurus.
e	13	
f	14	Tyburtius Valerius and Maximus Martyrs. Double Invitatory.
g	15	*The Keys of Rogations.*
A	16	
b	17	
c	18	
d	19	Alphege Archbiſhop and Martyr. Double Invitatory.
e	20	
f	21	
g	22	
A	23	George Martyr. Inferior Double, with Rulers of the Choir.
b	24	Translation of S. Wilfrid Archbiſhop. Double Feaſt. (York.)
c	25	Mark Evangeliſt. Inferior Double. Faſt. Greater Litany.
d	26	*Laſt of Eaſter.*
e	27	
f	28	Vitalis Martyr, with Rulers of the Choir. On this day was the Church of Sarum begun, A.D. MCCXX.
g	29	Departure of Noah from the Ark.
A	30	Deposition of S. Erkenwald Biſhop of London.

THE CALENDAR.

May *hath days* xxxi. *The Moon*, xxx.

b	1	Philip and James Apostles. Inferior Double.
c	2	
d	3	Finding of the Cross. Inferior Double. Memorial of the Martyrs Alexander, Eventius, Theodolus, and Juvenalis.
e	4	
f	5	
g	6	John Apostle and Evangelist before the Latin Gate. Triple Invitatory.
A	7	John Archbishop of Beverley, with Rulers of the Choir.
b	8	
c	9	Translation of S. Nicomede (aliter Nicholas), with Rulers of the Choir.
d	10	Gordian and Epimachus, Bishops and Martyrs. Double Invitatory. *First of Pentecost.*
e	11	
f	12	Nereus, Achilles, and Pancratius Martyrs. Double Invitatory.
g	13	The Sun in Gemini.
A	14	¶ *It is to be noted that the Feast of* S. Cedd *Bishop and Confessor ought always to be celebrated on the Sunday next before the Ascension of the Lord, with Rulers of the Choir. It is not of Sarum, but Synodal.*
b	15	
c	16	
d	17	
e	18	
f	19	Dunstan Archbishop and Confessor. Memorial of S. Potentiana.
g	20	S. Ethelbert King and Martyr.
A	21	
b	22	
c	23	
d	24	Feast of S. Saviour.
e	25	Aldhelm Bishop. Middle Lesson of S. Urbanus. Summer begins.
f	26	Augustine Apostle of the English. V. Bede Presbyter. Double Festival.
g	27	
A	28	Germanus Bishop and Confessor. Double Invitatory.
b	29	
c	30	
d	31	Petronilla Virgin non Martyr, *with Nocturns when it falls without the Octave of Trinity or of Corpus Christi.*

THE CALENDAR.

JUNE *hath days* xxx. *The Moon*, xxix.

e	1	Nicomede Martyr. Simple Invitatory.
f	2	Marcellinus and Peter. Double Invitatory.
g	3	
A	4	Petrocus Confeſſor.
b	5	Boniface and his Companions Martyrs. Double Invitatory.
c	6	
d	7	TRANSLATION OF S. WULSTAN Biſhop and Confeſſor.
e	8	Medardus and Gildardus Confeſſors. Simple Invitatory. WILLIAM Archbiſhop of York. Double Feaſt. (York.)
f	9	TRANSLATION OF S. EDMUND. Memorial, and the middle Leſſon of Primus and Felicianus Martyrs. Triple Invitatory.
g	10	
A	11	BARNABAS Apoſtle. Triple Invitatory.
b	12	Baſilides, Cyrinus, and Nabor. Double Invitatory.
c	13	*The Laſt of Pentecoſt*. Sun in Cancer. Solſtice.
d	14	Baſilius Biſhop and Confeſſor. Simple Invitatory.
e	15	Vitus, Modeſtus, and Creſcens. Double Invitatory.
f	16	Tranſlation of S. Richard. Memorial, and middle Leſſons of SS. Cyricus and Julita.
g	17	Botulph Abbot.
A	18	Marcus and Marcellinus Martyrs. Double Invitatory.
b	19	Gervaſius and Protaſius Martyrs. Double Invitatory.
c	20	TRANSLATION OF S. EDWARD King and Martyr.
d	21	Leofrid Abbot.
e	22	ALBAN Protomartyr.
f	23	ETHELDREDA Virgin, with Nocturns. Vigil.
g	24	NATIVITY OF S. JOHN Baptiſt. Inferior Double. Double Invitatory.
A	25	
b	26	John and Paul Martyrs. Double Invitatory.
c	27	
d	28	Leo Pope and Confeſſor, with Nocturns. Vigil.
e	29	PETER and PAUL Apoſtles. Inferior Double. Greater Double. (York.)
f	30	COMMEMORATION OF S. PAUL. Triple Invitatory.

JULY *hath days* xxxi. *The Moon*, xxx.

g	1	Octave of S. John Baptist. Double Invitatory.
A	2	VISITATION OF THE BLESSED MARY. Greater Double.
b	3	Swithin Bishop and Confessor. Memorial of SS. Processus et Martius. (York.)
c	4	TRANSLATION AND ORDERING OF S. MARTIN.
d	5	
e	6	Octave of Peter and Paul Apostles. Triple Invitatory.
f	7	TRANSLATION OF S. THOMAS Martyr. Inferior Double. ¶ *On the first Sunday after the Feast of S. Thomas is celebrated the* FEAST OF RELICS, *an Inferior Double.*
g	8	Grimbald Confessor non Pontif.
A	9	Everildis Virgin non Martyr.
b	10	The Seven Brothers Martyrs. Double Invitatory.
c	11	Translation of S. Benedict. Double Invitatory.
d	12	
e	13	
f	14	Sun in Leo. The dog days.
g	15	TRANSLATION OF S. SWITHUN AND HIS COMPANIONS.
A	16	Translation of S. Osmund Bishop and Confessor.
b	17	Kenelm King and Martyr. Double Invitatory.
c	18	Arnulph Bishop and Martyr. Double Invitatory.
d	19	
e	20	MARGARET Virgin and Martyr. Simple Invitatory.
f	21	Praxedes Virgin and Martyr. Simple Invitatory.
g	22	S. MARY MAGDELENE. Triple Invitatory. Memorial of S. Wandregesilla Abbot.
A	23	Apollinaris Bishop and Martyr. Simple Invitatory.
b	24	Christina Virgin and Martyr. Nocturns. Vigil.
c	25	JAMES Apostle. Inferior Double. Memorial of S. Christopher Martyr.
d	26	ANNE Mother of S. Mary. Triple Invitatory.
e	27	The Seven Sleepers. Double Invitatory. Martha Virgin.
f	28	Samson Bishop and Confessor. Memorial of S. Pantaleon Bishop and Martyr.
g	29	Felix, Simplicius, Faustus, and Beatus Martyrs. Double Invitatory.
A	30	Abdon and Sennes. Double Invitatory.
b	31	Germanus Bishop and Confessor. ¶ *If the Octave of the Visitation happen on a Sunday, nothing is done of the Octave unless a solemn Memorial. The Mass of the Visitation is said in the Chapel.*

THE CALENDAR.

AUGUST *hath days* xxxi. *The Moon*, xxx.

c	1	THE CHAINS OF S. PETER. Double Invitatory. Memorial of SS. Machabees.
d	2	Stephen Pope and Martyr. Double Invitatory.
e	3	FINDING OF STEPHEN Protomartyr and his Companions.
f	4	
g	5	S. MARY of the Snows. Oswald King and Martyr. Double Invitatory.
A	6	TRANSFIGURATION OF OUR LORD. Inferior Double. Sixtus Pope and Martyr. Memorial of Martyrs Felicissimus and Agapotus.
b	7	THE NAME OF JESUS. Greater Double. Donatus Bishop and Martyr; Memorial only.
c	8	Octave of Chains of S. Peter. Memorial of S. Cyriacus and his Companions Martyrs. Double Invitatory.
d	9	Romanus Soldier and Martyr; Memorial only. Vigil, with
e	10	LAURENCE Martyr. Triple Invitatory. [Nocturns.
f	11	Tyburtius Martyr. Double Invitatory. Memorial only.
g	12	
A	13	Hippolytus and his Companions Martyrs. Double Invitatory.
b	14	Octave of the Name of Jesus. Eusebius Presbyter and Confessor. Vigil.
c	15	ASSUMPTION OF THE BLESSED MARY. Principal Greater
d	16	The Sun in Virgo. [Double.
e	17	Octave of S. Laurence; Memorial only.
f	18	Agapotus Martyr; Memorial only.
g	19	Magnus Martyr; Memorial only.
A	20	
b	21	
c	22	Octave of the Assumption. Memorials of SS. Timotheus and Symphorianus and Apollinaris, with Nocturns.
d	23	Vigil.
e	24	BARTHOLOMEW Apostle. Inferior Double. Memorial of
f	25	Hilda Virgin and Martyr. [S. Audoenus.
g	26	
A	27	Ruffus Martyr. Double Invitatory.
b	28	AUGUSTINE Bishop and Doctor. Inferior Double. Memorial of S. Hermes.
c	29	DECOLLATION OF S. JOHN Baptist. Triple Invitatory. Memorial of S. Sabina.
d	30	Felix and Adauctus Martyrs. Double Invitatory.
e	31	Cuthberga Virgin non Martyr. Double Invitatory. Aidan Bishop and Confessor.

THE CALENDAR.

September *hath days* xxx. *The Moon,* xxix.

f	1	Egidius Abbot. Middle Leſſon and Memorial of S. Priſcus.
g	2	
A	3	
b	4	Translation of S. Cuthbert Biſhop and Confeſſor. Memorial of Bitinus Biſhop and Confeſſor.
c	5	Bertinus Abbot and Confeſſor, with Nocturns.
d	6	The dog days end.
e	7	Evercuus Biſhop and Confeſſor. Vigil, with Nocturns.
f	8	Nativity of Blessed Virgin. Greater Double. Memorial of Adrian Martyr.
g	9	Gorgonius Martyr.
A	10	Mauricius Biſhop and Confeſſor; Memorial only.
b	11	Prothus and Hyacinthus Martyrs; Memorial only.
c	12	
d	13	The Sun in Libra.
e	14	Exaltation of the Holy Cross. Inferior Double. Middle Leſſon and Memorial of SS. Cornelius and Cyprianus. Autumnal Equinox.
f	15	Octave of Nativity of Bleſſed Mary. Triple Invitatory. Memorial of S. Nicomede.
g	16	Editha Virgin and Martyr. Middle Leſſon and Memorial of Martyrs Euphemia, Lucina, and Geminianus.
A	17	Lambert Biſhop and Martyr. Simple Invitatory.
b	18	
c	19	
d	20	Vigil, with Nocturns.
e	21	Matthew Apoſtle and Evangeliſt. Inferior Double. Memorial of S. Laudus Biſhop and Confeſſor.
f	22	Maurice and his Companions Martyrs.
g	23	Tecla Virgin non Martyr, with Nocturns.
A	24	
b	25	Firminus Biſhop and Martyr. Simple Invitatory.
c	26	Cyprian Biſhop. Juſtina Virgin. Double Invitatory.
d	27	Coſmus and Damiian Martyrs. Double Invitatory.
e	28	
f	29	Michael Archangel. Inferior Double.
g	30	Jerome Preſbyter and Doctor. Inferior Double.

THE CALENDAR.

OCTOBER *hath days* xxxi. *The Moon*, xxx.

A	1	SS. REMIGIUS, GERMANUS, VEDASTUS, and BAVO Biſhops.
		Middle Leſſon of S. Melorus.
b	2	Leodegaire Biſhop and Martyr. S. THOMAS of Hereford
c	3	Biſhop and Confeſſor.
d	4	Francis Confeſſor non Pontif.
e	5	
f	6	Fidis Virgin and Martyr. Simple Invitatory.
g	7	Marcus, Marcellianus, and Apuleius. Martyrs. Double
		Invitatory.
A	8	Pelagia Matron.
b	9	DIONYSIUS AND HIS COMPANIONS Martyrs.
c	10	Gereon and his Companions Martyrs. Simple Invitatory.
		Paulinus of York Archbiſhop.
d	11	Nicaſius and his Companions Martyrs. Double Invitatory.
e	12	DEPOSITION OF S. WILFRID Archbiſhop of York. Inferior
		Double. (York.)
f	13	TRANSLATION OF S. EDWARD King and Confeſſor. Inferior
		Double.
g	14	Calixtus Pope. Double Invitatory. Sun in Scorpio.
A	15	WULFRAN Biſhop and Confeſſor.
b	16	S. MICHAEL in the Mount Tomb.
c	17	Tranſlation of S. Etheldreda Virgin and Martyr.
d	18	LUKE Evangeliſt. Inferior Double. Memorial of Juſtus
		Martyr.
e	19	Frideſwide Virgin non Martyr. FEAST DAY OF THE CHURCH
		OF YORK. Inferior Double.
f	20	Auſterberta Virgin non Martyr.
g	21	Eleven thouſand Virgins. Double Invitatory. Hilario Monk
A	22	non Pontif.
b	23	Romanus Archbiſhop and Confeſſor, with Nocturns.
c	24	
d	25	CRISPIAN and CRISPIANIANUS. Double Invitatory. TRANS-
e	26	LATION OF S. JOHN of Beverley. Inferior Double of York.
f	27	Vigil, cum Nocturns.
g	28	SIMON and JUDE Apoſtles. Inferior Double.
A	29	
b	30	German, Caprianus Biſhop and Confeſſor.
c	31	Quintinus Martyr, with Nocturns. Vigil.

NOVEMBER *hath days* xxx. *The Moon*, xxix.

d	1	ALL SAINTS. Greater Double.
e	2	COMMEMORATION OF ALL SOULS. Inferior Double. At Vespers of S. Mary, Memorial of S. Eustathius and Companions Martyrs.
f	3	WENEFRED Virgin and Martyr.
g	4	
A	5	
b	6	Leonard Abbot and Confessor.
c	7	Willebrod Bishop and Confessor.
d	8	The Four Crowned Martyrs. Double Invitatory.
e	9	Theodorus Martyr. Simple Invitatory.
f	10	
g	11	MARTIN Bishop and Confessor. Triple Invitatory. Memorial of S. Menna Martyr.
A	12	Sun in Sagittarius.
b	13	Britius Bishop and Confessor. Double Invitatory. Memorial of S. Martin.
c	14	Translation of S. Erkenwald Bishop and Confessor.
d	15	MACHUTUS Bishop and Confessor. Memorial of S. Martin.
e	16	DEPOSITION OF S. EDMUND Archbishop. Triple Invitatory.
f	17	HUGO Bishop and Confessor. Memorial of S. Anianus.
g	18	Octave of S. Martin. Double Invitatory.
A	19	
b	20	EDMUND King and Martyr.
c	21	
d	22	CECILIA Virgin and Martyr.
e	23	CLEMENT Pope and Martyr. Simple Invitatory. Memorial of S. Felicitas Virgin.
f	24	Chrysogonus Martyr. Simple Invitatory.
g	25	CATHERINE Virgin and Martyr.
A	26	Linus Pope and Martyr. Simple Invitatory.
b	27	
c	28	
d	29	Saturninus Bishop and Martyr, and Sisinius, with Nocturns. Vigil.
e	30	ANDREW Apostle. Inferior Double.

DECEMBER *hath days* xxxi. *The Moon*, xxx.

f	1	Crifantius and Dane Martyrs.
g	2	
A	3	
b	4	DEPOSITION OF S. OSMUND Bifhop and Confeffor.
c	5	
d	6	NICHOLAS Bifhop and Confeffor. Triple Invitatory.
e	7	Octave of S. Andrew. Double Invitatory.
f	8	CONCEPTION OF THE BLESSED MARY. Inferior Double.
g	9	
A	10	
b	11	
c	12	The Sun in Capricorn. Solftice.
d	13	Lucia Virgin and Martyr.
e	14	
f	15	
g	16	O Sapientia. (From this time there are no petitions at Vefpers.)
A	17	
b	18	
c	19	
d	20	Vigil, with Nocturns.
e	21	THOMAS Apoftle. Inferior Double.
f	22	
g	23	
A	24	Vigil.
b	25	NATIVITY OF OUR LORD JESUS CHRIST. Principal Greater Double.
c	26	STEPHEN Protomartyr. Inferior Double.
d	27	JOHN Apoftle and Evangelift. Inferior Double.
e	28	THE HOLY INNOCENTS Martyrs. Inferior Double.
f	29	THOMAS Archbifhop and Martyr. Inferior Double.
g	30	
A	31	SYLVESTER Pope and Confeffor. Inferior Double.

The Encheiridion,

OR

DAILY HOURS OF PRIVATE DEVOTION.

THE ENCHEIRIDION,

OR

HOURS OF DAILY PRIVATE DEVOTION.

¶ *The Manner to live well, devoutly, and savingly, every day, for all persons of common estate. Compiled by* Master John Quentyn, *Doctor in Divinity at Paris. Translated out of French into English by* Robert Copland, *Printer, at London.* A.D. 1531.

FOR to begin the manner of salutary and healthful living, and to come to perfection (though I have more need to be instructed myself than to teach others); yet practise these few lessons here following, to the utmost of your power. First, rise up at 6 o'clock in the morning at all seasons, and in your rising do as followeth: Thank our Lord for the rest that he gave you that night; commend you to God, to the fellowship of the blessed Virgin Mary, and all the Saints of Heaven. Secondly, beseech God that he preserve you that day from deadly sin, and so also at all other times; and pray Him, that all the works that others do for you, may be accepted to the laud of His Name, of His glorious Mother, and of all the Company of Heaven. When ye have arrayed you, say in your chamber Matins, Pryme, and Hours, if ye may; then go to the Church ere ye do any worldly works, if ye have no needful business, and abide in the Church a sufficient space of time, where ye shall meditate and thank God for His benefits. Think awhile on the goodness of God, and on His divine Power, and Virtue. Think what gift He hath given you to create you so nobly after His image, and likeness. Think also what grace He hath done to you in the Sacrament of Baptism; cleansing your soul from sin. Think how many times ye have offended Him, since ye were chriſtened. Think how forbearingly He hath awaited your return from ſin. Think from how many dangers He hath preſerved your body and ſoul. Think how ill ye have beſtowed the time that He hath given you for penitence; how many times He hath forgiven you in ſhrift, and how many times ye have fallen into ſin again. Think what pain ye had been in, now and ever, if God had taken you out of this world when ye were in deadly ſin. Think how dearly He bought you from peril of Satan, ſuffering continual pains in this world for the ſpace of 32 years; going barefoot, in cold and heat, ſuffering hunger and thirſt, and how many ſhameful injuries; and how dearly He redeemed you, giving for you His precious Body, His Blood and His Soul. And at this point conſider all the pains of His woful Paſſion, as God will give you grace. Think alſo what pain His dear and glorious Mother ſuffered all that while. Conſider His ſtrict judgement at the hour of your death. And touching this death, think often thereon, and that ye cannot eſcape it, nor know when, nor how, in what ſtate nor in what place, nor time, day nor hour it may be. Think what ſhall then become of the worldly goods that ye have gathered, and hoarded with great labour; and how loth ye ſhall be to leave them, and all your friends and kinsfolk, and that more when your ſoul in great pain ſhall leave your body to rot in the earth. Conſider what ſhall then become of your ſtrength, beauty, youth, health, and other riches of the body. Think what the poor ſoul ſhall do, when it goeth alone without company, where it was never. Think, what it will do when it ſeeth the horrible enemies that would drag it to perdition, if ye die in deadly ſin. Think what a woful journey it ſhall be when ye muſt yield a general reckoning of all your works, words, and thoughts, without exception of anything. Pray that God may give you grace. Think on the horrible pains of Hell, and on the cruel company of Devils; from which ye ſhall never have releaſe if ye die in deadly ſin. And think on the ineſtimable joys of the Saints in Heaven, the which our Lord hath promiſed you if ye live free from deadly ſin, and love Him above all things. And have ye a perfect hope, if ye live well, that ye ſhall come to that Glory. Amen.

¶ Theſe be the thoughts that I will that ye have in the Church. And if by any other reaſonable buſineſs ye may not be ſo long in the Church (as is ſaid heretofore), yield thanks to God for his goodneſs, and think on the reſidue in your houſe alone, or in the night if ye may. When ye are come from the Church, take heed to your houſehold or occupation till dinner-time; and in ſo doing think ſometimes that the pain that ye ſuffer in this world, is nothing in regard of the infinite Glory that ye ſhall have if ye take it meekly. Then take your refection or meal reaſonably, without exceſs or overmuch forbearing of your meat; for there is as much danger in too little as in too much. If ye faſt once in a week it is enough, beſide Vigils and Ember days, out of Lent. And if ye think the faſting be not good nor profitable, act by counſel. Reſt after your dinner an hour or half an hour, as ye think beſt, praying God that in that reſt He will promote your health, to the end that after it, ye may ſerve Him the more devoutly. The reſidue of the day beſtow in your buſineſs to the pleaſure of God. As touching your ſervice: ſay unto Terce before dinner, and make an end of all before ſupper; and when ye may, ſay a Commendation for all Chriſtian ſouls at leaſt on the Holy Days. And if ye have leiſure ſay them on other days. Shrive you every week to your Curate, except ye have great hindrance, and beware ye paſs not a fortnight except there be a very great hindrance. If ye be of ability, refuſe not your alms to the firſt poor body that aſketh it of you that day, if you think it needful. Take pains to hear and keep the Word of God. Confeſs you every day to God without fail, of ſuch ſins as ye know that ye have done that day. Conſider often, either by day, or night when ye awake, what our Lord did at that hour the day of His Bleſſed Paſſion, and where He was at that hour. ¶ Seek a good and faithful friend of good converſation to whom ye may diſcover your mind's ſecrets. Enquire and prove him well ere ye truſt in him, and when ye have well proved him do all by his counſel. Talk little, and follow virtuous company. Eſchew the fellowſhip of them that ye would not be like. After each work praiſe and thank God. Love Him above all things, and ſerve Him diligently. Do to none other but that ye would were done to you; love the well-being of another as your own. And in going to your bed have ſome good thought either of the Paſſion of Our Lord, or of your ſins, or of the future purgation, or ſome other good ſpiritual thoughts; and then I hope your living will be acceptable and pleaſing to God.

¶ *The beginning of The Holy Goſpel according to John.*

Glory be to Thee O Lord.

In the beginning was The Word, and The Word was with God, and The Word was God. All things were made by Him, and without Him was not anything made that was made. In Him was Life, and the Life was the Light of men; and the Light ſhined in darkneſs, and the darkneſs comprehended it not. There was a man ſent from God whoſe name was John; he came for a teſtimony, that he might bear teſtimony of the Light, that all men through him might believe. He was not that Light, but that he might bear witneſs of the Light; That was the true Light which lighteth every man that cometh into this world. He was in the world, and the world was made by him, and the world knew Him not. He came unto his own, and his own received Him not; but to as many as received Him, to them gave He power to become the Sons of God; unto them that believe in His Name; who were born not of bloods, nor of the will of the fleſh, nor of the will of man, but of God. And The Word was made Fleſh, and dwelt among us, and we beheld His Glory; the Glory as of The Only begotten of The Father, full of grace and truth. Thanks be to God.

Antiphon. Thee we invoke, Thee we adore, Thee we praiſe, Thee we glorify, O bleſſed Trinity!

℣. Bleſſed be The Name of The Lord,

℟. From this time forth now and ever for evermore.

Oriſon. O God! the Protector of them that truſt in Thee, without Whom nothing is ſtrong, nothing is holy; multiply upon us Thy mercy, that Thou being our Ruler, Thou our Guide, we may ſo paſs through good things temporal as not to loſe thoſe which are eternal, through Chriſt our Lord. Amen.

¶ *Here followeth The Holy Goſpel according to Luke.*

Glory be to Thee O Lord.

At that time The Angel Gabriel was ſent from God, to a city of Galilee called Nazareth, to a Virgin eſpouſed to a man whoſe name was Joſeph, of the houſe of David; and the name of the Virgin was Mary. And, entering in the Angel ſaid unto her, "Hail! full of grace; The Lord is with thee, bleſſed art thou among women." Whom when ſhe ſaw ſhe was troubled at his ſaying, and caſt in her mind what manner of ſalutation this ſhould be. And the Angel ſaid unto her, "Fear not, Mary; for thou haſt found favour with The Lord; behold thou ſhalt conceive in thy womb, and bring forth a Son, and thou ſhalt call His Name Jeſus. He ſhall be great, and He ſhall be called The Son of The Higheſt, and The Lord God ſhall give unto Him the throne of His Father David; and He ſhall reign over the houſe of Jacob for ever; and of His Kingdom there ſhall be no end." But Mary ſaid unto the Angel, "How ſhall this thing be, ſeeing I know not a man?" And the Angel anſwering ſaid unto her, "The Holy Ghoſt ſhall come upon thee, and the power of the Moſt Higheſt ſhall overſhadow thee, therefore alſo that Holy Thing which ſhall be born of thee, ſhall be called The Son of God. And behold Elizabeth, thy couſin, ſhe too hath conceived a ſon in her old age; and this is the ſixth month with her who is called barren; for there is not any word, which ſhall be impoſſible with God." But Mary ſaid, "Behold the handmaid of The Lord, be it unto me according to thy word."

Thanks be to God.

¶ *Here followeth the Holy Goſpel according to Matthew.*

Glory be to Thee O Lord.

When Jeſus was born in Bethleem of Judæa, in the days of Herod the King; Behold there came Magi from the Eaſt to Jeruſalem ſaying, "Where is he that is born King of the Jews, for we have ſeen his Star in the Eaſt, and are come with gifts to worſhip Him." But Herod the King hearing this was troubled, and all Jeruſalem with him. And gathering together all the Chiefs of the Prieſts and the Scribes of the people, he demanded of them where Chriſt ſhould be born; And they ſaid unto him, "In Bethleem of Judæa; for thus it is written by the prophet: And thou Bethleem in the land of Judah art by no means the leaſt among the princes of Judah, for out of thee ſhall come a Governor, who ſhall rule my people Iſrael." Then Herod when he had privily called the Magi, enquired of them diligently what time the Star appeared to them. And he ſent them to Bethleem, and ſaid, "Go and enquire diligently for The Child; and when ye ſhall have found Him, bring me word again, that I may come and worſhip Him alſo." Who, when they had heard the King, departed; and Lo! the Star which they had ſeen in the Eaſt went before them, until it came and ſtood over where The Child was. But ſeeing the Star, the Magi rejoiced with exceeding great joy; and entering into the houſe, they found The Child with Mary his Mother, and falling down before Him they worſhipped Him, and having opened their treaſures they offered unto Him gifts, Gold, Frankincenſe, and Myrrh. And having received a warning in dreams, that they ſhould not return to Herod, they returned into their country by another way.

Thanks be to God.

¶ *Here followeth The Holy Gospel according to Mark.*

Glory be to Thee O Lord.

At that time as the eleven disciples were reclining at meat, Jesus appeared unto them, and upbraided their unbelief and hardness of heart; because they had not believed them which had seen Him to have risen from the dead. And He said unto them, Go ye into the universal world and preach the Gospel to every creature. He that shall believe, and shall have been baptized, shall be saved, but he that believeth not shall be condemned. Moreover these signs shall follow them that believe: In My Name shall they cast out devils, they shall speak with new tongues, they shall take up serpents, and if they drink any deadly thing it shall not hurt them. They shall lay their hands on the sick, and they shall recover. So then The Lord Jesus after He had spoken to them was taken up into Heaven, and sitteth on the Right Hand of God. But they going forth preached everywhere, The Lord working with them, and confirming the Word with signs following.

Thanks be to God.

May our offences be blotted out by the words of the Gospel. Amen.

FOR THE MORNING.

¶ *THE LORD taught His Disciples this manner of Praying.*

UR Father, which art in Heaven, hallowed be Thy Name. Thy kingdom come. Thy will be done, as in Heaven so on earth. Give us this day our daily bread. And forgive us our debts, as we forgive our debtors. And lead us not into temptation; but deliver us from evil. Amen.

THE ANGELIC SALUTATION or Daily Memorial of the Incarnation.

HAIL, Thou that art full of Grace! The Lord is with thee. Blessed art thou among women, and Blessed is the Fruit of thy womb, Jesus! Amen.

THE APOSTLES' CREED.

I BELIEVE in God The Father Almighty, Maker of Heaven and Earth: and in Jesus Christ His Only Son our Lord; Who was conceived by The Holy Ghost, born of The Virgin Mary, suffered under Pontius Pilate, was crucified, dead, and buried; He descended into Hell; the third day He rose again from the dead, He ascended into Heaven, and sitteth at the right hand of God The Father Almighty; from whence He shall come to judge the quick and the dead.

I believe in The Holy Ghost; The Holy Catholic Church; The Communion of Saints; The Forgiveness of Sins; The Resurrection of the Flesh, and Life everlasting. Amen.

HYMN.

Jam Lucis orto Sydere.

THE Star of Light hath risen, and now
To God in suppliant prayer, we bow,
That He, the Fount of endless Light,
Would guide our daily walk aright.

May tongue and hand abstain from ill,
No empty thoughts our bosoms fill,
Pure Truth within our mouths abide
And Love in every heart reside.

As wane the hours, O Chrift! at hand
Our ever watchful champion ftand;
From ravening foes with fure defence
To guard each inlet of the fenfe.

Grant that the employment of our days
Be e'er fubfervient to Thy praife;
That all things in Thy fear begun,
May through Thy favouring help be done.

Let not the flefh with tyrant fway
Miflead the recreant foul aftray;
But abftinence each paffion calm
And all our rebel pride difarm.

Glory to God The Father be,
Like Glory, Only Son! to Thee,
And to The Holy Paraclete
Now and through ages infinite.
Amen.

Tu Trinitatis Unitas.

Thou Trinity in Unity!
Great Ruler of the world! to Thee
We chant our canticles of Praife,
O liften to our early lays.

Now joyful from the couch we rife,
While twilight veils the filent fkies;
O make our mental failings whole,
Thou Great Phyfician of the Soul!

If aught of fin this night defiled
The foul, by Satan's arts beguiled,
Regard from Heaven, Thy dwelling place,
And cleanfe it by Thy fpecial Grace.

Let purenefs every frame poffefs,
No laggard floth our hearts opprefs,
Nor fin's cold leprofy with ill,
The fervour of our fpirits chill.

Redeemer! in Thy faving might
Illume us with Thy healthful light;
That in our walk from day to day,
From Thee we never more may ftray,

Lord! Holy Virgin born! to Thee
Eternal Praife and Glory be;
With Father and with Holy Ghoft,
Long as eternity fhall laft! Amen.

¶ *These prayers following are to be faid ere ye depart out of your chamber at your uprifing.*

O Holy Trinity! be Thou my helper. In Thy Name, O God! will I lift my hands. O triumphal Crofs of The Paffion of our Lord Jefus Chrift! Jefus! Nazarene! King of the Jews! Son of God! have mercy upon me! In the Name of The Father, and of The Son, and of The Holy Ghoft! By the fign of The Holy Crofs ✠, deliver us from our enemies, O God our Saviour!

O most gracious God and merciful Father! I give Thee thanks and praife, O Lord Jefu Chrift! Almighty everlafting God! Who in the night paft haft guarded, protected, and vifited me, thine unworthy fervant, and haft brought me fafe and unharmed to the beginning of this day;

ſo alſo for Thine other benefits, which of Thine own Goodneſs alone Thou haſt conferred upon me. O merciful God, I entreat Thee of Thy clemency to grant, that I may ſo paſs this day in Thy ſervice, with humility, diſcretion, devotion, and loving-kindneſs, that in all my doings I may be enabled to perform unto Thee my due and propitiatory ſervice; and make me ever to live in Thy favour, and I commend unto Thee my body and ſoul all the days of my life, through The Same Jeſus Chriſt our Lord. Amen.

¶ *When thou firſt goeſt out of thy houſe, bleſs thy going thus:—*

O Triumhphal Croſs of our Lord Jeſus Chriſt! Behold the Sign of the Life-giving Croſs of The Lord! Begone, ye adverſaries, In The Name (✠) of The Father, and of The Son, and of The Holy Ghoſt. Amen.

Oriſon.

God, Who by the leading of a Star didſt guide the Eaſtern Magi in ſafety to Thy cradle, to venerate Thee with myſtical gifts; graciouſly beſtow Thy remembrance upon me thy ſervant, and guide me in all the places whither I am going, with all quickneſs, joy, grace, and peace, without any hindrance from adverſity: And do Thou, our true Sun, our true Star, our true Light of lights, Who didſt lead them by the meſſage of an Angel back to their own country, bring me again to my home, whole and unhurt, in all peace and ſafety and proſperity, by Thy ſuccour, Who liveſt and reigneſt God, world without end. Amen.

A good bleſſing, when ye go forth on a ſtage or journey, ſay thus:—

The Imperial Majeſty bleſs me! The Royal Divinity protect me! The Everlaſting Deity guard me! The Glorious Unity cheriſh me! The Infinite Trinity defend me! The ineſtimable Goodneſs direct me! The Might of The Father guide me! The Wiſdom of The Son quicken me! The Virtue of The Holy Ghoſt enlighten me! Alpha and Omega, God and Man! May this benediction be unto me health and protection, now and for evermore. Amen. Our Father, Hail Thou!

When thou enterest into The Church, say thus:—

O Lord! in the multitude of Thy mercy I will enter into Thy House, I will worship in Thy Holy Temple, and I will give thanks unto Thy Name.

O Lord! guide me in Thy righteousness, because of mine enemies, direct my way before Thy face.

¶ *When thou beginnest to pray, begin thus, kneeling:—*

Depart from me, ye wicked, and I will search out the Commandments of my God. Take away from me, O Lord, all mine iniquities, that I may be worthy with pure mind to enter into The Holy of Holies. Come, O Lord! and visit me in Thy peace, that I may rejoice before Thee with a perfect heart. O Lord! open Thou my lips to bless Thy Name. Cleanse my heart from vain and evil thoughts, that I may worthily deserve to be heard in the presence of Thy Divine Majesty. Thou art worthy, O Lord! my God! to receive Glory, and Honour, and Power, for Thou hast created all things, and for Thy pleasure they are and were created. Salvation and Honour unto my God, Who sittest upon the Throne, and to The Lamb! Alleluya.

O Good Jesu! Thou knowest, and canst secure, and dost desire, the good of my soul; I, Thy miserable creature, neither know nor can obtain it. Do Thou of Thine ineffable kindness dispose of me as Thou knowest to be according to Thy will and for my benefit. Amen.

O Lord God! let my prayer ascend up unto Thee, and I beseech Thee that it return not unto me void; but according as is Thy will and Thou knowest, have mercy upon me in all my necessities of mind and body. Amen. Jesu! Jesu! Jesu! be to me a Jesus! Amen.

For Protection.

O God! the Author and Lover of Peace, Whom to know is to live, Whom to ſerve is to reign; protect Thy ſuppliant from all aſſaults; that we who truſt in Thy defence may not fear the arms of any adverſary, through Chriſt our Lord. Amen.

O Holy Lord! Almighty Father! Eternal God! Who haſt ſafely brought me to the beginning of this day, defend me therein by Thy might; and grant that in this day I fall not into any ſin, neither run into any kind of danger, but that all my words may be uttered, my thoughts and actions be directed, to fulfil Thy Righteouſneſs, through Chriſt our Lord. Amen.

O Lord God, I beſeech Thee, to direct, ſanctify, and govern my heart and body in Thy law, and in the works of Thy commandments, ſo that, both now and ever, by Thy help I may be worthy of health and ſalvation, through Chriſt our Lord. Amen.

O Jesu! Son of the living God, Creator of all things, help me that I be not occupied nor delighted with vain imaginations. Amen.

O Jesu! Son of God! Who waſt ſilent before Pontius Pilate, reſtrain my tongue, until I conſider how and what I ought to ſpeak. Amen.

O Jesu! Son of God! Who waſt bound for me, govern my hands and all my members, that all my actions may be over-ruled for my good, and Thy Glory. Amen.

Againſt carnal deſires.

O Lord! deliver my ſoul from carnal deſires and from all remembrance of evil, that what I may have ſeen or heard from the wicked of this world, I may never think of, nor ſpeak of to others; and grant me, O Lord, ſo to live here on this earth, in all holy converſation, that I may never be ſeparated from Thee, and may be enabled worthily to intercede with Thee, for myſelf, and for all my relations and friends, Who liveſt and reigneſt with The Father and The Holy Ghoſt, God, world without end. Amen.

Againſt evil thoughts.

Almighty and moſt merciful God! favourably regard my petitions, and deliver my heart from the temptation of wicked thoughts, that I may be found worthy to become a dwelling-place for Thy Holy Spirit, through Chrift our Lord. Amen.

Againft temptation of the flefh.

O Lord Jefu Chrift! King of Virgins! Lover of Chaftity! cleanfe me and fhield my heart from all the weapons and fnares of the enemy. Extinguifh in me all the flames of concupifcence; implant true humility, tranquillity, and patience, in my breaft. Inflame my affections with the fires of love; that hating every way of iniquity, I may ferve Thee with a chafte body and a pure heart, and pleafe Thee all the days of my life. Amen.

For thy friend living.

O God! Who doft juftify the wicked! and wouldeft not the death of a finner; I Thy fuppliant befeech Thy Majefty gracioufly to protect thy fervant *N.*, who trufts in Thy mercy, with Thy celeftial help, and keep him under Thy continual protection; that he may ever rightly ferve Thee, and by no temptations be feparated from Thee, through Chrift our Lord. Amen.

God! Who through the Grace of Thy Holy Spirit doft pour the gifts of charity unto the hearts of thy faithful people; grant to thy fervants and handmaidens, for whom we befeech Thy clemency, health both of mind and body; that they may love Thee with their whole ftrength, and, with entire fatisfaction may perform thofe things which are pleafing unto Thee, through Chrift our Lord. Amen.

In tribulations.

Juft art Thou, O Lord! and true are Thy judgements! Do unto Thy fervant according to Thy Great Mercy.

O God! Who defpifeft not the fighing of the contrite, nor fpurneft the grief of the forrowful, be prefent with our prayers, which in this our tribulation we offer up to Thy compaffion: befeeching Thee mercifully to look upon us, and to grant unto us the wonted heed of Thy pity; fo that whatever evil the malice of Satan or man worketh againft us be brought to naught, and by the Providence of Thy Goodnefs may be defeated;

and hurt by no adversities but delivered from all tribulation and anxiety, we may be truly comforted, and render thanks unto Thee in Thy Holy Church through Christ our Lord. Amen.

For friends in sickness or necessity.

ALMIGHTY and everlasting God! The Eternal Salvation of believers, the only help of human infirmity, upon Whose will every moment of life dependeth; hearken unto me who intreat the help of Thy compassion for Thy servant *N.*; that health and prosperity being restored to him, he may return to Thee the offering of thanksgiving in Thy Holy Church; and being guided according to Thy great mercy in the way of eternal salvation, may, through Thy gift, desire what is pleasing unto Thee, and be made perfect in all virtue, through Christ our Lord. Amen.

Almighty and everlasting God! The Consolation of the sorrowful, the Strength of the afflicted, may the prayers of all that cry unto Thee in any tribulation or distress enter into Thine ears, so that in all their necessities they may rejoice in the help of Thy mercy, through Christ our Lord. Amen.

For thy Father and Mother dead.

GOD, Who hast commanded us to honour our parents, of Thy great goodness have mercy upon the souls of my father and mother, and grant that I may hereafter live with them in the joys of everlasting Glory, through Christ our Lord. Amen.

For thy friend that is dying or lately dead.

O ALMIGHTY and everlasting God! The Preserver of souls, Who dost chastise those whom Thou lovest, and correct every son whom Thou receivest; we intreat Thee to receive into the bosom of Thy patriarch Abraham the soul of Thy servant *N.*; may he be presented without spot of sin before Thee by the hands of Thy holy Angels, and be admitted to the fellowship of all Thy Saints and elect; so that no guilt of the flesh may hurt or pain him; but the pity of Thy compassion may absolve him from all his offences, through Chriſt our Lord. Amen.

For our benefactors quick and dead.

We entreat Thee, O Lord Jeſu, for Thy mercy's ſake, that Thy wrath may be turned away from us, and Thine anger from this place and this Thy holy houſe; for we have ſinned againſt Thee, and committed iniquity before Thee, and have done nothing that is righteous in Thy ſight. Succour us, we beſeech Thee, and have pity upon the ſouls of all our benefactors, both the living and the dead; and for the benefits which they have conferred upon us on earth, may they obtain eternal rewards in the Heavens.

℣. We adore Thee, O Chriſt, and bleſs Thee, for by Thy Holy Croſs Thou haſt redeemed the world. Have compaſſion upon us.

℟. Who in Thy clemency didſt ſuffer for us.

For all the faithful departed.

Absolve, we beſeech Thee, O Lord! the ſouls of Thy ſervants and handmaidens, our relations, our neighbours, our friends, our benefactors, as well as the ſouls of all the faithful departed from the chains of their ſins; that in the Glory of the Reſurrection they may be raiſed up to life and breath among Thy Saints and Elect, through Chriſt our Lord. Amen.

We beſeech Thee, O Lord! that the prayers of Thy ſuppliants may profit the ſouls of all Thy ſervants and handmaidens, that Thou mayeſt free them from all their ſins and make them partakers of Thy redemption, through Chriſt our Lord. Amen.

For the King.

O God of kingdoms! and chief Protector of a Chriſtian ſtate! Grant to Thy ſervant *N.*, our Queen, a triumph over her enemies, that ſhe who hath been conſecrated by Thy Providence may ever be powerful and ſecure under Thy protection, through Chriſt our Lord. Amen.

For the Biſhops.

Almighty and everlaſting God, Who alone doeſt great wonders, ſend down upon our

Bishops and Curates and all the congregations committed to their charge the healthful spirit of Thy Grace; and that they may truly please Thee pour upon them the continual dew of Thy blessing, through Christ our Lord. Amen.

For true Penitence.

Almighty and everlasting God, I intreat Thee, suffer me not to perish in my sins, but since I am Thy Creature, grant me space of life, and the opportunity and will to live righteously; so that before the day of my death I may in true penitence attain to please Thee The living and true God, Who livest and reignest The Only God and Lord for ever and ever. Amen.

A Penitential Prayer of S. Anselm.

O Lord, my God, although I have so behaved as to be guilty in Thy sight, can I so have acted as to be no longer Thy creature? If I have sullied my purity, have I exhausted Thy mercy? If I have committed that for which Thou mightest justly condemn me, Thou hast not lost that by which Thou art wont to save. O Lord! verily my conscience deserves condemnation, but Thy compassion exceeds all mine offences. Spare me, therefore, O Lord! since this is neither impossible for Thy Power, nor unbecoming Thy Justice, nor unwonted to Thy Clemency. For what is Jesus but Saviour! Therefore, O Jesu, Who art my Maker, destroy not me whom Thou hast redeemed, nor condemn me whom in Thy goodness Thou hast created. Let not me Thy workmanship perish in mine iniquity. Favourably regard in me that which is Thine, and abolish that which is mine own; Who with God The Father and The Holy Ghost livest and reignest God, world without end. Amen

¶ *Confession.*

In The Name of The Father, and of The Son, and of The Holy Ghost! Amen.

I confess to Thee, O Lord, Jesu Christ! all my sins that I have committed from my childhood even until this hour, whether knowingly or ignorantly, by day, or by night, either ſleeping or waking, in word or in deed, in thought or in neglect, through the aſſaults of the Devil or the frailty of my fleſh, againſt Thy Divine will; beſeeching Thee that Thy wrath may not come upon me, but that Thy grace may viſit me now and evermore. May the Benediction of God The Father, The Son, and The Holy Ghoſt be upon me! May the interceſſions of the holy Mother of God, of S. Michael the Archangel, S. John the Baptiſt, S. John the Evangeliſt, S. Peter and S. Paul, and of all the holy Apoſtles, help me; and may all the Saints and elect of God pray for me, that I may be worthy with them to poſſeſs the kingdom of God. Amen.

OUR FATHER.

HEARKEN, O Lord! I beſeech Thee, to the prayer of Thy ſuppliant, and ſpare the ſins which I confeſs unto Thee; and of Thy goodneſs beſtow upon me pardon as well as peace, through Chriſt our Lord. Amen.

GOD! Who art the Saviour of the living, Who wouldeſt not the death of a ſinner, nor rejoiceſt in the perdition of the wicked, I humbly intreat Thee to grant me pardon of all mine offences. May I weep for them when they have been committed, and never again be guilty of them; that when my laſt day and the end of my life ſhall arrive, the Angel of Holineſs may receive me, and carry me purified from all my ſins into Thy preſence, through Chriſt our Lord. Amen.

Oriſon of S. Gregory for the Morning.

O LORD God Almighty! Ruler of all things! Who art Trinity in The Son, and in The Father, along with The Holy Spirit; Who ever art, and waſt before all things, and ſhalt be throughout all things, God Bleſſed for evermore! I commend my ſoul into the hands of Thy power, that Thou mayeſt keep it by day and by night in every hour and moment of my life. Have mercy upon me, O God of Angels! Guide me, O King of Archangels! Preſerve me for the prayers of the Patriarchs, for the merits of the Prophets, the ſupplications of Thine Apoſtles, for the victories of Martyrs, for the faith of Confessors, for the chastity of Virgins, for the intercessions of all Thy Saints and elect, who have pleased Thee from the beginning of the world. May Holy Abel pray for me who first of all men was crowned with martyrdom; May Holy Enoch pray for me who walked with God and was translated from the world; May Holy Noah pray for me whom for his righteousness The Lord preserved in the flood; May faithful Abraham entreat for me who first believed God and his faith was counted unto him for righteousness; May Holy Isaac intercede for me who was obedient to his father even unto death, as a type of our Lord Jesus Christ, Who was offered up to The Father for the salvation of the world. May happy Jacob beseech for me who saw the Angels of God coming unto his aid; May Joseph beloved of his father pray for me whom his brethren sold; May Holy Moses petition for me with whom The Lord spake face to face; May Holy David pray for me whom Thou choosedst, O Lord! after Thine own heart; May Elias the Prophet supplicate for me whom Thou didst exalt in a fiery chariot even unto Heaven; May Elisha the Prophet pray for me who raised up the dead after his decease; May Holy Isaiah pray for me whose lips were cleansed with celestial fire; May blessed Jeremiah help me whom Thou didst sanctify in his mother's womb; May Holy Ezekiel the Prophet implore for me who saw the wonderful visions of God; May Holy Daniel supplicate for me, beloved of God who solved the dreams of the King and rightly interpreted them, and was delivered from the den of Lions; May the three Children, Shadrach, Meshach, and Abednego, who were delivered from the furnace; May the twelve Prophets, Hosea, Joel, Amos, Abakuk, Obadiah, Micah, Jonah, Nahum, Zephaniah, Haggai, Zachariah, and Malachi; May all the Apostles of Jesus Christ intreat for me; with Peter, Paul, Andrew, John, Thomas, James, Philip, Matthew, James, Bartholomew, Symeon, Thaddeus Matthias, and all the holy disciples of our Lord Jesus Christ. May all the Martyrs and Confessors, Virgins, and all the elect of Christ intercede for me, that I may be able to overcome all the temptations of the world. Expel from me, O Lord! the lust of gluttony, and give me the virtue of abstinence; banish from me the spirit of fornication, and grant me the love and fervour of chastity; extinguish covetousness within me, and grant me voluntary poverty; restrain me from anger, and kindle in me sweetness of temper and the love of God and my neighbour. Cut off from me, O Lord! the sorrow of this world, and increase within me spiritual joy. Quell the arrogance of my mind, and bestow on me compunction of heart; lessen my pride and perfect in me true humility, for I am an unworthy and miserable man. Who shall deliver me from the body of this death except Thy Grace, O Lord Jesu Christ? for I am a very exceeding sinner, and innumerable are my faults, and I am not worthy to be called Thy servant. Awaken tears in me, soften my hard and stony heart, and kindle in me the fire of Thy fear and love who am but a dead dog! deliver my soul from all the snares of the enemy, and preserve me in Thy good pleasure; teach me to do Thy will, Thou that art my God! To Thee be all Honour and Glory throughout infinite ages of ages. Amen.

¶ *Orison of S. Augustine.*

O God! be favourable to me a sinner, and be my keeper all the days and nights of my life! God of Abraham! God of Isaac! God of Jacob! have mercy upon me, and send to my help Holy Michael The Archangel to guard and protect me from all mine enemies. Holy Archangel Michael! keep me from all peril that may not offend in that tremendous judgement! O Holy Michael Archangel! by the Grace which thou hast obtained, I intreat thee by the might of The Only begotten Son of God, our Lord Jesus Christ, deliver me from the peril of death. O Holy Gabriel! Holy Raphael! All ye holy Angels and Archangels of God, succour me! All ye hosts of Heaven, I intreat ye to give me help and strength, that no enemy may prevail to injure me in the way, neither by fire nor by water nor by sudden death, nor may destroy nor hurt me sleeping or waking. Behold the Cross ✠ of The Lord! Begone, ye adversaries; The Lion of the tribe of Judah hath conquered! The Root of David! Alleluya. Saviour of the world! save us; Who by Thy Cross and Thy Blood hast redeemed us! Be our helper, we intreat Thee, O our God! Holy God! Holy Mighty! Holy Immortal! have mercy upon us! Holy God! Holy Mighty! Holy and Immortal! have mercy upon us! Cross ✠ of Christ, save us; Cross ✠ of Christ, protect us; Cross ✠ of Christ, defend us; in The Name of The Father, and of The Son, and of The Holy Ghost. Amen.

Orison of S. Thomas Aquinas.

Grant me, O merciful God! fervently to desire, wisely to search out, truly to acknowledge, and perfectly to fulfil such things as are well-pleasing unto Thee, to the praise and Glory of Thy Name. Order my worldly condition and all that Thou requirest me to do. Grant that I may know Thy will, and give me strength to perform it as I ought, and as is expedient for my soul. May my path before Thee, O Lord! be safe, upright and perfect; falling not away either in prosperity or in adversity; so that I may render thanks unto Thee in prosperity and may patiently endure adversity; that in the one I may not be lifted up and in the other never be cast down. May I rejoice and grieve at nothing but what concerns Thy Glory. May I seek to please none and fear to displease none beside Thee. May all transitory things appear vile to me in comparison of Thee, O Lord! and may all that is Thine be dear unto me, and Thou, O God! more than all things. May I be weary of the joy which is without Thee, and desire not anything beside Thee. Let all toil delight me that is for Thee, and may all repose be wearisome which is not in Thee. Grant that I may continually direct my heart unto Thee, and with all purpoſe of amendment think with ſorrow upon my ſhortcomings. Make me, O God! unfeignedly humble; joyful without levity, ſad without dejection, grave without moroſeneſs, active without frivolity, truthful without duplicity; fearing Thee without deſpair, truſting in Thee without preſumption. May I reprove my neighbour without diſſimulation, edify him by word and example without pride, be obedient without gainſaying, patient without murmuring, continent without depravity. Give me, O God! Thou beloved, a very watchful heart which no curious imaginations may lead aſtray from Thee; a noble heart which no unworthy affection may draw backward; a ſteadfaſt heart which no tribulation can break; a free heart which no violent aſſault ſhall betray unto captivity. Beſtow upon me, O Lord! my God, underſtanding to know Thee, diligence to ſeek Thee, wiſdom to find Thee, a deportment which may pleaſe Thee, perſeverance in faithfully waiting upon Thee, and truſtfulneſs in embracing Thee unto the end; ſo to be afflicted by Thy pains in penitence here, and ſo to uſe the benefits of Thy grace in this my pilgrimage, that I may attain to the fruition of Thy joys and rewards in the regions of Glory, Who liveſt and reigneſt God, world without end. Amen.

Oriſon.

O Lord Jeſu Chriſt! make me to love Thee fervently and perſeveringly; make me to feel with what a boundleſs love Thou haſt loved me, O Lord Jeſu Chriſt! I deſire to love Thee, which without Thine aid I cannot do. Make me to die to Thy love; give me, O Lord my God! a reverent, humble, modeſt, obedient, ſtrenuous, grateful love, having a conſtant ſenſe of Thy benefits and favours which Thou doſt beſtow upon me and others. O Thou! Crucified for me! may Thy love fix in me the nails and thorns of Thy Paſſion. Crucify me with Thyſelf! O Love! moſt profound, moſt glorious, when ſhall I be wholly inebriate with Thee? When ſhall I viſibly behold Thee? When ſhall I ſalute Thee? When familiarly embrace Thee? When ſhall I be ſo joined unto Thee that I may offend Thee in nothing, and never can be ſeparated from Thee? How long ſhall I be an exile from Thy preſence? To be without Thee is baniſhment unto me! continual ſorrow, and as it were an eternal death! Who liveſt and reigneſt. Amen.

O Good Jeſu! may all the time paſt of my life which I have ſpent in ſo evil a manner be forgotten before Thee, and grant that the reſidue of theſe my years may be to Thine honour, fruitful toward Thee, and profitable to my neighbour. Who liveſt and reigneſt. Amen.

Oriſon to The Father.

O Lord! Holy Father! Almighty and Eternal God! to that holy keeping and remembrance whereto Thou didſt commend The Moſt Glorious Spirit of our Lord Jeſu Chriſt Thy Son, when Thou didſt ſend Him from Heaven unto Earth; and to that holy keeping and remembrance whereto Thou didſt commit the glorious Mother and the Perſon of Thy Son, hanging upon the bleſſed Croſs, to John the Apoſtle and Evangeliſt; and to that keeping and power whereunto, in the Ninth Hour of Good Friday, Thou didſt commend Thy Sacred Soul and yield It up unto Thy Father, ſaying, Into Thine hands I commend My Spirit! [and in the preſence of Thy Very Body and Blood] O Lord Jeſu Chriſt! I alſo commend my ſoul and my body, my mind and my thoughts, my words and my deeds, and all my prayers; my father, my mother, my brethren and ſiſters, and all my friends, beſeeching on our behalf Thy moſt loving mercy; that Thou wouldeſt grant to us ſinners pardon of our ſins, eſcape and deliverance from thoſe which are preſent, and ſecurity and caution as to the future; ſtrong perſeverance in, and a devout will towards, Thy Faith; in all our proſperity in this world, wiſdom and humility; in the good things of Thy grace, abundance of all ſpiritual gifts, charity and perfect patience; to all our friends and benefactors, mercy and everlasting Glory; to our enemies, contrition and pardon; and alike to them and us space for true penitence and amendment of life, the grace and consolation of Thy Holy Spirit and perseverance in good works; so that by Thee, Whose Sacred Body and Blood we adore on earth, we may be joined unto God in the Heavens, and that our enemies, visible or invisible, may never hurt us, either waking or sleeping, by themselves or by any other; and Thy mercy may ever prevent and follow us. Amen.

Vouchsafe, O Lord, Almighty God! to receive these prayers, which I an unworthy sinner desire to offer unto Thee, to the Honour of Thy Most Holy Name and of all Thy Saints, for myself a miserable sinner, and for all my neighbours, friends, relations, benefactors, and those who are commended to my charge, for the numberless sins we have committed, and for the souls of the faithful departed. Grant we beseech Thee, Almighty God, that these prayers may profit to us all for the salvation of the body, and the cure of the soul; to the doing of true penitence in this life, and to the obtaining of Glory and Life eternal hereafter. Amen.

The Glorious Passion of our Lord
Christ Jesus, The Incarnate Word,
Deliver us from guilt and sadness,
And bring us to the Paradise of gladness!

Into Thy hands, most beloved Son of God, and to Thy sweet loving-kindness, I commend this day and at all times my body and my soul, the amendment of my ways, my entire life and death, my resurrection, and my judgement wherein I must give account for all I have done in this world. To Thee I commend all the prayers which I an unworthy sinner desire to offer up unto Thee. God be merciful to me a sinner! and after Thy good knowledge and will have pity upon me. Send Thy holy Angel both now and ever to be my guardian and defence, and grant that hereafter, along with all the faithful departed, I may be found worthy to obtain eternal rewards at Thy hand, through The Same Jesus Christ our Lord, The Mediator of God and man, and The Redeemer of the world, Who with Thee liveth and reigneth God throughout all ages world without end. Amen.

O Lord! we beseech Thee, prevent all our doings with Thy favour and further them by Thy help, so that all our works may begin, and all our undertakings end in Thee, through Christ our Lord. Amen.

Christ! King of grace, Thy servants bless,
And with Thyself our hearts possess;
So to Thy Glory, all our days,
We'll give the tribute of our praise.

Lord! Holy Virgin born! to Thee
All Glory everlasting be;
To Father and to Holy Ghost,
Long as Eternity shall last. Amen.

Orison.

Be present, O Lord! with my supplication, and dispose the way and actions of Thy servant in the prosperity of Thy Salvation; that among all the changes of my path and of this life I may ever be protected by Thy help, through Christ our Lord. Amen.

O Lord! favourably receive my prayers, that being delivered from all adversity and error I may serve Thee in safety and freedom, and grant us Thy Peace in our time, through our Lord Jesus Christ, Thy Son, Who with Thee liveth and reigneth in the Unity of The Holy Ghost, God world without end. Amen.

May God The Father Who created all things out of nothing bless me; may The Son of God keep me, Who with His own Blood restored lost man; may The Holy Ghost enlighten me; the infusion of whose loving consolation may it ever comfort me! The Most Holy Trinity deliver me from all evil, preserve and strengthen me in all well doing, and bring me at the last to eternal Life! Amen.

O Lord Jesu Christ! hearken unto my prayer, and fulfil my desire for my good, and the praise of Thy Name.

Bless we The Lord.
Thanks be to God. Amen.

¶ *Memorials for the Morning.*

On Sunday of The Holy Trinity.

Our Hope, our Salvation, our Honour, O Blessed Trinity!

℣. Blefs we The Father and The Son, with The Holy Ghoft.

℟. Let us praife and highly exalt Him for ever.

Almighty and everlafting God! I Thy fuppliant befeech Thee that Thou wouldeft make me fo firmly and faithfully to believe, fo truthfully and fimply to confefs The Holy Trinity in this world, that in the life to come I may be enabled perfectly to know and with all joy face to face to behold The Same, Who liveft and reigneft God world without end. Amen.

℣. May the fouls of the faithful departed, through the mercy of God, reft in peace. Amen.

℟. Bleffed be the moft fweet Name of our Lord Jefus Chrift and of the fweeteft Virgin Mary His Mother, and may all the Company of Heaven be bleffed now and for ever and for evermore. Amen.

On Monday of the Faithful Departed.

I AM The Refurrection and The Life, faith The Lord. He that believeth in Me though he were dead yet fhall he live, and whofo liveth and believeth in Me fhall never die. Amen.

℣. Eternal reft grant them, O Lord!

℟. And may perpetual light fhine upon them.

℣. May their fouls dwell in good things.

℟. And their feed inherit the earth.

GOD Who didft form man from the duft of the earth after Thy likenefs, to make good the lofs of the Angels, and didft fuffer death upon the Crofs to reftore him when fallen, fhew pity I befeech Thee on the fouls of all the faithful departed by mitigating Thy juftice with mercy; fo that the works of Thy hands, which Thou haft created frail and prone to finfulnefs, be not condemned for their fins in the flefh, Who liveft and reigneft God, world without end. Amen.

MAY the fouls of the faithful departed, through the mercy of God, reft in peace. Amen.

Tuesday of The Holy Spirit.

Come, O Holy Spirit! fulfil the hearts of Thy faithful ones and kindle in them the fire of Thy love. Alleluya.

℣. Send forth Thy Spirit and they ſhall be created.

℟. And Thou ſhalt renew the face of the earth.

Grant, we beſeech Thee Almighty God, that the radiance of Thy Brightneſs may ſhine forth upon us, ſo that the beams of Thy Light through the illumination of Thy Holy Spirit may confirm our hearts and renew them, by Thy Grace through Chriſt our Lord. Amen.

On Wedneſday of Saints.

The Saints ſhall be joyful in Glory; they ſhall rejoice in their beds.

℣. Wonderful is God in His Saints.

℟. And Glorious in His Majeſty.

O Lord! we beſeech Thee, mercifully regard our infirmities, and all the evils which we juſtly deſerve, for the interceſſions of all Thy Saints, do Thou mercifully avert from us, through Chriſt our Lord. Amen.

O Lord! we beſeech Thee, purify our conſciences by Thy Viſitation; ſo that when Jeſus Chriſt Thy Son our Lord ſhall come with all His Saints, He may find in us a manſion prepared for Himſelf, through The Same Jeſus Chriſt our Lord. Amen.

Of Angels.

The Son of the Supreme King all the heavenly citizens do praiſe, to Whom Cherubim and Seraphim continually do cry, Holy! Holy!

℣. Bleſs ye The Lord, all ye His Angels.

℟. Ye ſervants of His, that do His pleaſure.

O God! Who in the beginning didſt create divers orders of bleſſed Spirits to know Thine Everlaſting Divinity, and after the fall of mankind didſt wonderfully redeem mankind whom He had deceived in order to make good their loſs; grant unto us ſo to be fulfilled with the gifts of Thy Grace by the Spirit of Thy Mouth that going on from ſtrength to ſtrength we may be enabled to attain to the happy ſociety of the choirs of Thy bleſſed Angels, through Chriſt our Lord. Amen.

Thursday of The Blessed Sacrament.

My Flesh is meat indeed, and My Blood is drink indeed. Whoso eateth My Flesh and drinketh My Blood abideth in Me and in Him saith The Lord.

℣. He gave them meat from Heaven.

℟. Man did eat Angels' food.

O God! Who unto us in a wonderful Sacrament hast left the Memorial of Thy Passion; grant to us, we beseech Thee, so to venerate the Sacred Mysteries of Thy Body and Blood that we may evermore perceive in ourselves the fruit of Thy Redemption, through Christ our Lord. Amen.

Friday of The Holy Cross.

Christ crucified, to the Jews a stumbling block and to the Greeks foolishness; but unto them which are called both Jews and Greeks, Christ The Power of God and The Wisdom of God.

℣. We praise Thee, O Christ! and we bless Thee.

℟. For by Thy Cross Thou hast redeemed the world.

O Lord Jesu Christ! Son of The living God! Who for the redemption of mankind didst vouchsafe to ascend the wood of The Cross, that the whole world which lay in darkness might be enlightened; we beseech Thee, pour such light into our souls and bodies that we may be enabled to attain to that Light which is eternal, and through the merits of Thy Passion and Wounds, may after death joyfully enter within the gates of Paradise, Who with The Father and. Amen.

Saturday of The Incarnation.

O wonderful exchange! The Creator of mankind taking upon Him a living Body vouchsafed to be born of The Virgin Mary, and proceeding forth as Man, bestowed upon us His Divinity!

℣. Beautiful is His Form before the sons of men.

℟. Grace is poured forth upon Thy lips.

Almighty and everlasting God, Who by the co-operation of Thy Holy Spirit didst wonderfully prepare the Body and Soul of the Blessed Virgin and Mother Mary to become a fit habitation for Thy Son, grant that we who have been gladdened by His Incarnation, by His merits and intercession, may be delivered from all the evils which threaten us, and from everlasting death, Who livest and reignest God, world without end. Amen.

℣. May the souls of the faithful departed, through the mercy of God, rest in peace. Amen.

℟. Blessed be the most sweet Name of our Lord Jesus Christ, and of the sweetest Virgin Mary His Mother, and may all the Company of Heaven be blessed, now and for ever and for evermore. Amen.

¶ *A general and devout prayer for the good state of our Mother Church militant here on Earth.*

Almighty and merciful God! King of Heaven and Earth! I a suppliant beseech Thy clemency, that for the intercessions and sake of the glorious Mother of God ever Virgin, and of all Thy Saints, Angels, Patriarchs, Prophets, Apostles, Martyrs, Confessors, Virgins, Widows, and of all the citizens of Heaven, Thou wouldest keep all the Ecclesiastical Order, our Bishops, Kings, and Princes, Thy servants and handmaidens, and this place, along with the Universal Catholic Church, in all sanctity and peace. And that all who are connected with us by consanguinity, relationship, friendship, protection, and giving of alms, and all Christians, Thou wouldest cleanse from vices and sins, and adorn with virtue. Grant us peace and health both of mind and body; banish from us our enemies visible and invisible; favour us with temperate weather, bestow upon us the fruits of the earth, expel from us carnal desires, restore health to the sick, grant restoration to the fallen, to the faithful who are travelling by sea or land a prosperous journey and a harbour of safety, joy to those that are in tribulation, relief to the oppressed; and bestow on our enemies, and on those who are at discord with us, and on ourselves, true charity.

Give to our rulers peace; correct the erring, convert the unbelieving, increase holy faith in Thy Church, destroy the simoniacal heresy, and all heresies and schisms in Thy Catholic Church; and grant unto all the faithful, living and departed, eternal life, and also rest in the land of the living, through Christ our Lord. Amen.

TO THY GUARDIAN ANGEL.

A Prayer to thy proper Angel.

Angele qui meus es custos pietate Supernâ.

Dear Angel Guardian, given by
  Heaven's kind care for my direction,
O succour, shield, and guide me,
  thus consigned to Thy protection!
Cleanse Thou my soul from guilt
  and shame, all stain of sin expelling;
Be e'er my comrade and life's lamp
  in this mine earthly dwelling.
O Thou sweet Angel friend! who
  ever nigh me stayest,
Yet never aught unto mine outward
  senses sayest,
In soul and body I beseech Thee to
  defend me;
For 'tis Thy gracious task thus
  lovingly to tend me.

Kind Angel! Herald of my God on
  high Who reigneth;
Rule all my words and actions as
  His will ordaineth.
Intreat for me, thou Angel blest of
  God my Maker,
That I of Christ's sweet promises
  may be a meet partaker! Amen.

A Prayer to thy proper Angel.

O Holy Angel of God! Minister of the Celestial Kingdom, whom God Almighty hath appointed for my guardian; by His Majesty and Mercy I humbly entreat thee to preserve my mind and my body and all my senses from wicked and unlawful desires, from hurtful, vain, and impure thoughts, from the wiles of malignant spirits, from defilement of mind and body, and from the snares of mine enemies visible and invisible, who seek after my soul; and be to me a faithful guardian wheresoever I go, by day and by night, in every hour and minute. Keep me pure in mine actions, and strengthen in me the fear and love of Jesus Christ, and all holy desires. Help me ever to speak and do and think the will of God; make me to know mine end and the number of my days; and after this miserable and fleeting life, conduct my soul to eternal felicity, where it may rejoice with God and all His Saints eternally, by the help of our Lord Jesus Christ, to Whom be Honour and Glory, world without end. Amen.

To thy proper Angel a devout prayer.

O Glorious Angel! to whom our blessed Lord of His most merciful Grace hath given me to keep, to thee I a sinful creature cry and call with heart and mind, beseeching thee ever to be a singular comfort to me in all my necessity. Suffer me never to be overcome with temptation or evil affections; but help me that by Grace I may ever proceed in virtuous living. At the hour of my death be present, that my ghostly enemy may have no power over me, and afterward bring me into bliss, where with thee I may live and for ever praise my Saviour. Amen.

A Prayer to thy proper Angel.

O good kind Angel! ordained to my governance, I know well my feebleness and ignorance. Well also do I wot that I have no strength to do God's service but only of His Grace, and of thy busy keeping. The knowledge that I have cometh naught of myself, but of what God will send me by thy good persuasion. Now, good gracious Angel, I ask thee humbly mercy; for little heed have I taken of thy good office; but now I thank thee as I can, with good heart, beseeching thee to keep me truly this day and evermore, sleeping and waking, with sure defence and holy teaching. Shield and protect me from bodily harm; defend and guard me from ghostly perils to God's worship and the saving of my soul. Teach me and influence my senses to spend very much in God's worship and pleasing; feed me with devotion and the savour of ghostly sweetness; strengthen me when need is, againſt my ghoſtly enemies, and ſuffer me not to loſe the grace that is granted me, but of thy worthy office, keep me in God's ſervice to my life's end; and after the paſſing away of the body, preſent my ſoul unto The Merciful God; for though I fall all day by my own frailty, I take thee to witneſs that I ever hope in His Mercy. God I worſhip, and for thee alſo, after His holy teaching, I thank Him with grateful devotion. Amen.

Salve mi Angelice!

Hail, mine Angel pure and bright!
Hail, thou bleſſed Spirit!
Fulneſs of celeſtial light
Thou who doſt inherit;
Viewing e'er in perfect joy
God's unclouded Viſion,
And of Him, without alloy,
Haſt complete fruition.

When thy brethren proud of will,
Were to ruin driven,
Grace Divine preſerved thee ſtill
Loyal unto Heaven;
And with virtues firm and free,
Wondrouſly anointed;
And a guardian unto me
Frail and weak, appointed.

Now I bend my knees, and haſte
Reverently to greet thee,
And with ſuppliant hands upraiſed
Fervently intreat thee,
That this day, with keeping ſure,
Thou wouldſt be my warder,
And, from ghoſtly foes ſecure
All my doings order.

From all perils be my frame
By thy proweſs guarded,
Blemiſhes of ſin and ſhame
From my ſoul diſcarded;
In each place and time of need
From the foe protect me,
And in thought, and word, and deed,
And in act, direct me.

For my welfare kindly pray,
Let not ſloth enſlave me;
O reſtore me when I ſtray,
And from falling ſave me;
All rebellions of the ſenſe
Paſt and preſent quelling,
And from heart and fleſh offence
Now and e'er expelling.

Aid and cheer me, and condole
With me, when in ſadneſs;
Kindle, cleanſe, illume my ſoul
With all holy gladneſs;
Teach, aſſiſt me, and incite
To endure temptation;
Guide me in life's path aright,
Till I reach Salvation.

Grace aſk for me when I pray,
For forgiveneſs yearning;
And joy with me in the way,
When from error turning;
So ſhall I, till life's laſt cloſe,
Be God's faithful ſervant,
And a truſt in Him repoſe
Ever ſure and fervent.

When I die, to ſoothe me ſpeed,
Sweeteſt comfort giving;
And, from every peril freed,
Bring me with the living
Heavenward to the Courts of Day,
Where without ceſſation
God is praiſed; and where for aye
Is true conſolation. Amen.

Orison to our Lord Jesus Christ.

O Lord Jesus Christ! be Thou nigh at hand to defend me; within me, that Thou mayest refresh me; around me, that Thou mayest preserve me; before me, that Thou mayest guard me; beneath me, that Thou mayest lift me up; above me, that Thy bounteous right hand may bless me. Thou One, yet Triune! protect me for evermore, In The Name of The Father, and of The Son, and of The Holy Ghost. ✠ Holy Michael be my coat of mail! Holy Gabriel be my helmet! Holy Raphael be my shield! Holy Uriel be my helper! Holy Cherubim be my health! Holy Seraphim be my truth! All holy Angels and Archangels preserve me, protect and defend me, and bring me to Life eternal. Amen.

O most sweet Jesu! breathe into my heart a most devoted love for Thee, contempt of the world, hatred for sin, a longing for my celestial country, perseverance in penitence, which may no evil desires interrupt, until Thy compassion bring it to due effect. Amen.

¶ FOR THE HOURS.

At the Third Hour.

O ALMIGHTY Lord God! Who after the darkness of the night hast caused me to arrive at the Third Hour of this day, preserve me therein in every hour and in every moment of time; and of Thy great goodness grant that I may continue safe and unharmed, in soul and in body, throughout the same, through our Lord.

O Lord Jesu Christ! Who at the Third Hour of the day wast led to the pain of The Cross for the salvation of the world; I humbly beseech Thee to blot out mine offences, so that I may find pardon with Thee for my past misdeeds, and may continually watch against them in future, Who with The Father.

At the Sixth Hour.

O Lord Jesu Christ! Who at the Sixth Hour of the day wast uplifted on The Cross of suffering, for the salvation of the world, and thereon didst shed forth Thy precious Blood for the remission of our sins; I humbly beseech Thee, that through the merits of Thy Passion and Wounds, I, after death, may be found worthy to enter rejoicing into the gate of Paradise, Who with The Father.

¶ *Say this prayer devoutly at None in Memorial of The Passion and Death of Christ.*

℟. It became darkness when The Jews had crucified Jesus; and about the Ninth Hour He cried out with a loud voice, Eloi! Eloi! Lama Sabacthani? that is, My God! My God! why hast Thou forsaken me? and bowing His Head He gave up the Ghost. Then one of the soldiers with a spear pierced His Side, and forthwith came thereout Blood and Water.

℣. And the veil of the Temple was rent from the top even to the bottom, and the whole earth trembled.

℟. And bowing His Head He gave up the Ghost.

Orison.

O Lord Jesu Christ! Son of The living God! Who for the salvation of mankind wast made to drink of Gall and Vinegar on the Cross, when Thou, all things being finished, didst expiring on that Cross commit Thy Spirit into the hands of The Father; so, in the hour of my death, I commend my spirit into the hands of Thy pity, that Thou mayest receive it in peace, and command it to be added to the choirs of Thine Elect, Who now livest and reignest, with God The Father in The Unity of The Holy Ghost, God world without end. Amen.

Our Father.

ℭ DEVOTIONS FOR THE EVENING.

GOOD Jeſus! enlighten mine eyes that I ſleep not in death: neither let mine enemy ſay, I have prevailed againſt him.

Into Thine hands, O Lord! I commend my ſpirit: for Thou haſt redeemed me O Lord! Thou God of Truth.

I ſpake with my tongue, Lord! let me know mine end and the number of my days: that I may be certified how long I have to live.

Thou haſt broken my bonds in ſunder: I will offer unto Thee the ſacrifice of praiſe, and will call upon The Name of The Lord.

Shew a token upon me for good, that they who hate me may ſee it and be aſhamed: for Thou, Lord, haſt holpen me and comforted me.

The Light of Thy countenance hath ſhined forth upon us, O Lord! Thou haſt given joy to my heart.

They who trouble me will rejoice if I be moved: but I have put my ſure truſt in Thy mercy.

Glory be to The Father.

As it was in the beginning.

Let all Thy works acknowledge Thee O Lord! and Thy Saints praiſe Thee.

I will ſing unto The Lord Who hath given me good things;

And I will praiſe The Name of The Lord Moſt High.

O Jeſu dulciſſime.

O SWEETEST Jeſu! Saviour dear!
Kind Jeſu! to my prayer give ear!
With me, this night, O Lord! abide
In peace reclining at my ſide,
While ſlumber ſhall my ſenſes ſteep;
That ſo my heart may never ſleep,
But with Thee holy vigil keep;
And Thou may'ſt all my ſpirit fill;
Though abſent, yet be preſent ſtill,
To guard me ſafe from every ill.
My warder let Thine Angel be;
The Croſs from peril keep me free,
That Satan far away may flee,
And Jeſus only ſtay with me.
O gather thoſe I love to reſt
Within Thy kind and ſheltering breaſt;
Nor me, nor them in life forſake,
But us to Thy protection take
For ever, ſleeping and awake.
Amen.

Grates peracto jam die.

MY thanks for this completed day
To Thee, O God! I meekly pay;
And as the glooms of night deſcend,
Before Thy footſtool ſuppliant bend.

Forgiveneſs for the day's offence
To me Thy penitent diſpenſe;
And while mine eyes to ſlumber yield,
My ſoul from deadly peril ſhield.

For Satan round our earthly home
Doth as a ravening lion roam;
From him beneath Thy ſheltering wings
Protect Thy ſervant, King of Kings!

O when ſhall that bright morn appear
Which hath no eve, our hearts to cheer!
O when that home, thoſe peaceful bowers
Which know no grief, no foe, be ours!

Glory to God The Father be,
Like Glory, Only Son! to Thee;
And to Thee, Spirit Paraclete!
Now and through ages infinite.
Amen.

Te lucis ante terminum.

To Thee, before the cloſe of Day,
Creator of the worlds, I pray,
With all Thy wonted clemency,
Our Princely Guard and Keeper be.

Far may unholy viſions fly,
No fiend of Darkneſs venture nigh;
Do Thou repel the infernal Foe,
And peace and purity beſtow.

Almighty Father, hear my cry,
Through Jeſus Chriſt Our Lord Moſt High;
Who with The Holy Ghoſt and Thee
Doth reign throughout Eternity!
Amen.

On Feſtivals.

Salvator Mundi Domine!

O Saviour of the world! whoſe might
Hath ſaved me in the day that's paſt;
Protect me through the coming night,
And ſave me, long as Time ſhall laſt.

Thy gracious promiſe now fulfil,
And mercy to my prayer accord;
O blot out all my deeds of ill,
And lighten Thou our darkneſs, Lord!

May ſlumber ne'er the ſoul oppreſs,
No ghoſtly foe my reſt invade;
Nor be this frail and mortal fleſh
In aught to ſin or ſhame betrayed.

Reſtorer of our every ſenſe!
O grant me, from the heart I pray,
Devout and pure from all offence
To ariſe with the returning day.

To God The Father Glory be;
Like Glory to His Only Son;
And Spirit Paraclete! to Thee,
While endleſs years their courſes run. Amen.

Abide with us, O Lord!
For it is evening, and the day is far ſpent.

May my evening prayer aſcend up unto Thee, O Lord!
And Thy mercy deſcend upon me.

Preſerve me, O Lord!
As the apple of an eye protect me under the ſhadow of Thy wings.

I render thanks to Thee, O Lord! Almighty God! Who haſt given me to reach this Veſper hour; and I humbly beſeech Thee that the lifting up of my hands unto Thee, may in Thy ſight be an acceptable evening ſacrifice, Through our Lord. Amen.

Lord! have mercy.
Chriſt! have mercy.
Lord! have mercy.

OUR FATHER.

I ſaid I will confeſs my ſins unto The Lord: and ſo Thou forgavedſt the iniquity of my tranſgreſſion.

O Lord Jeſu Chriſt! I acknowledge that I have grievouſly offended, and I deſire through Thy Grace to amend my ways. Have mercy upon me for Thy bitter Paſſion's ſake. Amen.

ℭ *CONFESSION.*

I CONFESS to Thee, O Lord God! Almighty Creator of Heaven and Earth! all my ſins which I have ever committed from my childhood even to this hour, whether knowingly or ignorantly, and eſpecially what I have done his day in deed, thought, word, or neglect, againſt Thy Divine Majeſty. To Thee alone, O Lord! I confeſs from my heart, and I intreat forgiveneſs; for my ſins are innumerable; and moſt humbly I beſeech Thee to pardon all mine offences, whatſoever they be Thou knoweſt me to have been guilty of. Kindle, moreover, within me the flame of Thy love and fear; and grant me a real amendment of my whole life, together with true Hope, Faith, and Charity! O merciful, O kind, O ſweet Jeſu! Son of Mary!

God of Mercy! God of Pity! God of Goodneſs! pardon and have compaſſion upon me Thy ſervant; vouchſafe graciouſly to receive my ſupplications, and of Thy great kindneſs and long-ſuffering forgive me all the ſins and crimes into which I have fallen; grant me ſpace for penitence, and rivers of tears, ſo that I may receive at Thy hand remiſſion of all my tranſgreſſions through Chriſt our Lord. Amen.

ALMIGHTY and Everlaſting God! Who on Hezekiah the King of the Jews, when he intreated with tears Thy pity, didſt beſtow a longer period of life; grant to me, Thy ſervant, at leaſt ſuch a length of days as may ſuffice me to deplore my ſins, ſo that I may be found worthy to obtain pardon and grace of Thy compaſſion through our Lord Jeſus Chriſt. Amen.

O Triumphal Title, 'Jeſus of Nazareth The King of the Jews!' Behold the Sign of the life-giving Croſs of The Lord ✠. Begone, ye adverſaries! The Lion of the Tribe of Judah, The Root of David, hath conquered! Alleluya.

Be unto us, O Lord! a tower of ſtrength;

From the face of the enemy.

O Lord! hear my prayer;

And let my crying come unto Thee.

I beſeech Thee, O Lord Jeſus Chriſt! to grant me love of Thee without meaſure; the performance of Thy promiſes without ſtint; and a burning zeal for Thee without reſtriction. Amen.

O Lord God! Father Almighty! Who haſt promiſed rewards to the righteous and pardon to the penitent; Who wouldeſt not the death of a ſinner, nor rejoiceſt in the perdition of tranſgreſſors; I humbly entreat Thee for the Wounds and Merits of Thine Only begotten Son Jeſus Chriſt, and for the ſake of The Holy Mother of God, and of all Thy Saints and Elect, of Thine own great mercy, to beſtow upon me, Thy ſervant, remiſſion of all my ſins. Bring me to that penitence for which Thou didſt ſave David, and didſt look graciouſly upon the weeping Peter, and didſt cleanſe Mary Magdalene. O Lord Jeſu Chriſt! expel from my heart all that offends Thee; and pour into my heart ſuch charity, that I may be enabled perfectly to love and to fear Thee, and may never think of or deſire anything that I am not certain will pleaſe Thee, O Lord! May the bleſſed Virgin Mary, the Temple of The Lord, the Sanctuary of The Holy Ghoſt, all Holy Archangels and Angels appointed for my keeping, intercede for me, with all the Apoſtles, Martyrs, Confeſſors, Virgins, Saints, and Elect of God, when I ſhall be preſented for judgement before the tribunal of the Eternal King.

I commend unto Thee, moſt merciful Chriſt Jeſus, all who love me, or care for me; all who afford me help, all who are indebted to me, and all my relations and friends. And, even for mine enemies I beſeech Thee, that Thou wouldeſt convert them unto peace; and cauſe them to attain to true penitence. I intreat Thee, O Lord Jeſu Chriſt! mercifully to viſit, comfort, and direct all who are mindful of me, or who have commended themſelves to my unworthy prayers, or who have done me any charity or kindneſs; as well as all who are connected with me by relationſhip, friendſhip, or the affection of faith, whether they ſtill exiſt in the body or have departed this life; that they may faithfully ſerve Thee, and may be defended from all adverſities; and, with me, abſolve them from all pains, and bring us to everlaſting reſt; and for this I eſpecially ſupplicate Thee, that when the day of my death ſhall come, Thou, Who giveſt judgement againſt the accuſers, wilt become my defender, Who art bleſſed for ever and ever. Amen.

For The Holy Spirit.

The love of God is ſhed abroad in our hearts by His Spirit that dwelleth in us. Alleluya.

O God! to Whom every heart lieth open, every will ſpeaketh, and from Whom no ſecret is hid, cleanſe the thoughts of my heart by the inſpiration of Thy Holy Spirit, that I may be enabled perfectly to love Thee and meetly to praiſe Thee, through Chriſt our Lord. Amen.

Almighty and Eternal God! Who doſt write the righteouſneſs of Thy law in the hearts of believers with the finger of Thy Holy Spirit; grant unto me an increaſe of Faith, Hope, and Charity; and that I may attain Thy promiſes, enable me to love that which Thou doſt command, through Chriſt our Lord. Amen.

For Divine Wiſdom.

The Law of The Lord is an undefiled law, converting the ſoul; The teſtimony of The Lord is ſure, giving wiſdom unto the ſimple.

God! Who, by Wiſdom co-eternal with Thee, didſt create man out of nothing, and didſt mercifully reſtore him when fallen; grant, I beſeech Thee, that, The Same Wiſdom inſpiring my mind, I may love Thee with my whole ſoul, and run after Thee with my whole heart, through Chriſt our Lord. Amen.

In tribulation of heart.

O LORD! I beſeech Thee, pardon mine offences, grant unto me Thy mercy; and, appeaſed by the interceſſions of my lips, look upon my humiliation, looſe my chains, blot out my miſdeeds, comfort me in my trials, drive away all adverſity, and, beſtowing effect upon my petitions, evermore favourably hear me, through Chriſt our Lord. Amen.

[*For other Collects, ſee the Morning Office.*]

Oriſon to The Father.

O FATHER of Heaven God! have mercy upon me. O Holy Lord! Almighty Father! Eternal God! Who before all worlds didſt ineffably beget The Son Co-equal, Co-ſubſtantial, and Co-eternal with Thee; and with Him and with The Holy Spirit proceeding from Thee and from The Same Son, didſt wonderfully create Heaven, Earth, and all things whatſoever exiſt, viſible and inviſible; I render thanks to Thee, I adore Thee, I praiſe Thee, I bleſs Thee, I magnify Thee. Be favourable to me, a moſt miſerable ſinner, and deſpiſe me not who am the work of Thy hands; but deliver, ſave, and help me, for Thy Name's ſake, Who liveſt and reigneſt God world without end. Amen.

Oriſon to The Son.

O SON! Redeemer of the world! God! have mercy upon me. O Lord Jeſu Chriſt! Son of the living God! Who art True and Almighty God, Brightneſs and Image of The Father, and Life eternal, to Whom along with The Eternal Father and The Holy Ghoſt belongeth equal Honour, the Same Glory, Co-eternal Majeſty, and One Subſtance; I give thanks to Thee, I adore Thee, I praiſe Thee, I bleſs Thee, I glorify Thee. Suffer me not to periſh, I beſeech Thee, but ſave and help me, for Thy Holy Name's ſake, Who liveſt and reigneſt with God. Amen.

Orison to The Holy Spirit.

O Holy Ghoſt! God! have mercy upon me! O Lord, Holy Ghoſt! God, Who, exiſting Co-equal, Conſubſtantial, and Co-eternal with The Father and The Son, doſt from Them ineffably proceed; and Who upon The Same our Lord Jeſus Chriſt in the form of a dove, and upon His holy diſciples in fiery tongues didſt deſcend! I give thanks to Thee, I adore Thee, I praiſe Thee, I bleſs Thee, and I glorify Thee. Drive from me, I beſeech Thee, the darkneſs of all mine iniquities, and kindle and perfect in me the light of Thy mercy, and the fire of Thy moſt holy love, Who liveſt and reigneſt God. Amen.

Almighty and everlaſting God! I give Thee thanks Who of Thy grace haſt vouchſafed to preſerve me to this hour; and I intreat Thee that all the ſins that I have committed this day, in thought, ſpeech, deed, or look, through the deceitfulneſs of the world, the fleſh, or the Devil, Thou, for the ſake of Thy Paſſion and Croſs, wouldeſt mercifully forgive me. Vouchſafe to keep me from all impurity of mind and body, that I may riſe again in ſafety to praiſe The Name of Thy Majeſty, and may be enabled to ſerve Thee with goodwill, a pure heart, and a chaſte body, with true gladneſs and giving of thanks. Amen.

I give Thee thanks, O Holy Father Almighty! Eternal God! Who not for mine own merits, but of Thy moſt holy Grace, haſt vouchſafed to keep me, Thine unworthy ſervant, ſafe throughout this day. Of Thy goodneſs, O moſt merciful God, I intreat Thee, that I may ſo paſs through the enſuing night with a pure heart and body, that ariſing in the morning I may be enabled to perform unto Thee a grateful and obedient ſervice, through Chriſt our Lord. Amen.

O Lord! Who didſt work out Thy Salvation in the midſt of the earth, with Whom darkneſs is not dark, but the night is as clear as the day; enlighten our darkneſs, I beſeech Thee, ſo that, paſſing a peaceable and quiet night, in the morning hours we may riſe again to Thy praiſes, through Chriſt our Lord. Amen.

O Almighty and Eternal God! enlighten our night, I beſeech Thee, and make us, Thy ſervants, to ſleep from our ſins, that we may be awake to the virtues of the Angels, and ſafe from all the darkneſs of iniquity, may through Thy help be found worthy to attain to the clear light of the perfect day, through Chriſt our Lord. Amen.

O God! The Ruler and Protector of all things, Who didſt divide the light from the darkneſs, I thy ſuppliant earneſtly intreat Thee, that throughout the darkneſs of the coming night, Thy right hand may defend us, ſo that we may riſe up again rejoicing in the light of the morning, through Chriſt our Lord. Amen.

For Saturday Evening.

O God! Who doſt illumine the night, and again reſtoreſt the day after darkneſs, grant to us Thy ſervants that we may paſs this night without any hindrance from Satan; and in the morning hours, returning to Thy holy Altar, may render unto Thee, The living and true God, praiſes and thankſgivings, through Chriſt our Lord. Amen.

Againſt Mortality and Sickneſs.

Visit us, O Lord! I intreat Thee, and defend this habitation againſt all the aſſaults of the enemy; and baniſh him far away from us. May Thy Holy Angels keep it and thoſe who dwell in it in peace, and evermore bleſs us; and may they defend us Thy ſervants from all ſudden peſtilence, and unforeſeen and eternal death, through Chriſt our Lord. Amen.

O God! The Strength of all them that put their truſt in Thee, favourably receive my ſupplications; and becauſe our mortal infirmity without Thee can do nothing, grant me the help of Thy grace, that in fulfilling Thy commandments I may pleaſe Thee both in will and deed, through Chriſt our Lord. Amen.

O God! Who didſt give Thine Holy Spirit to Thine Apoſtles, grant unto Thy ſervant the performance of his petitions; and on us to whom Thou haſt given Faith, beſtow alſo Peace, through our Lord Jeſus Chriſt, Thy Son, Who with Thee liveth and reigneth in The Unity of The Holy Ghoſt God, world without end. Amen.

To The Holy and Undivided Trinity; To the Crucified Humanity of our Lord Jeſus Chriſt; To the very happy fruitfulneſs of the bleſſed Virgin Mary, be everlaſting Glory from every creature through infinite ages of ages. Amen.

MEMORIALS FOR THE EVENING.

On Sunday of The Holy Trinity.

THEE dutifully praiſe, Thee adore, Thee glorify, all Thy creations, O Bleſſed Trinity!

℣. Bleſs we The Father, and The Son, with The Holy Ghoſt.

℟. Let us praiſe and highly exalt Him for ever.

Almighty and Everlaſting God! Who haſt given unto us Thy ſervants, grace on the Confeſſion of a true Faith to acknowledge the Glory of The Eternal Trinity, and in the Power of The Divine Majeſty to worſhip The Unity, we beſeech Thee that by our ſteadfaſtneſs in the ſame Faith we may ever be defended from all adverſities, Who liveſt and reigneſt God, world without end. Amen.

MAY the ſouls of the faithful departed, through the mercy of God, reſt in peace. Amen.

℟. Bleſſed be The moſt ſweet Name of our Lord Jeſus Chriſt, and of the ſweeteſt Virgin Mary His Mother, and may all the Company of Heaven be bleſſed, now and for evermore. Amen.

On Monday of the Faithful Departed.

I HEARD a voice from Heaven ſaying, Bleſſed are the dead which die in The Lord.

℣. Eternal reſt grant them, O Lord!

℟. And may perpetual light ſhine upon them.

Almighty and Everlaſting God, Who ruleſt over the living and doſt pity all the lead whom Thou foreknowest should be Thine in faith and good works; I humbly beseech Thee that all Those for whom I purpose to offer my prayers whether this present world still retain them in the flesh, or the future having put off their bodies hath received them, may by the intercessions of all Thy Saints be found worthy of obtaining the clemency of Thy compassion and the pardon of their sins, and may attain to joys everlasting, through Christ our Lord. Amen.

On Tuesday of The Holy Spirit.

Come, O Holy Spirit! fulfil the hearts of Thy faithful ones and kindle in them the fire of Thy Love. Alleluya.

℣. Send forth Thy Spirit and they shall be created.

℟. And Thou shalt renew the face of the earth.

O Lord! we beseech Thee let The Comforter Who proceedeth from Thee enlighten our minds and lead us as Thy Son hath promised into all truth, through The Same Jesus Christ our Lord.

O Lord! we beseech Thee let the Virtue of Thy Holy Spirit ever be with us, to amend and cleanse our hearts, and also to defend us against all adversities, through Christ our Lord. Amen.

On Wednesday of Saints.

Oh! how glorious is the Kingdom in which with Christ rejoice All His Saints; clothed in white robes they follow The Lamb whithersoever He goeth.

℣. The voice of joy and exultation

℟. Is in the dwellings of the righteous.

Grant, we beseech Thee Almighty God, that in the Resurrection of our Lord Jesus Christ with All His Saints we may in very deed receive our portion, through The Same Jesus Christ our Lord. Amen.

Of Angels.

The Angel of the Lord tarrieth round about them that fear Him and delivereth them.

℣. In the sight of the Angels I will sing Psalms unto Thee, My God!

℞. I will worſhip toward Thy Holy Temple, and give thanks unto Thy Name.

O God! Who doſt graciouſly permit ſome of Thy holy Angels to aſſiſt Thee, and in Thy Goodneſs doſt command them here on earth to miniſter unto men; Grant that Thine Angel, to whoſe charge Thou haſt committed me, may ſo guide me into all good, conſtantly incite me to virtue, and mightily deliver me from the gulph of ſin, that, in the ſtrict judgement, when one fold ſhall be made of men and of Angels, I, under this Thy ſhepherd, may be found worthy to be numbered among the ſheep of Thy flock, through Chriſt our Lord. Amen.

On Thurſday of the Holy Sacrament of the Altar.

O Sacred Feaſt! wherein Chriſt is received; the memory of His Paſſion is brought to our remembrance; our ſouls are filled with grace, and a pledge of eternal Glory is given unto us! Alleluya.

℣. Thou didſt give them Bread from Heaven.

℞. Having in Itſelf every delight.

O God! Who didſt form us after Thy likeneſs, and doſt renew us by Thy precepts and by Thy Sacraments; Grant that we may ever be fulfilled with the perpetual fruition of Thy Divinity, which the reception of The precious Body and Blood of Thy dear Son doth pre-figure to us here upon earth, Through the Same Jeſus Chriſt our Lord. Amen.

On Friday of the Holy Croſs.

But it behoveth us to glory in The Croſs of our Lord Jeſus Chriſt; wherein is our Salvation, our Life, our Reſurrection, by which we were redeemed and delivered.

℣. Chriſt was for us made obedient unto death, even The Death of The Croſs.

℞. Wherefore God hath highly exalted Him, and hath given Him a Name Which is above every name. Alleluya.

O Lord Jeſu Chriſt! Son of The living God! Who didſt deſcend from Heaven from the boſom of The Father unto this earth, and on the Tree of The Croſs didſt endure Five Wounds and ſhed forth Thy moſt precious Blood for the remiſſion of my ſins; I humbly beſeech Thee that at the Day of Judgement I may be placed at Thy Right Hand, and be found worthy to hear of Thee thoſe moſt ſweet words, Come, ye bleſſed of My Father, inherit the kingdom, Who liveſt and reigneſt God, world without end. Amen.

O Lord Jeſu Chriſt! Son of The living God! put Thy Paſſion, Croſs, and Death between Thy judgements and my ſoul, now and in the hour of my death; and vouchſafe to grant mercy and grace to the living, reſt and pardon to the dead, to Thy Holy Church peace and concord, and to me a ſinner everlaſting life and glory, Who with The Father and The Holy Ghoſt liveſt and reigneſt God, world without end. Amen.

On Saturday of The Incarnation.

Fear not thou, Mary, ſaid the Angel; thou haſt found favour with The Lord. Behold, thou ſhalt conceive and bring forth a Son. Alleluya.

℣. There ſhall come forth a Rod from the root of Jeſſe.

℟. And a Flower from his ſtem ſhall grow up.

O Lord! we beſeech Thee, ſtabliſh in our minds the Sacraments of The True Faith; that we who confeſs that Very God and Man was conceived by the Virgin Mary, by the power of His ſaving Incarnation, Nativity, Paſſion, Reſurrection, Aſcenſion, and by the Coming of The Holy Ghoſt, may through the Grace of The Same Holy Ghoſt, riſe again from the death of the ſoul, and finally attain the Heavenly and Eternal Country, through The Same Jeſus Chriſt our Lord. Amen.

℣. May the ſouls of the faithful departed, through the mercy of God, reſt in peace. Amen.

℟. Bleſſed be The moſt ſweet Name of our Lord Jeſus Chriſt, and of the ſweeteſt Virgin Mary, His Mother; and may all the Company of Heaven be bleſſed now and for ever and for evermore. Amen.

¶ *Here follow*

DEVOTIONS ON THE INCARNATION

COMMONLY CALLED

THE HOURS OF THE BLESSED VIRGIN MARY.

¶ *Prayer before The Hours.*

Open my mouth, O Lord! to bleſs Thy Holy Name, and purify my heart from all vain thoughts, that I may be worthy to be heard before The Face of Thy Divine Majeſty, Through.

¶ *AT MATINS.*

O Lord! open Thou my lips;

And my mouth ſhall ſhew forth Thy praiſe.

O God! make ſpeed to ſave me.

O Lord! make haſte to help me.

Glory be to The Father.

As it was in the beginning.

Invitatory.

Hail! thou that art full of Grace, The Lord is with thee; Bleſſed art thou among women, and bleſſed is The Fruit of thy womb, Jeſus!

O come let us ſing unto The Lord; let us heartily rejoice in The God of our Salvation.

Let us come before His preſence with thankſgiving: and ſhew ourſelves glad in Him with Pſalms.

Hymn.

Quem Terra Pontus Æthera.

The God Whom Earth and Sea and Sky
Revere, adore, and magnify,
Who o'er the threefold ſyſtem reigns
The Virgin Mary's womb contains.

The King Whom Sun and Moon obey.
Submiſſive to His ſovereign ſway,
A Maiden filled with Grace Divine
Doth in her ſpotleſs boſom ſhrine.

The nations of the world admire;
An Angel's words the germ inſpire;
A Virgin by her ear conceives,
And brings forth That her heart believes.

O Mother! Thou with honour deck'd
Didſt Heaven's eternal Architect,
Whoſe hands creation's courſe diſpoſe,
E'en as a ſacred Ark, encloſe.

By Heaven's ambaſſador thou'rt bleſt,
The Holy Ghoſt hath filled thy breaſt;
The long-deſired of earth is come,
And with thee finds a ſaintly home.

How glorious, Lady! is thy ſame;
Sublimer than the ſtars thy name;
Who greatly favoured, didſt indeed
Thy Maker at thy boſom feed.

What Eve in ſorrow rent away,
Thine Offspring doth to man repay;
That mourners may a reſt attain
Thou'rt made Heaven's window
unto men.

Gate of The Eternal King of Might!
Refulgent Portal of The Light!
Life through a Virgin is beſtowed;
Ye ranſomed nations hail your God!

Lord! Holy Virgin born! to Thee
All Glory everlaſting be;
To Father and to Holy Ghoſt,
Long as eternity ſhall laſt. Amen.

℣. God choſe her and predeſtined her.

℟. And cauſed her to dwell in His tabernacle.

Somno refectis artubus.

My limbs with grateful ſleep refreſhed,
With gladneſs I ariſe from reſt;
Look down and bleſs my words and
ways,
O Father! as I hymn Thy praiſe.

Thee ſhall my earlieſt accents ſing,
To Thee my ſoul her homage
bring;
That ſo my actions all may be,
O Holy Lord! begun in Thee.

Now darkneſs yields unto the light,
The Day Star hath diſperſed the
night;
So may the guilt which darkneſs
brought,
Melt in Thy radiant beams to
naught.

Suppliant before Thy face I fall,
On Thee to cleanſe my heart I call,
That ſo my tongue may hymn Thy
love,
For ever in Thy Courts above.

Lord! Holy Virgin born! to Thee
Eternal Praiſe and Glory be;
To Father and to Holy Ghoſt
Long as eternity ſhall laſt. Amen.

Summæ Deus clementiæ.

Great God of boundleſs mercy!
hear;
Thou Framer of this earthly ſphere!
One, in Eternity of Might!
In Whom The Immortal Three
unite!

O liſten to my thankful lays
Of mingled penitence and praiſe;
And ſet my heart from error free,
More fully to rejoice in Thee!

My reins and heart in pity heal,
And with Thy chaſtening fires anneal;
Gird Thou my loins, each paſſion
quell,
And every ſordid luſt expel.

Now as mine anthems, upward borne,
Awake the ſilence of the morn;
Enrich me with Thy gifts of Grace
From Heaven Thy bliſsful dwelling-place.

Moſt gracious Father! grant my
prayer;
Co-equal Only Son! give ear;
Who with Thee! Spirit Paraclete!
Reign throughout ages infinite!
Amen.

Psalm viii.—*Domine, Dominus noſter.*

O Lord our Governour! how excellent is Thy Name

in all the world; Thou that hast set Thy Glory above the Heavens!

Out of the mouth of very babes and sucklings hast Thou ordained strength, because of thine enemies: that Thou mightest still the enemy, and the avenger.

For I will consider Thy Heavens, even the works of Thy fingers: the Moon and the stars which Thou hast ordained.

What is man that Thou art mindful of him: and the son of man that Thou visitest him?

Thou madest him lower than the Angels: to crown him with glory and worship.

Thou makest him to have dominion of the works of Thy hands: and Thou hast put all things in subjection under his feet.

All sheep and oxen: yea, and the beasts of the field;

The fowls of the air: and the fishes of the sea: and whatsoever walketh through the paths of the sea.

O Lord our Governour! how excellent is Thy Name in all the world.

Psalm xix.—*Cœli enarrant.*

The Heavens declare The ·lory of God: and the firmament sheweth His handywork.

One day telleth another: and one night certifieth another.

There is neither speech nor language: but their voices are heard among them.

Their sound is gone out into all lands: and their words into the ends of the world.

In them hath He set a tabernacle for the Sun: which cometh forth as a bridegroom out of his chamber, and rejoiceth as a giant to run his course.

It goeth forth from the uttermost part of the Heaven: and runneth about unto the end of it again: and there is nothing hid from the heat thereof.

The law of The Lord is an undefiled law, converting the soul: the testimony of The Lord is sure and giveth wisdom unto the simple.

The statutes of The Lord are right and rejoice the heart: the commandment of The Lord is pure and giveth light unto the eyes.

The fear of The Lord is clean and endureth for ever:

the judgements of The Lord are true, and righteous altogether.

More to be desired are they than gold, yea, than much fine gold: sweeter also than honey, and the honey-comb.

Moreover, by them is Thy servant taught: and in keeping of them there is great reward.

Who can tell how oft he offendeth: O cleanse Thou me from my secret faults.

Keep Thy servant also from presumptuous sins, lest they get the dominion over me: so shall I be undefiled, and innocent from the great offence.

Let the words of my mouth, and the meditation of my heart: be alway acceptable in Thy sight.

O Lord!: my Strength, and my Redeemer.

Psalm xxiv.—*Domini est terra.*

The Earth is The Lord's, and all that therein is: the compass of the world, and they that dwell therein.

For He hath founded it upon the seas: and prepared it upon the floods.

Who shall ascend into the hill of The Lord: or who shall rise up in His Holy Place?

Even he that hath clean hands, and a pure heart: and that hath not lift up his mind unto vanity, nor sworn to deceive his neighbour.

He shall receive the blessing from The Lord: and righteousness from The God of his salvation.

This is the generation of them that seek Him: even of them that seek Thy face, O Jacob!

Lift up your heads, O ye gates, and be ye lift up, ye everlasting doors: and The King of Glory shall come in.

Who is The King of Glory?: it is The Lord strong and mighty, even The Lord mighty in battle.

Lift up your heads, O ye gates, and be ye lift up, ye everlasting doors: and The King of Glory shall come in.

Who is The King of Glory?: even The Lord of Hosts, He is the King of Glory.

Antiphon.

Blessed art thou among women, and blessed is The Fruit of thy womb.

℣. The Holy Mother of God, ever Virgin,

℟. Intercede for us unto The Lord our God.

Our Father.

Psalm xlv.—*Eructavit cor meum.*

My heart is inditing of a good matter: I ſpeak of the things which I have made unto The King.

My tongue is the pen: of a ready writer.

Thou art fairer than the children of men: full of grace are Thy lips, becauſe God hath bleſſed Thee for ever.

Gird Thee with Thy ſword upon Thy thigh, O Thou moſt Mighty: according to Thy worſhip and renown.

Good luck have Thou with Thine honour: ride on, becauſe of the word of truth, of meekneſs, and righteouſneſs; and Thy right hand ſhall teach Thee terrible things.

Thine arrows are very ſharp, and the people ſhall be ſubdued unto Thee: even in the midſt among the King's enemies.

Thy ſeat, O God! endureth for ever: the ſceptre of Thy kingdom is a right ſceptre.

Thou haſt loved righteouſneſs, and hated iniquity: wherefore God, even Thy God, hath anointed Thee with the oil of gladneſs above Thy fellows.

All Thy garments ſmell of myrrh, aloes, and caſſia: out of the ivory palaces, whereby they have made Thee glad.

Kings' daughters were among Thy honourable women: upon Thy right hand did ſtand the Queen in a veſture of gold, wrought about with divers colours.

Hearken, O daughter, and conſider, incline thine ear: forget alſo thine own people, and thy father's houſe.

So ſhall The King have pleaſure in thy beauty: for He is thy Lord God, and worſhip Thou Him.

And the daughter of Tyre ſhall be there with a gift: like as the rich alſo among the people ſhall make their ſupplication before thee.

The King's daughter is all glorious within: her clothing is of wrought gold.

She ſhall be brought unto The King in raiment of needlework: the virgins that be her fellows ſhall bear her company, and ſhall be brought unto thee.

With joy and gladneſs ſhall they be brought: and ſhall enter into The King's palace.

Inſtead of thy fathers thou ſhalt have children: whom

thou mayest make princes in all lands.

I will remember Thy Name from one generation to another : therefore shall the people give thanks unto Thee world without end.

Psalm xlvi.—*Deus noster refugium.*

God is our hope and strength: a very present help in trouble.

Therefore will we not fear, though the earth be moved : and though the hills be carried into the midst of the sea.

Though the waters thereof rage and swell : and though the mountains shake at the tempest of the same.

The rivers of the flood thereof shall make glad the City of God: the holy place of the tabernacle of The Most Highest.

God is in the midst of her, therefore shall she not be removed: God shall help her, and that right early.

The heathen make much ado, and the kingdoms are moved : but God hath shewed His Voice, and the earth shall melt away.

The Lord of Hosts is with us : The God of Jacob is our refuge.

O come hither, and behold the works of The Lord : what destruction He hath brought upon the earth.

He maketh wars to cease in all the world: He breaketh the bow, and knappeth the spear in sunder, and burneth the chariots in the fire.

Be still then, and know that I am God: I will be exalted among the heathen, and I will be exalted in the earth.

The Lord of hosts is with us : The God of Jacob is our refuge.

Psalm lxxxvii.—*Fundamenta ejus.*

Her foundations are upon the holy hills: The Lord loveth the gates of Sion more than all the dwellings of Jacob.

Very excellent things are spoken of thee : thou City of God.

I will think upon Rahab and Babylon : with them that know me.

Behold ye the Philistines also : and they of Tyre, with the Morians ; lo, there was He born.

And of Sion it shall be reported that He was born in her : and The Most High shall stablish her.

The Lord ſhall rehearſe it when He writeth up the people: that He was born there.

The ſingers alſo and trumpeters ſhall he rehearſe: All my freſh ſprings ſhall be in thee.

Psalm xcvi.—*Cantate Domini.*

O sing unto The Lord a new ſong: ſing unto The Lord, all the whole earth.

Sing unto The Lord, and praiſe His Name: be telling of His ſalvation from day to day.

Declare His honour unto the heathen: and His wonders unto all people.

For The Lord is great, and cannot worthily be praiſed: He is more to be feared than all gods.

As for all the gods of the heathen, they are but idols: but it is The Lord that made the heavens.

Glory and worſhip are before Him: power and honour are in His ſanctuary.

Aſcribe unto The Lord, O ye kindreds of the people: aſcribe unto The Lord worſhip and power.

Aſcribe unto The Lord the honour due unto His Name: bring preſents, and come into his courts.

O worſhip The Lord in the beauty of Holineſs: let the whole earth ſtand in awe of Him.

Tell it out among the heathen that The Lord is King: and that it is He who hath made the round world ſo faſt that it cannot be moved; and how that He ſhall judge the people righteouſly.

Let the heavens rejoice, and let the earth be glad: let the ſea make a noiſe, and all that therein is.

Let the field be joyful, and all that is in it: then ſhall all the trees of the wood rejoice before The Lord.

For He cometh, for He cometh to judge the earth: and with righteouſneſs to judge the world, and the people with His truth.

Psalm xcvii.—*Dominus regnavit.*

The Lord is King, the earth may be glad thereof: yea, the multitude of the iſles may be glad thereof.

Clouds and darkneſs are round about Him: righteouſneſs and judgement are the habitation of His ſeat.

There ſhall go a fire before Him: and burn up His enemies on every ſide.

His lightnings gave ſhine unto the world: the earth ſaw it, and was afraid.

The hills melted like wax at the preſence of The Lord: at the preſence of The Lord of the whole earth.

The Heavens have declared His righteouſneſs: and all the people have ſeen His Glory.

Confounded be all they that worſhip carved images, and that delight in vain gods: worſhip Him, all ye gods.

Sion heard of it, and rejoiced: and the daughters of Judah were glad, becauſe of Thy judgements, O Lord!

For Thou, Lord, art higher than all that are in the earth: Thou art exalted far above all gods.

O ye that love The Lord, ſee that ye hate the thing which is evil: The Lord preſerveth the ſouls of His ſaints; He ſhall deliver them from the hand of the ungodly.

There is ſprung up a light for the righteous: and joyful gladneſs for ſuch as are true-hearted.

Rejoice in The Lord, ye righteous: and give thanks for a remembrance of His holineſs.

Pſalm xcviii.—*Cantate Domino.*

O sing unto The Lord a new ſong: for He hath done marvellous things.

With His own Right Hand, and with His holy arm: hath He gotten himſelf the victory.

The Lord declared His ſalvation: His righteouſneſs hath He openly ſhewed in the ſight of the heathen.

He hath remembered His mercy and truth toward the houſe of Iſrael: and all the ends of the earth have ſeen the ſalvation of our God.

Shew yourſelves joyful unto The Lord, all ye lands: ſing, rejoice, and give thanks.

Praiſe The Lord upon the harp: ſing to the harp with a pſalm of thankſgiving.

With trumpets alſo, and ſhawms: O ſhew yourſelves joyful before The Lord The King.

Let the ſea make a noiſe, and all that therein is: the round world, and they that dwell therein.

Let the floods clap their hands, and let the hills be joyful together before The Lord for He is come to judge the earth,

With righteousness shall He judge the world: and the people with equity.

Psalm xxi.—*Domine, in virtute tua.*

The King shall rejoice in Thy strength, O Lord!: exceeding glad shall He be of thy salvation.

Thou hast given Him His heart's desire: and hast not denied Him the request of His lips.

For Thou shalt prevent Him with the blessings of goodness: and shalt set a crown of pure gold upon His head.

He asked life of Thee, and Thou gavest Him a long life: even for ever and ever.

His honour is great in Thy salvation: glory and great worship shalt Thou lay upon Him.

For Thou shalt give Him everlasting felicity: and make Him glad with the joy of Thy countenance.

And why? because the King putteth his trust in The Lord: and in the mercy of The Most Highest He shall not miscarry.

All Thine enemies shall feel Thy hand: Thy right hand shall find out them that hate Thee.

Thou shalt make them like a fiery oven in time of Thy wrath: The Lord shall destroy them in His displeasure, and the fire shall consume them.

Their fruit shalt thou root out of the earth: and their seed from among the children of men.

For they intended mischief against Thee: and imagined such a device as they are not able to perform.

Therefore shalt Thou put them to flight: and the strings of Thy bow shalt Thou make ready against the face of them.

Be Thou exalted, Lord, in Thine own strength: so will we sing, and praise Thy power.

Psalm xxvii.—*Dominus illuminatio.*

The Lord is my light, and my salvation; whom then shall I fear: The Lord is the strength of my life; of whom then shall I be afraid?

When the wicked, even mine enemies, and my foes, came upon me to eat up my flesh: they stumbled and fell.

Though an host of men

were laid againſt me, yet ſhall not my heart be afraid : and though there roſe up war againſt me, yet will I put my truſt in Him.

One thing have I deſired of The Lord, which I will require : even that I may dwell in the houſe of The Lord all the days of my life, to behold the fair beauty of The Lord, and to viſit His temple.

For in the time of trouble He ſhall hide me in His tabernacle : yea, in the ſecret place of His dwelling ſhall He hide me, and ſet me up upon a rock of ſtone.

And now ſhall He lift up mine head : above mine enemies round about me.

Therefore will I offer in His dwelling an oblation with great gladneſs : I will ſing, and ſpeak praiſes unto The Lord.

Hearken unto my voice, O Lord! when I cry unto Thee : have mercy upon me, and hear me.

My heart hath talked of Thee, Seek ye My Face : Thy Face, Lord, will I ſeek.

O hide not Thou thy Face from me : nor caſt Thy ſervant away in diſpleaſure.

Thou haſt been my ſuccour : leave me not, neither forſake me, O God of my ſalvation!

When my father and my mother forſake me : The Lord taketh me up.

Teach me Thy way, O Lord! : and lead me in the right way, becauſe of mine enemies.

Deliver me not over into the will of mine adverſaries : for there are falſe witneſſes riſen up againſt me, and ſuch as ſpeak wrong.

I ſhould utterly have fainted : but that I believe verily to ſee the goodneſs of The Lord in the land of the living.

O tarry Thou The Lord's leiſure : be ſtrong, and He ſhall comfort thine heart; and put thou thy truſt in The Lord.

Leſſon I.—Isaiah ii.

There ſhall come forth a Rod from the root of Jeſſe, and a Flower from his root, ſhall grow up. And The Spirit of The Lord ſhall reſt upon Him; The Spirit of Wiſdom, and Underſtanding; The Spirit of Counſel and Ghoſtly Strength; The Spirit of Knowledge and Piety; and The Spirit of the Fear of The Lord, shall fill Him. Thus saith the Lord.

℟. The Angel Gabriel was sent to Mary, a Virgin espoused to Joseph, announcing to her the Word; and the Virgin trembled at the light. Fear not, Mary! thou hast found favour with The Lord; Behold, thou shalt conceive, and bring forth; and He shall be called The Son of The Highest.

℣. And The Lord God shall give unto Him the throne of His father David, and He shall reign over the House of Jacob for evermore. And He shall be called The Son of The Highest.

Lesson II.

He shall not judge after the sight of His eyes, nor reprove after the hearing of His ears; but with righteousness shall He judge the poor, and reprove with equity for the meek of the earth. And He shall smite the earth with the rod of His mouth, and with the breath of His lips shall He slay the wicked. And righteousness shall be the girdle of His loins, and faithfulness the cincture of His reins. Thus saith The Lord.

℟. Hail! thou that art full of grace; The Lord is with thee. The Holy Ghost shall come in upon thee, and the Virtue of The Most Highest shall overshadow thee; wherefore that Holy Thing which shall be born of thee, shall be called The Son of God.

℣. How shall this thing be, seeing I know not a man? And the Angel answering said unto her,

The Holy Ghost shall come in upon thee, and the Virtue of The Most Highest shall overshadow thee; wherefore that Holy Thing which shall be born of Thee shall be called The Son of God.

Lesson III.—Isaiah vii.

The Lord spake unto Achaz, saying, Ask thee a sign of The Lord thy God, in the depth of Hell or in the height above. And Achaz said, I will not ask, neither will I tempt The Lord. And He said, Hear ye now, O house of David! is it a small thing for you to weary men, that ye be weary of thy God alſo? Therefore The Lord Himſelf ſhall give you a Sign: Behold, a Virgin ſhall conceive, and bear a Son. His name ſhall be called Emmanuel. Butter and honey ſhall He eat, that He may know to refuſe the evil and to chooſe the good. Thus ſaith The Lord.

℟. Receive The Word, O Virgin Mary! which unto thee from The Lord by the Angel hath been ſent. Thou ſhalt conceive by thine ear, thou ſhalt bring forth God and Man, that thou mayeſt be called Bleſſed among all women.

℣. Thou ſhalt bring forth a Son; but of thy virginity thou ſhalt ſuffer no hurt; thou ſhalt be with child, yet abide a mother inviolate.

℟. That thou mayeſt be called Bleſſed among all women.

℣. Glory be to The Father, and to The Son, and to The Holy Ghoſt.

℟. That thou mayeſt be called Bleſſed among all women.

Other Lessons.

Leſſon I.

The Angel Gabriel was ſent by God to a city of Galilee, the name of which was Nazareth, to a Virgin eſpouſed to a man whoſe name was Joſeph, of the houſe of David; and the name of the Virgin was Mary. To Mary then, a Virgin, is Gabriel ſent, who is called "The Might of God." He came to announce Him Who vouchſafed to appear in humility, to ſubdue the powers of the air. Concerning Whom it is ſaid by the Pſalmiſt, "The Lord ſtrong and mighty," "The Lord Mighty in battle," And again, "The Lord of Hoſts, He is The King of Glory."

℟. The Angel Gabriel was ſent (*ante, p.* 56).

Leſſon II.

By the Might of God, then, was He to be announced, Who, The Lord of Hoſts ſtrong and mighty in battle, came to war againſt the powers of the air. For many cauſes did The Lord will to be born, not of a ſimple Virgin, but of an eſpouſed one. In the firſt place, that by the lineage of Joſeph (whoſe kinſwoman Mary was) the family of Mary might be known alſo; for it is not the cuſtom of Scripture to detail the genealogy of women. For of both it may be underſtood when it is ſaid Of the houſe of David.

℟. Hail! thou that art *(ante, p. 56)*.

Leſſon III.

Again, that ſhe might not be ſtoned as an adultereſs by the Jews, preferring that ſome ſhould doubt of His origin, rather than of the chaſtity of His parents; at the ſame time depriving immodeſt virgins of all pretence for ſaying that the Mother of The Saviour was ſlandered by falſe ſuſpicions. In the third place, that when going into Egypt, and thence returning, ſhe might have the comfort of a huſband, who might become at once the guardian and the witneſs of her very entire virginity. In the fourth place, that her Offspring might not be diſcloſed to the Devil, and he might not know Him as born of a Virgin, and perhaps as more eminent than other men might fear to betray Him to death.

℟. Receive The Word *(ante, p. 57)*.

Leſſon I.

St. Auguſt. Sermon 35, *De Sanctis* 3.

Let us ſpeak, deareſt brethren, ſomething in praiſe of the moſt ſacred Virgin Mary. But what ſhall we who are ſo little, who are ſuch dwarfs in ſtrength, what can we ſpeak in her praiſe, when even if all our members were turned into tongues we ſhould not ſuffice to praiſe her. For ſhe is ſublimer than the Heavens, deeper than the abyſs, of whom we attempt to ſpeak. For God, Whom creation cannot contain, ſhe carried in her immaculate womb. For ſhe only it is who hath been found worthy to be called the Mother and Spouſe of Chriſt. She was the means of reſtoring the ruin of our firſt mother. She was the channel of Redemption to loſt man.

℟. Holy and immaculate Virginity! with what praiſes to addreſs thee I know not. For Him, Whom the Heavens cannot contain, thou haſt carried in thy boſom.

℣. Bleſſed art thou among women, and bleſſed is The Fruit of thy womb.

For Him, Whom the Heavens cannot contain, thou haſt carried in thy boſom.

Leſſon II.

For the mother of our race brought woe into the world; the Mother of our Lord Jeſus Chriſt brought forth Salvation to the world. Eve augmented our ſin; Mary was the means of increaſing our righteouſneſs. Eve by ſlaying injured us; Mary by quickening helped us: the one wounded, the other healed; for ſhe in a wonderful and ineffable manner, brought forth The Saviour of all men, and of herſelf. For how holy muſt have been that Virgin to whom The Holy Spirit vouchſafed to come! How beautiful, whom God choſe for His Spouſe! How chaſte, that ſhe ſhould be a Virgin after giving birth. For ſhe was the Temple of God, a Fountain ſealed, a Gate cloſed in the Houſe of The Lord. Upon her, as I have ſaid, The Holy Ghoſt deſcended; her did the Virtue of The Moſt High overſhadow. She was undefiled by man, fruitful in child-bearing. A Virgin at her breaſt nurturing the Food of God and men. Deſervedly, then, is The Moſt Bleſſed Virgin Mary extolled with eſpecial praiſes by us, who was the ſource of this wonderful benefit to the world, and was laſtly ſo exalted to celeſtial dignity that ſhe received The Word, Who was in the beginning with God, from His ſupernal Throne in Heaven.

℟. Bleſſed art thou, Virgin Mary, who didſt bear The Lord, The Creator of the world; who didſt bring forth Him Who made thee and for evermore abideſt a Virgin.

℣. Hail! thou that art full of grace, The Lord is with thee.

Who didſt bring forth Him Who made thee and evermore abideſt a Virgin.

Leſſon III.

O happy Mary! and moſt worthy of all praiſe! O glorious Mother! O ſublime Parent! to whoſe boſom the Author of Heaven and earth is entrusted. O happy kisses impressed by the lips of the Babe! when among the many tokens of His early infancy, as a true Son of thine, He sported with thee. Yet true God, and begotten of God His Father, He ruled thee. For thou conceiving in time, didst bring forth thy Maker, Who was before all time thy Creator. O happy Birth! joyous to Angels, longed for by Saints, necessary to the lost, profitable to us exiles; Who after many injuries, in that Flesh which He had taken upon Him, was at the last beaten with stripes, made to drink vinegar and gall, nailed to the Cross, that by suffering He might shew Himself to be true Man.

℟. For thou art happy, O holy Virgin Mary! and most worthy of praise, for from thee hath arisen The Sun of Righteousness, Christ our God!

℣. May'st thou pray for the people and the clergy, and intercede for the devout female sex. May all perceive thy assistance who celebrate thy memory.

For from thee hath arisen The Sun of Righteousness, Christ our God!

Glory be to The Father.

Christ our God.

Lesson I.

There stood near the Cross of Jesus, His Mother, and the sister of His Mother, Mary the wife of Cleophas, and Mary Magdalene. When therefore He saw His Mother and the Disciple standing near whom He loved, He said unto His Mother, 'Woman, behold thy Son!' Then He said to the Disciple, 'Behold thy Mother.' And from that Hour the Disciple took her to his own home.

℟. Holy and immaculate *(ante, p. 58)*.

Alleluya.

Lesson II.

This verily is that Hour of which Jesus when about to turn the water into wine spake to His Mother, What to Me and thee is it, O Lady? Mine Hour is not yet come. He foretold that Hour, then, which had not yet come, wherein about to die, He would acknowledge of Whom

He was born, according to His mortality. For then when about to perform divine things, he reprehended her as unknown and the Mother not of His Divinity, but of His infirmity. But now when He was ſuffering human things, He commended her with human affection of whom He had been made Man. For then He, Who had created Mary, was exerciſing His power; but now He, Whom Mary had brought forth, was hanging on The Croſs.

℟. Bleſſed art thou *(ante, p. 59)*.
Alleluya.

Leſſon III.

A MORAL leſſon is, then, here taught us, which He admoniſheth us to perform. And by His own example, The Good Teacher inſtructed His diſciples that good children ſhould take care of their parents. So that the Tree upon which His dying limbs were nailed became alſo the chair of the Inſtructor to teach us. From this wholeſome doctrine the Apoſtle Paul taught, when he ſaid, If any man provide not for his own, eſpecially for them of his own houſehold, he denieth the faith, and is worſe than an infidel. For what is ſo much of a man's own houſe, as parents to their ſons, or ſons to their parents? Of this moſt ſalutary precept, He Himſelf, The Maſter of Saints, ſet us an example here in His own Perſon, when He provided another ſon for her inſtead of Himſelf; not, as being God, for a ſervant whom He had created and ruled, but, as being Man, for a Mother of whom He had been born, and whom He was leaving behind Him.

℟. For thou art happy, *(ante, p. 60)*.
Alleluya.

The Canticle of S. Ambroſe and S. Auguſtine.

THEE God we praiſe: Thee The Lord we confeſs.

Thee Eternal Father: All the Earth doth worſhip.

To Thee all Angels: To Thee the Heavens and the univerſal Powers;

To Thee Cherubim and Seraphim with ceaſeleſs voice do cry;

Holy, Holy, Holy: Lord God of Sabaoth.

Full are the Heavens, and the Earth: of the Majesty of Thy Glory.

Thee the glorious Choir of the Apostles,

Thee the laudable Company of Prophets,

Thee the Martyrs' white-robed Army doth praise.

Thee throughout the orb of the world: The Holy Church doth confess;

The Father of Infinite Majesty,

Thy Venerable, True, and Only Son,

Also The Holy Ghost, The Paraclete.

Thou art King of Glory: O Christ!

Thou of The Father: art The everlasting Son.

Thou, when taking upon Thee to deliver man: didst not abhor the Virgin's womb.

Thou having overcome the sting of Death: hast opened to believers the Kingdom of Heaven.

Thou at the Right Hand of God sittest: in the Glory of The Father.

Our Judge we believe that Thou shalt come to be.

We therefore pray Thee help Thy servants: whom Thou hast redeemed with Thy precious Blood.

Make them to be numbered with Thy Saints: in Glory everlasting.

Give Salvation unto Thy people O Lord!: and bless thine heritage.

And govern them: and lift them up even for evermore.

Day by day: we magnify Thee.

And we praise Thy Name for ever: and for ever and ever.

Vouchsafe O Lord! in this day: to keep us without sin.

Have mercy upon us O Lord!: have mercy upon us.

Let Thy mercy O Lord! be upon us: like as we have put our trust in Thee.

In Thee O Lord! have I trusted: let me not be confounded for ever.

¶ *At LAUDS.*

O GOD! make speed to save me.

O Lord! make haste to help me.

Glory be to The Father.

As it was in the beginning.

Psalm xciii.—*Dominus regnavit.*

The Lord is King, and hath put on glorious apparel: The Lord hath put on His apparel, and girded Himſelf with ſtrength.

He hath made the round world ſo ſure: that it cannot be moved.

Ever ſince the world began hath Thy ſeat been prepared: Thou art from everlaſting.

The floods are riſen, O Lord! the floods have lift up their voice: the floods lift up their waves.

The waves of the ſea are mighty, and rage horribly: but yet The Lord, Who dwelleth on high, is mightier.

Thy teſtimonies, O Lord! are very ſure: holineſs becometh Thine houſe for ever.

Psalm c.—*Jubilate Deo.*

O be joyful in The Lord, all ye lands: ſerve The Lord with gladneſs, and come before His preſence with a ſong.

Be ye ſure that The Lord He is God: it is He that hath made us and not we ourſelves; we are His people, and the ſheep of His paſture.

O go your way into His gates with thankſgiving, and into His courts with praiſe: be thankful unto Him, and ſpeak good of His Name.

For The Lord is gracious, His mercy is everlaſting: and His truth endureth from generation to generation.

Psalm lxiii.—*Deus, Deus, meus.*

O God! Thou art my God: early will I ſeek Thee.

My ſoul thirſteth for Thee, my fleſh alſo longeth after Thee: in a barren and dry land where no water is.

Thus have I looked for Thee in holineſs: that I might behold Thy power and glory.

For Thy loving-kindneſs is better than the life itſelf: my lips ſhall praiſe Thee.

As long as I live will I magnify Thee in this manner: and lift up my hands in Thy Name.

My ſoul ſhall be ſatisfied, even as it were with marrow and fatneſs: when my mouth praiſeth Thee with joyful lips.

Have I not remembered Thee in my bed: and thought upon Thee when I was waking?

Becauſe Thou haſt been my helper: therefore under the

ſhadow of Thy wings will I rejoice.

My ſoul hangeth upon Thee: Thy Right Hand hath upholden me.

Theſe alſo that ſeek the hurt of my ſoul: they ſhall go under the earth.

Let them fall upon the edge of the ſword: that they may be a portion for foxes.

But the King ſhall rejoice in God; all they alſo that ſwear by Him ſhall be commended: for the mouth of them that ſpeak lies ſhall be ſtopped.

Psalm lxvii.—*Deus miſereatur.*

God be merciful unto us, and bleſs us: and ſhew us the light of His countenance, and be merciful unto us;

That Thy way may be known upon earth: Thy ſaving health among all nations.

Let the people praiſe Thee, O God!: yea, let all the people praiſe Thee.

O let the nations rejoice and be glad: for Thou ſhalt judge the folk righteouſly, and govern the nations upon earth.

Let the people praiſe Thee, O God!: let all the people praiſe Thee.

Then ſhall the earth bring forth her increaſe: and God, even our own God, ſhall give us His bleſſing.

God ſhall bleſs us: and all the ends of the earth ſhall fear Him.

Psalm xcii.—*Bonum eſt confiteri.*

It is a good thing to give thanks unto The Lord: and to ſing praiſes unto Thy Name, O Moſt Higheſt.

To tell of Thy loving-kindneſs early in the morning: and of Thy truth in the night-ſeaſon;

Upon an inſtrument of ten ſtrings, and upon the lute: upon a loud inſtrument, and upon the harp.

For Thou, Lord, haſt made me glad through thy works: and I will rejoice in giving praiſe for the operations of Thy hands.

O Lord, how glorious are Thy works: Thy thoughts are very deep.

An unwiſe man doth not well conſider this: and a fool doth not underſtand it.

When the ungodly are green as the graſs, and when all the workers of wickedneſs do flouriſh: then ſhall they be deſtroyed for ever; but Thou, Lord, art The moſt Higheſt for evermore.

For Lo! Thine enemies, O Lord! Lo! Thine enemies ſhall periſh: and all the workers of wickedneſs ſhall be deſtroyed.

But mine horn ſhall be exalted like the horn of an unicorn: for I am anointed with freſh oil.

Mine eye alſo ſhall ſee his luſt of mine enemies: and mine ear ſhall hear his deſire of the wicked that ariſe up againſt me.

The righteous ſhall flouriſh like a palm-tree: and ſhall ſpread abroad like a cedar in Libanus.

Such as are planted in the Houſe of The Lord: ſhall flouriſh in the courts of the Houſe of our God.

They alſo ſhall bring forth more fruit in their age: and ſhall be fat and well-liking.

That they may ſhew how true The Lord my Strength is: and that there is no unrighteouſneſs in Him.

Canticle of the Three Children.

Benedicite omnia opera.

BLESS ye The Lord all ye works of The Lord: praiſe Him and highly exalt Him for ever.

Bleſs ye The Lord all ye Angels of The Lord: bleſs ye The Lord O ye Heavens.

Bleſs ye The Lord all ye Waters that are above the Heavens: bleſs ye The Lord all ye Powers of The Lord.

Bleſs ye The Lord O ye Sun and Moon: bleſs ye The Lord all ye Winds of God.

Bleſs ye The Lord O ye Fire and Heat: bleſs ye The Lord O ye Winter and Summer.

Bleſs ye The Lord O ye Dews and Hoar Froſt: bleſs ye The Lord O ye Froſt and Cold.

Bleſs ye The Lord O ye Ice and Snows: bleſs ye The Lord O ye Nights and Days.

Bleſs ye The Lord O ye Light and Darkneſs: bleſs ye The Lord O ye Lightnings and Clouds.

Let The Earth bleſs The Lord: praiſe Him and highly exalt Him for ever.

Bleſs ye The Lord O ye Mountains and Hills: bleſs ye The Lord all ye growing Things upon the earth.

Bleſs ye The Lord O ye

Fountains : bleſs ye The Lord O ye Seas and Floods.

Bleſs ye The Lord ye Whales and all that move in the Waters : bleſs ye The Lord all ye Fowls of Heaven.

Bleſs ye The Lord all ye Beaſts and Cattle : bleſs ye The Lord O ye Children of men.

Let Iſrael bleſs The Lord : praiſe Him and highly exalt Him for ever.

Bleſs ye The Lord O ye Prieſts of The Lord : bleſs ye The Lord O ye Servants of The Lord.

Bleſs ye The Lord O ye Spirits and Souls of the righteous : bleſs ye The Lord all ye Holy and Humble in heart.

Bleſs ye The Lord O Ananias, Azarias, and Miſael : praiſe Him and highly exalt Him for ever.

Bleſs we The Father and The Son with The Holy Ghoſt : let us praiſe Him and highly exalt Him for ever.

Bleſſed be Thou O Lord ! in the firmament of Heaven : worthy to be praiſed and glorious and highly exalted for ever.

Psalm cxlviii.—*Laudate Dominum.*

O praise The Lord of Heaven : praiſe Him in the height.

Praiſe Him, all ye Angels of His : praiſe Him, all His Hoſt.

Praiſe Him, Sun and Moon : praiſe Him, all ye ſtars and light.

Praiſe Him, all ye Heavens : and ye waters that are above the Heavens.

Let them praiſe the Name of The Lord : for He ſpake the word, and they were made ; He commanded, and they were created.

He hath made them faſt for ever and ever : He hath given them a law which ſhall not be broken.

Praiſe The Lord upon earth : ye dragons, and all deeps ;

Fire and hail, ſnow and vapours : wind and ſtorm, fulfilling His word ;

Mountains and all hills : fruitful trees and all cedars ;

Beaſts and all cattle : worms and feathered fowls ;

Kings of the earth and all people : princes and all judges of the world ;

Young men and maidens, old men and children, praiſe

the Name of The Lord: for His Name only is excellent, and His praiſe above heaven and earth.

He ſhall exalt the horn of His people; all His Saints ſhall praiſe Him: even the children of Iſrael, even the people that ſerveth him.

Psalm cxlix.—*Cantate Domino.*

O sing unto The Lord a new ſong: let the congregation of Saints praiſe Him.

Let Iſrael rejoice in Him that made him: and let the children of Syon be joyful in their King.

Let them praiſe His Name in the dance: let them ſing praiſes unto Him with tabret and harp.

For The Lord hath pleaſure in His people: and helpeth the meek-hearted.

Let the Saints be joyful with glory: let them rejoice in their beds.

Let the praiſes of God be in their mouth: and a two-edged ſword in their hands;

To be avenged of the heathen: and to rebuke the people.

To bind their kings in chains: and their nobles with links of iron.

That they may be avenged of them as it is written: ſuch honour have all His Saints.

Psalm cl.—*Cantate Domino.*

O praiſe God in His Holineſs: praiſe Him in the firmament of His Power.

Praiſe Him in His noble acts: praiſe Him according to His excellent greatneſs.

Praiſe Him in the ſound of the trumpet: praiſe Him upon the lute and harp.

Praiſe Him in the cymbals and dances: praiſe Him upon the ſtrings and pipe.

Praiſe Him upon the well-tuned cymbals: praiſe Him upon the loud cymbals.

Let every thing that hath breath: praiſe The Lord.

Glory be to The Father.

As it was in the beginning.

Antiphon.

O wonderful exchange! The Creator of Mankind, taking upon him a living body, vouchſafed to be born of a Virgin, and proceeding forth as Man, beſtowed upon us His Divinity.

Chapters.

Now it is high time to awake out of ſleep, for now is our ſalvation nearer than when we believed. The night is far ſpent, the day is at hand; let us therefore caſt off the works of darkneſs and put on us the Armour of Light.

The kindneſs of God our Saviour hath appeared unto all men; teaching us that denying ungodlineſs and worldly luſts, we ſhould live ſoberly, righteouſly and godly in this preſent world.

O the depth of the riches of the wiſdom and knowledge of God! for of Him and to Him and through Him are all things. To Him be Glory for evermore. Amen.

Bleſſing, and Glory, and Wiſdom, and Thankſgiving, and Honour, and Power, and Might, be unto our God for ever and ever. Amen.

As ſtrangers and pilgrims abſtain from fleſhly luſts which war againſt the ſoul; having your converſation honeſt among the Gentiles, that by your good works which they behold they may glorify God

Be ye followers of God as dear children, and walk in love as Chriſt alſo hath loved us, and gave Himſelf for us, an Offering and a Sacrifice to God for a ſweet-ſmelling ſavour.

If ye then be riſen with Chriſt ſeek thoſe things which are above where Chriſt ſitteth at the Right Hand of God. Set your affections on things above, not on things on the earth; for ye are dead, and your life is hid with Chriſt in God.

If a man love Me he will keep My words, and My Father will love him, and we will come unto him and make Our abode with him.

The Comforter which is The Holy Ghoſt Whom The Father will ſend in My Name He ſhall teach you all things.

Now ye are no more ſtrangers and pilgrims but fellow citizens with the Saints and of the Houſehold of God, and are built upon the foundation of the Apoſtles and Prophets, Jeſus Chriſt Himſelf being the Head Corner-ſtone.

Hymn.

Maria Mater Domini.

O Mary! Mother of Thy Lord!
The Father's Son, Eternal God;
As all thy bleſſedneſs we ſing,
May He to us deliverance bring.

Him God of God, Divinely born
Thou didſt bring forth, The Only
 Son;
And He who ne'er began to be,
Exiſtence yet derived from thee.

This was the fair and wondrous Birth
For ever celebrate on earth,
Which far-eyed Prophet Seers of old
In ſacred uniſon foretold.

Now is the Archangel Gabriel ſent
A Herald from the firmament;
The Son of God, Elect, he names,
And thus Heaven's beniſon pro-
 claims.

"Hail Mary! evermore renowned,
With God's eternal favour crowned;
Thou by The Spirit ſhalt conceive,
And bring forth That thou doſt be-
 lieve.

And thou, O Virgin! bleſt ſhall be
Through ages everlaſtingly;
How honoured, and how paſſing fair,
All generations ſhall declare.

For He Who framed the worlds doth
 reſt
An inmate of thy ſacred breaſt;
He in thy ſpotleſs boſom lies,
Whom Earth and Heaven cannot
 compriſe."

Born for our ſakes, from Heaven a-
 bove
He came, and ſaved us by His love;
For us the Croſs of Death He bore,
And we through Him live evermore.

Lord, Holy Virgin born! to Thee
All Glory everlaſting be;
To Father and to Holy Ghoſt,
Long as eternity ſhall laſt! Amen.

Œterna Cœli Gloria.

Eternal Glory of the Heaven!
Thou ſureſt hope to mortals given!
Son of the Higheſt! God moſt bleſt!
Pure Offspring of a Virgin chaſte;

Uplift us with Thine Arm of might;
So may our ſouls riſe clear and bright;
So with the praiſe of God inflame
And ſpeak thankſgivings to His
 Name.

Refulgent beams the Morning Star
And ſcatters orient light afar,
The darkneſs of the night departs,
O Holy Light illume our hearts;

Within our ſenſes ever dwell,
All worldly darkneſs thence expel;
Long as the days of life endure
Preſerve our minds devout and pure.

The Faith of old by Saints poſſeſſed
Root deep within our inmoſt breaſt;
Let Hope with joy triumphant glow,
And Charity in fervour grow.

To God The Father Glory be,
Like Glory, Only Son! to Thee,
And to The Spirit Paraclete
Now and through ages infinite.
Amen.

Jeſu dulcedo cordium.

Jesu! delight of every heart! [art;
Life's Fountain, Lamp of ſouls Thou
Who doſt all other joys exceed
Contenting every wiſh and need!

Be with us, Lord! our mental gloom
With all Thy Holy Light illume;
Diſperſe the oppreſſive ſhades of ni
Creation with Thy ſweetneſs fi

When Thou unto the ravished heart
Dost Thy celestial Truth impart,
How mean earth's vanities appear;
But loving Charity, how dear!

O Jesus! cause us here below
The riches of Thy Truth to know;
Then in Thy blissful presence place,
To see Thy Glory face to face.

Thy sweetness they alone discern
Who with Thy love celestial burn;
Blest! who are kindled with that fire
And naught beyond that bliss desire.

Light of our promised Paradise!
Jesu! Thou Sun of Grace arise!
Chase all our clouds of grief away,
And cheer us with Thy glorious Day.
Amen.

ℭ *The Canticle of Zechariah.*

Benedictus.—Luke i. 68.

Blessed be The Lord God of Israel: for He hath visited and redeemed His people;

And hath raised up a mighty salvation for us: in the house of His servant David;

As He spake by the mouth of His holy Prophets: which have been since the world began;

That we should be saved from our enemies: and from the hands of all that hate us;

To perform the mercy promised to our forefathers: and to remember His holy Covenant;

To perform the oath which He sware to our forefather Abraham: that He would give us;

That we being delivered out of the hand of our enemies: might serve Him without fear;

In holiness and righteousness before Him: all the days of our life.

And Thou, Child, shalt be called the Prophet of The Highest: for thou shalt go before the face of The Lord to prepare His ways;

To give knowledge of salvation unto His people: for the remission of their sins,

Through the tender mercy of our God: whereby the Day-spring from on high hath visited us;

To give light to them that sit in darkness, and in the shadow of death: and to guide our feet into the way of peace.

Glory be to The Father.

Antiphon.

The Holy Spirit shall descend upon thee, Mary! Fear not, having in thy womb The Son of God. Alleluya.

Blessed is the womb that

bare Thee and the paps which Thou hast sucked.

℣. O Lord! shew Thy mercy upon us.

℟. And grant us Thy salvation.

Orison.

O Lord God! we beseech Thee, grant that we Thy servants may rejoice in continual health both of mind and body; and helped by the glorious intercessions of The Blessed Mary ever Virgin, and of All Thy Saints, may be delivered from present sorrow, and at the last attain to eternal joys, Through Christ our Lord. Amen.

O God! Who by the Message of an Angel didst will Thy Word to take upon Him flesh in the womb of the Blessed Virgin; grant to us Thy supplicants, that we who truly believe her to be the Mother of God, may with Thee be assisted by her intercessions, Through The Same our Lord Jesus Christ. Amen.

Antiphon.

Behold! Mary hath brought forth a Saviour; Whom when John saw, he exclaimed, saying, Behold The Lamb of God! Behold Him! that taketh away the sin of the world. Alleluya.

Or this,—

The Root of Jesse hath sprouted forth, there hath arisen a Star from Jacob; a Virgin hath brought a Saviour; we praise Thee O our God!

℣. Beautiful is His form before the sons of men.

℟. Full of Grace are Thy lips.

O Lord we beseech Thee, may the sacred splendour of the Incarnation, Nativity, Resurrection, and Ascension of Thy Son and of the coming of The Holy Ghost with genial beams enlighten our hearts; that we may be enabled to be rid of the darkness of this world, and by their means attain to the land of everlasting brightness Through The Same.

Of The Holy Ghost.

Antiphon.

Come, O Holy Ghost! fulfil the hearts of Thy faithful ones and kindle in them the fire of Thy love.

℣. Send forth Thy Spirit and they ſhall be created.

℟. And Thou ſhalt renew the face of the earth.

God Who didſt teach the hearts of Thy faithful people by The Enlightening of Thy Holy Spirit; grant us by The Same Spirit to have a right judgement in all things, and ever to rejoice in His Holy conſolation Through Chriſt our Lord. Amen.

Of the Holy Trinity.

Antiphon.

DELIVER us, ſave us, juſtify us, O Bleſſed Trinity!

℣. Let The Name of The Lord be bleſſed,

℟. From this time forth even for evermore.

Almighty and everlaſting God! Who haſt given unto us Thy ſervants in the confeſſion of a true faith to acknowledge The Glory of The Eternal Trinity, and in the Power of The Majeſty to worſhip The Unity, we beſeech Thee that by our ſteadfaſtneſs in the ſame Faith we may evermore be defended from all adverſities, Who liveſt and reigneſt God world without end. Amen.

Of the Holy Croſs.

Antiphon.

BUT us it behoveth to glory in The Croſs of our Lord Jeſus Chriſt.

℣. Let all the Earth worſhip Thee O God.

℟. And ſing pſalms unto Thy Name.

God! Who didſt aſcend Thy Holy Croſs and enlighten the darkneſs of the world, do Thou vouchſafe to enlighten our hearts and bodies O Saviour of the world, Who liveſt and reigneſt with God The Father. Amen.

In Lent.

Antiphon.

BE ye converted unto me with all your heart, and with faſting and weeping and mourning, ſaith The Lord.

℣. We have ſinned with our fathers.

℟. We have done amiſs and dealt wickedly.

O Lord! we beſeech Thee mercifully hearken to our prayers, and ſpare all thoſe who confeſs their ſins unto Thee, that of Thy goodneſs Thou mayeſt beſtow upon them pardon as well as peace, Through.

In Easter-tide.
Antiphon.

The Crucified hath arisen from the dead, He hath redeemed us. Alleluya.

℣. Tell ye among the nations

℟. That The Lord hath reigned from the Tree.

God! Who for our sake didst will Thy Son to undergo the suffering of The Cross that Thou mightest expel from us the power of the Enemy, grant to us Thy servants that we may ever live in the joys of His Resurrection Through The Same Jesus Christ our Lord. Amen.

Of Holy Michael Archangel.
Antiphon.

O Michael Archangel! come to help the people of God.

℣. In the sight of the Angels I will sing psalms to Thee my God.

℟. I will worship in Thy Holy Temple and give thanks unto Thy Name.

O God! Who disposest the ministrations of Angels and men in a wonderful order, mercifully grant, that by them who are always ready to do Thee service in Heaven, we may ever be protected in our life upon earth, Through Christ our Lord. Amen.

Of S. John Baptist.
Antiphon.

Among the sons of women there hath not arisen a greater than John Baptist, who prepared the way of The Lord.

℣. There was a man sent from God,

℟. Whose name was John.

Grant we beseech Thee Almighty God that Thy family may walk in the way of salvation; and following the exhortations of the blessed Forerunner John, may attain in safety unto Him Whom he foretold, our Lord Jesus Christ Thy Son, Who with Thee. Amen.

Of S. Peter and S. Paul Apostles.
Antiphon.

Peter the Apostle and Paul the Teacher of the Gentiles; they taught us Thy law O Lord!

℣. Their sound hath gone out into all lands,

℟. And their words unto the ends of the earth.

God! Whose right hand upheld the blessed Apostle Peter when walking on the waves, that he should not be swallowed up, and delivered his fellow Apostle Paul when thrice shipwrecked from the depths of the sea, favourably hearken unto us; and grant that for the sake of both these Thy servants we may obtain of Thee the glories of eternity Through Christ our Lord. Amen.

Of S. Paul Apostle.

Antiphon.

O Glorious Light of all the Churches! more splendid than the Sun; O truly Apostolical and sublime Star! Holy Paul! who didst pour forth the bright beams of the Eternal King upon the darkness of The Gentiles; who whilst yet on earth didst explore the secrets of the Heavens, and foresaw those things which it is not lawful for man to utter! thither may we attain after the death of the body, whom thou hast brought to acknowledge the light of The Truth.

℣. Their sound hath gone out, &c.

God! Who didst teach the universal world by the preaching of the blessed Apostle Paul, grant to us we beseech Thee; that after the example of him whose memory (or Conversion) we this day celebrate, we may at the last attain unto Thee, Through Christ our Lord. Amen.

Of S. Andrew Apostle.

Antiphon.

O Andrew! servant of Christ, worthy Apostle of God, cousin of Peter, comrade in his suffering!

℣. The Lord loved Andrew

℟. In the savour of sweetness.

O Lord! we Thy suppliants beseech Thy Majesty, that like as blessed Andrew the Apostle became a preacher and ruler in Thy Church, so with Thee he may for us be a perpetual intercessor Through Christ our Lord. Amen.

Of S. John the Evangelist.

Antiphon.

This is John Who upon the bosom of The Lord in The Supper leaned. Blessed Apostle! to whom were revealed the heavenly secrets.

℣. Very honourable is the blessed Evangelist S. John;

℟. Who upon the bosom of The Lord in The Supper leaned.

O Lord! we beseech Thee, mercifully to cast light upon Thy Church; that it being enlightened with the doctrine of Thy blessed Apostle and Evangelist S. John may at length attain to the rewards which are everlasting Through Christ our Lord. Amen.

Of S. Laurence Martyr.

Antiphon.

The Deacon Laurence worked a good work who through the sign of the Holy Cross enlightened the blind, and gave the alms of the Church to the poor.

℣. He dispersed abroad, he gave to the poor.

℟. His righteousness remaineth for ever and ever.

Grant we beseech Thee Almighty God that we may extinguish the flames of our vices, Who didst grant to the blessed Laurence to vanquish the torment of his burnings Through Christ our Lord. Amen.

S. Bartholomew.

Almighty and Everlasting God! Who hast given unto us to rejoice this day with holy joy in the Festival of Thine Apostle Bartholomew; grant unto Thy Church to love what he believed, and to preach what he taught, Through.

Of S. Stephen Protomartyr.

Antiphon.

Stephen saw the Heavens opened; he saw and entered in. Blessed was he to whom Heaven was disclosed.

℣. With glory and honour hast Thou crowned him, O Lord!

℟. And hast set him over the works of Thy hands.

Grant to us we beseech Thee O Lord! to imitate what we reverence; that we may learn also to love our enemies by the example of Thy First Martyr, who knew how to pray even for his persecutors unto our Lord Jesus Christ Thy Son, Who with Thee liveth and reigneth world without end. Amen.

Of S. Mary Magdalene.

Antiphon.

MARY anointed the feet of Jesus and wiped them with the hair of her head, and the house was filled with the odour of the ointment.

℣. Mary's sins were forgiven her.

℟. For she loved much.

Grant to us, most gracious Father! that like as the blessed Mary Magdalene by loving Thine Only Begotten above all things obtained pardon; so with her, from Thy mercy we may obtain eternal felicity Through Christ our Lord.

Of All Saints.

Antiphon.

BEHOLD, The Lord shall come and All His Saints with Him, and there shall be in that day a great light. Alleluya.

℣. Behold, The Lord shall appear in the white clouds.

℟. And with Him thousands of His Saints.

O Lord, we beseech Thee purify our consciences by Thy Visitation, so that when Jesus Christ Thy Son our Lord shall come with All His Saints He may find in us a mansion prepared for Himself, Who with Thee liveth and reigneth in The Unity of The Holy Ghost God, world without end. Amen.

Or this,—

Antiphon.

THE Saints shall be joyful in Glory, they shall rejoice in their beds.

℣. Wonderful is God in His Saints.

℟. And Glorious in His Majesty.

Grant we beseech Thee, O Lord! that All Thy Saints may continually pray for us and do Thou vouchsafe ever favourably to hear them Through Christ our Lord. Amen.

Or these:—

Antiphons.

THY Saints, O Lord, shall flourish as the lily. Alleluya. And like as the odour of balsam shall they be before Thee. Alleluya.

Ye Saints and just ones rejoice in The Lord. Alleluya. You hath God chosen as His heritage, for ever. Alleluya.

Within the veil Thy Saints do cry, O Lord! Alleluya, Alleluya, Alleluya.

℣. The voice of joy and exultation

℟. Is in the tabernacles of the righteous. Alleluya.

Grant we beseech Thee, Almighty God, that in the Resurrection of our Lord Jesus Christ, with All His Saints we may in very deed receive our portion, Who with Thee liveth and reigneth in The Unity of The Holy Ghost, God world without end. Amen.

Antiphon.

PRAISE The Lord All ye Saints of His, ye that fear The Lord both small and great; For our Lord God Omnipotent reigneth; Let us rejoice and be glad and give glory to Him.

℣. Ye Saints and just ones rejoice in The Lord.

℟. You hath God chosen as His heritage for ever.

Orison of All Saints.

ALL ye Saints pray for us! O most merciful God! Almighty Creator! Who art Trine and One, Supreme and Infinite, by Whose commands the Universe is governed! have mercy upon us sinners. Spare the offenders. Spare the suppliants. In Thy compassion look not upon our faults but upon the holiness of Thy Saints. Regard, O Lord Jesu Christ! The Virginity and humility of Mary of Thee exceedingly beloved, the perseverance of the Angels, the faith of Patriarchs, the hope of Prophets, the blood of Martyrs, the diligence of Teachers, the zeal of Confessors, the tears of Penitents, the purity of Virgins, the chastity of Matrons, the fairness of Innocents well-pleasing unto Thee. For their sake O most Merciful Lord Jesu Christ! be propitious unto us wretched sinners, and inspire us with saving penitence; that neither harmful pleasures nor any perverse habit may ever oppress us; but may we rather have foretaste of the sweetness of Thy love and perseverance in Thy service; so that at Thy coming in Thy fearful judgement we may be found watching, and with Thy Saints and Elect may be esteemed worthy to receive a portion in the blessed life through The Same Jesus Christ our Lord. Amen.

For Peace.

Antiphon.

GIVE Peace in our days, O Lord! Because there is none

other that fighteth for us, except Thou, our God!

℣. O Lord, let there be Peace in Thy Strength.

℟. And abundance in Thy towers.

O God! of Whom are all holy desires, all right counsels, and all just works; give unto Thy servants that Peace which the world cannot give, that both our hearts may be set to obey Thy commandments, and we being freed from the fear of our enemies may pass our time in quietness under Thy protection, Through our Lord Jesus Christ Thy Son Who with Thee. Amen.

Bless we The Lord.

Thanks be to God.

Our Father.

Hail, thou that art highly favoured.

ℭ *For all the faithful departed.*

O God! The Creator and Redeemer of all the faithful; grant remission of all their sins to the souls of Thy servants and handmaidens; and the pardon which they have ever desired, by our pious supplications may they obtain, Through Christ our Lord. Amen.

May they rest in peace. Amen.

ℭ *At PRIME.*

O God! make speed to save me.

O Lord! make haste to help me.

Glory be to The Father.

As it was in the beginning.

Hymn.

O Dei Sapientia.

O wisdom of The God of Grace!
Pervading all things mightily,
The frailties of man's fallen race
Restoring with sweet clemency;

Thou deignedst human flesh to assume,
And e'en a death of pain to endure;
Proceeding from a Virgin's womb,
From all our guilt for ever pure.

Thou didst with joy that Mother crown,
Her holy Inmate, ere Thy Birth;
Then bright with blessings and renown
Arise a Star upon the earth.

And O! what gifts of love are Thine,
So sure, so blissful, and so free;
Whereby, with sweetness all divine,
Thou drawest every heart to Thee.

All Glory, Lord, to Thee be given,
Who waſt of Virgin Mother born;
And with The Father high in Heaven,
And Holy Ghoſt art ever One.
Amen.

Jam orto lucis ſidere.

The Star of Light hath riſen, and now
To God in ſuppliant prayer we bow;
May He in every work and way,
From harm preſerve us through the day.

May He reſtrain our tongues in peace,
And make the din of ſtrife to ceaſe;
And kindly ſhield and cloſe our eyes
From gazing on Earth's vanities.

O may our inmoſt hearts be pure,
From folly, word and thought ſecure;
Let temperance all our pride diſpel,
And every carnal paſſion quell;

So when the light ſhall fade away,
And night ſucceed the waning day,
We by the world unſtained, may raiſe
To Heaven our thankful ſongs of praiſe.

To God the Father Glory be!
Like Glory, Only Son! to Thee!
And to The Spirit Paraclete,
Now and through ages infinite.
Amen.

Psalm xxiii.—*Dominus regit me.*

The Lord is my ſhepherd: therefore can I lack nothing.

He ſhall feed me in a green paſture: and lead me forth beſide the waters of comfort.

He ſhall convert my ſoul: and bring me ſorth in the paths of righteouſneſs, for His Name's ſake.

Yea, though I walk through the valley of the ſhadow of death, I will fear no evil: for Thou art with me; Thy rod and Thy ſtaff comfort me.

Thou ſhalt prepare a table before me againſt them that trouble me: Thou haſt anointed my head with oil, and my cup ſhall be full.

But Thy loving-kindneſs and mercy ſhall follow me all the days of my life: and I will dwell in the Houſe of The Lord for ever.

Psalm xxv.—*Ad te, Domine, levavi.*

Unto Thee, O Lord! will I lift up my ſoul; my God, I have put my truſt in Thee: O let me not be confounded, neither let mine enemies triumph over me.

For all they that hope in Thee ſhall not be aſhamed: but ſuch as tranſgreſs without a cauſe ſhall be put to confuſion.

Shew me Thy ways, O Lord!: and teach me Thy paths.

Lead me forth in Thy truth, and learn me: for Thou art The God of my ſalvation; in

Thee hath been my hope all the day long,

Call to remembrance, O Lord! Thy tender mercies: and Thy loving-kindneſſes, which have been ever of old.

O remember not the ſins and offences of my youth: but according to Thy mercy think Thou upon me, O Lord! for Thy goodneſs.

Gracious and righteous is The Lord: therefore will He teach ſinners in the way.

Them that are meek ſhall He guide in judgement: and ſuch as are gentle, them ſhall He learn His way.

All the paths of The Lord are mercy and truth: unto ſuch as keep His covenant, and His teſtimonies.

For Thy Name's ſake, O Lord!: be merciful unto my ſin, for it is great.

What man is he that feareth The Lord: him ſhall He teach in the way that He ſhall chooſe.

His ſoul ſhall dwell at eaſe: and his ſeed ſhall inherit the land.

The ſecret of The Lord is among them that fear Him: and He will ſhew them His covenant.

Mine eyes are ever looking unto The Lord: for He ſhall pluck my feet out of the net.

Turn Thee unto me, and have mercy upon me: for I am deſolate and in miſery.

The ſorrows of my heart are enlarged: O bring Thou me out of my troubles.

Look upon mine adverſity and miſery: and forgive me all my ſin.

Conſider mine enemies, how many they are: and they bear a tyrannous hate againſt me.

O keep my ſoul and deliver me: let me not be confounded, for I have put my truſt in Thee.

Let perfectneſs and righteous dealing wait upon me: for my hope hath been in Thee.

Deliver Iſrael, O God!: out of all his troubles.

Psalm xxvi.—*Judica me Domine.*

Be Thou my Judge, O Lord! for I have walked innocently: my truſt hath been alſo in The Lord, therefore ſhall I not fall.

Examine me, O Lord! and prove me: try out my reins and my heart.

For Thy loving-kindneſs is ever before mine eyes: and I will walk in Thy truth.

I have not dwelt with vain perſons : neither will I have fellowſhip with the deceitful.

I have hated the congregation of the wicked : and will not ſit among the ungodly.

I will waſh my hands in innocency, O Lord ! : and ſo will I go to Thine Altar ;

That I may ſhew the voice of thankſgiving : and tell of all Thy wondrous works.

Lord, I have loved the habitation of Thine Houſe : and the place where Thine Honour dwelleth.

O ſhut not up my ſoul with the ſinners : nor my life with the blood-thirſty ;

In whoſe hands is wickedneſs : and their right hand is full of gifts.

But as for me, I will walk innocently : O deliver me, and be merciful unto me.

My foot ſtandeth right : I will praiſe The Lord in the congregations.

Psalm liv.—*Deus, in nomine.*

Save me, O God ! for Thy Name's ſake : and avenge me in Thy ſtrength.

Hear my prayer, O God ! : and hearken unto the words of my mouth.

For ſtrangers are riſen up againſt me : and tyrants, which have not God before their eyes, ſeek after my ſoul.

Behold ! God is my helper : The Lord is with them that uphold my ſoul.

He ſhall reward evil unto mine enemies : deſtroy Thou them in Thy truth.

An offering of a free heart will I give Thee, and praiſe Thy Name, O Lord ! ; becauſe it is ſo comfortable.

For He hath delivered me out of all my trouble : and mine eye hath ſeen His deſire upon mine enemies.

Psalm cxviii.—*Confitemine Domino.*

O give thanks unto The Lord, for He is gracious : becauſe His mercy endureth for ever.

Let Iſrael now confeſs, that He is gracious : and that His mercy endureth for ever.

Let the houſe of Aaron now confeſs : that His mercy endureth for ever.

Yea, let them now that fear The Lord confeſs : that His mercy endureth for ever.

I called upon The Lord in trouble : and The Lord heard me at large.

The Lord is on my ſide : I will not fear what man doeth unto me.

The Lord taketh my part with them that help me : therefore ſhall I ſee my deſire upon mine enemies.

It is better to truſt in The Lord : than to put any confidence in man.

It is better to truſt in The Lord : than to put any confidence in princes.

All nations compaſſed me round about : but in the Name of The Lord will I deſtroy them.

They kept me in on every ſide, they kept me in, I ſay, on every ſide : but in The Name of The Lord will I deſtroy them.

They came about me like bees, and are extinct even as the fire among the thorns : for in The Name of The Lord I will deſtroy them.

Thou haſt thruſt ſore at me, that I might fall : but The Lord was my help.

The Lord is my ſtrength, and my ſong : and is become my ſalvation.

The voice of joy and health is in the dwellings of he righteous : the right hand of The Lord bringeth mighty things to paſs.

I ſhall not die but live : and declare the works of The Lord.

The Lord hath chaſtened and corrected me : but He hath not given me over unto death.

Open me the gates of righteouſneſs : that I may go into them and give thanks unto The Lord.

This is the gate of The Lord : the righteous ſhall enter into it.

I will thank Thee, for Thou haſt heard me : and art become my Salvation.

The ſame Stone which the builders refuſed : is become the Headſtone in the corner.

This is The Lord's doing : and it is marvellous in our eyes.

This is the Day which The Lord hath made : we will rejoice and be glad in it.

Help me now, O Lord ! : O Lord ! ſend us now proſperity.

Bleſſed be He that cometh in The Name of The Lord : we have wiſhed you good luck, ye that are of The Houſe of The Lord.

God is The Lord Who hath ſhewed us light: bind the ſacrifice with cords, yea, even unto the horns of The Altar.

Thou art my God, and I will thank Thee: Thou art my God, and I will praiſe Thee.

O give thanks unto The Lord, for He is gracious: and His mercy endureth for ever.

Glory be to The Father.

Antiphon.

O WONDERFUL Exchange! The Creator of man taking upon Him a living body, vouchſafed to be born of a Virgin, and proceeding forth as Man, beſtowed upon us His Divinity!

The Creed.

WHOSOEVER will be ſaved.

¶ *On Sundays from the firſt Sunday in Advent to Eaſter.*

Antiphon.

THEE, God The Father Unbegotten, Thee The Son Only-begotten, Thee Spirit! Holy Paraclete! Holy and undivided Trinity! with our whole heart and mouth we do confeſs, we do praiſe, and we bleſs; to Thee be glory for evermore.

On other Sundays.

THEE dutifully praiſe, Thee adore, Thee glorify, all Thy creatures, O Bleſſed Trinity!

In Double Feaſts.

THANKS to Thee, O God! thanks to Thee, The True One Trinity, One and Supreme Deity, Holy and One Unity!

In Week-days.

GLORY to Thee, O Trinity! Co-equal One Deity! both before all ages and now and for evermore.

In the Week of Holy Trinity.

O BLESSED and Benedict and Glorious Trinity! Father, Son, and Holy Ghoſt.

Chapters.

IN all things I ſought reſt; and in the inheritance of The Lord I will dwell. Then The Creator of all things commanded and ſpake unto me, and He Who created me reſted in my tabernacle.

To The King Eternal, Immortal, Inviſible, The Only God, be Honour and Glory for ever and ever. Amen.

O Lord! be gracious unto us for we have waited for Thee; be Thou our Arm every morning, our Salvation alſo in the time of trouble.

Love Peace and Truth, ſaith The Lord God Almighty.

One Lord, One Faith, One Baptiſm, One God and Father of us all, Who is above all, and through all, and in us all. To Him be Glory for evermore.

Let every man be ſwift to hear, ſlow to ſpeak, ſlow to wrath: and lay apart all filthineſs and ſuperfluity of naughtineſs, and receive with meekneſs the engrafted Word which is able to ſave your ſouls.

℟. Hail! thou that art full of grace; The Lord is with thee.

℣. Bleſſed art thou among women, and bleſſed is The Fruit of thy womb.

The Lord is with thee.

Glory be to The Father.

Hail! thou that art full of grace, The Lord is with thee.

Reſponſory.

Jesu Chriſt! Son of The living God! Have mercy upon us.

Thou Who of a Virgin didſt vouchſafe to be born. Have mercy.

Thou Who on this day to the world didſt appear. Have mercy.

Thou Who didſt ariſe from the dead. Have mercy.

Thou Who ſitteſt at The Right Hand of The Father.

Have mercy upon us.

Glory be to The Father, and to The Son, and to The Holy Ghoſt.

Jeſu Chriſt! Son of The living God! Have mercy upon us.

Ariſe, O Lord! and help us.

And deliver us for Thy Name's ſake.

Lord have mercy.

Chriſt have mercy.

Lord have mercy.

Our Father.

The Apoſtle's Creed.

I believe in God.

Let my mouth be filled with Thy praiſe, that I may ſing Thy Glory, and all the day long Thy greatneſs.

O Lord! turn Thy face away from my ſins. And blot out all mine iniquities.

Create in me a clean heart, O God! And renew a right ſpirit within me.

Caſt me not away from Thy Face; and take not Thy Holy Spirit from me.

Reſtore to me the joy of Thy ſalvation;

And ſtabliſh me with Thy Chief Spirit.

Deliver me, O Lord! from the evil man; Reſcue me from the wicked man.

Reſcue me from mine enemies, O my God! And deliver me from them that riſe up againſt me.

O deliver me from the workers of iniquity: And ſave me from the men of blood.

So will I ſing Pſalms unto Thy Name for ever and ever; That day by day I may perform my vows.

Hear us, O God our Salvation! The Hope of all the confines of the earth, and in the ſea afar off.

O God! make ſpeed to ſave me;

O Lord! make haſte to help me.

Holy God! Holy Mighty! Holy and Immortal!

Lamb of God! Who takeſt away the ſins of the world. Have mercy upon us.

Bleſs The Lord, O my ſoul! And all that is within me His Holy Name.

Bleſs The Lord, O my ſoul! And forget not all His benefits.

Who forgiveth all thine iniquities; And healeth all thine infirmities.

Who redeemeth thy life from deſtruction; Who crowneth thee with mercy and compaſſion.

Who ſatisfieth thy deſire with good things; and reneweth thy youth as the eagle's.

Confeſſion.

I CONFESS to God, the Bleſſed Mary, and All the Saints, I have ſinned exceedingly in thought, word, and deed, of mine own fault, of my grievous fault; I beſeech All The Saints and Elect of God to pray for me.

Almighty God have mercy upon me, and forgive me all my ſins; deliver me from all evil, preſerve and ſtrengthen me in all goodneſs, and bring me to everlaſting life. Amen.

The Almighty and Merciful God grant me Abſolution and Remiſſion of all my ſins; ſpace for true penitence, amendment of life, and the grace and consolation of The Holy Spirit. Amen.

Hear, O Lord! I beseech Thee, the prayers of Thy suppliant, and spare all those who confess their sins unto Thee, that of Thy goodness Thou mayest bestow upon them pardon and peace, Through Christ our Lord. Amen.

O God! be Thou turned; and Thou shalt quicken us: And Thy people shall rejoice in Thee.

O Lord! shew Thy mercy upon us: And grant us Thy salvation.

Vouchsafe, O Lord! in this day: to keep us without sin.

Have mercy upon us, O Lord!: have mercy upon us.

Let Thy mercy, O Lord! be upon us: like as we have put our trust in Thee.

Arise, O Lord! and help us: and deliver us for Thy Name's sake.

O Lord, God of Hosts! convert us: and shew us Thy Countenance, and we shall be saved.

O Lord! hear my prayer; And let my crying come unto Thee.

Let us pray.

Orison in all Double Feasts.

In this hour of the day fulfil me, O Lord! with Thy mercy; that so rejoicing throughout this day I may find delight in Thy praises, through our Lord Jesus Christ Thy Son, Who with Thee liveth and reigneth in The Unity of The Holy Ghost God, world without end. Amen.

On other days.

O Holy Lord! Almighty Father! Eternal God! Who hast brought me to the beginning of this day, preserve me therein by Thy might; and grant that in this day I fall not away into any sin, neither run into any danger; but may all my doings be ordered by Thy governance, to do always Thy righteousness, Through our Lord.

May Holy Mary, Mother of our Lord God Jesus Christ, and All The Saints, Just Men, and Elect of God, intercede and pray for me, a sinner, to The Lord our God: that I may be worthy to obtain help and salvation from Him Who in perfect Trinity liveth and reigneth God, world without end. Amen.

Let Thy mercy come upon us, O Lord! Thy ſalvation according to Thy word.

And look down upon Thy ſervants and upon Thy works: And guide their children.

And let the Brightneſs of The Lord our God be upon us; and direct Thou the work of our hands upon us; O proſper Thou our handywork.

Oriſon in Double Feſtivals.

Almighty and Everlaſting God, direct all my actions according to Thy good will; ſo that through The Name of Thy beloved Son I may be enabled to abound in good works, Who with Thee liveth and reigneth.

On other days.

O Lord God! vouchſafe I beſeech Thee to direct, ſanctify, and govern, my heart and body in Thy law and in the works of Thy commandments; ſo that, both here and for ever, by Thy help I may be worthy of health and ſalvation: Through our Lord Jeſus Chriſt Thy Son, Who with Thee.

Bleſs we The Lord.
Thanks be to God.

Psalm cxxi.—*Levavi oculos.*

I will lift up mine eyes unto the hills: from whence cometh my help.

My help cometh even from The Lord: Who hath made Heaven and Earth.

He will not ſuffer thy foot to be moved: and He that keepeth thee will not ſleep.

Behold! He that keepeth Iſrael: ſhall neither ſlumber nor ſleep.

The Lord Himſelf is thy keeper: The Lord is thy defence upon thy right hand;

So that the Sun ſhall not burn thee by day: neither the Moon by night.

The Lord ſhall preſerve thee from all evil: yea it is even He that ſhall keep thy ſoul.

The Lord ſhall preſerve thy going out and thy coming in: from this time forth and for evermore.

Glory be to The Father and to The Son: and to The Holy Ghoſt;

As it was in the beginning is now and ever ſhall be: world without end. Amen.

Lord have mercy.
Chriſt have mercy.
Lord have mercy.

OUR FATHER.

O Lord! ſhew Thy mercy upon us,

And grant us Thy ſalvation.

Preſerve Thy ſervants and handmaidens,

My God, who put their truſt in Thee.

O Lord! ſend them help from Thy Holy Place,

And defend them out of Syon.

Be unto us O Lord! a Tower of Strength,

From the face of the enemy.

O Lord! hear my prayer,

And let my crying come unto Thee.

Let us pray.

Be preſent O Lord! with my ſupplications, and diſpoſe the way of Thy ſervants in the proſperity of Thy ſalvation; that among all the changes of our way and of this life, we may ever be protected by Thy help Through our Lord Jeſus Chriſt Thy Son, Who with Thee liveth and reigneth in the Unity of The Holy Ghoſt God world without end. Amen.

Bleſs we The Lord.
Thanks be to God. Amen.

ℂ *At TERCE.*

O GOD! make ſpeed, *and the reſt.*

Hymn.

Creator Spirit! Power Divine!
Come viſit all the Souls of Thine;
With Heaven descending Grace pervade,
The breaſts which Thou Thyſelf haſt made.

Remember, for Thy people's ſake,
Thou, Lord, didſt once our nature take;
And of the Virgin undefiled
Waſt born in fleſh, an infant Child.

Lord! Holy Virgin born, to Thee
All Glory everlaſting be,
To Father and to Holy Ghoſt
Long as eternity ſhall laſt! Amen.

Or this,—

Come Holy Ghoſt! Who ever One
Art, with the Father and the Son;
E'en now Thine influence ſweet inſtil,
And deign our boſoms to fulfil.

May lips, tongue, mind, ſtrength, ſenſe, proclaim
The Honour of the Eternal Name;
The Fire of Love its flame impart,
To kindle every human heart.

Most Gracious Father! hear our
prayer!
Co-equal Only Son! give ear;
Who with Thee, Spirit Paraclete!
Reign throughout ages infinite.
Amen.

PSALM cxx.—*Ad Dominum.*

WHEN I was in trouble I called upon The Lord: and He heard me.

Deliver my soul, O Lord! from lying lips: and from a deceitful tongue.

What reward shall be given or done unto thee, thou false tongue: even mighty and sharp arrows, with hot burning coals.

Wo is me, that I am constrained to dwell with Mesech! and to have my habitation among the tents of Kedar.

My soul hath long dwelt among them: that are enemies unto peace.

I labour for peace, but when I speak unto them thereof: they make them ready to battle.

PSALM cxxi.—*Levavi oculos.*

I WILL lift up mine eyes unto the hills: from whence cometh my help.

My help cometh even from The Lord: Who hath made heaven and earth.

He will not suffer thy foot to be moved: and He that keepeth thee will not sleep.

Behold! He that keepeth Israel: shall neither slumber nor sleep.

The Lord Himself is thy keeper: The Lord is thy defence upon thy right hand;

So that the Sun shall not burn thee by day: neither the Moon by night.

The Lord shall preserve thee from all evil: yea, it is even He that shall keep thy soul.

The Lord shall preserve thy going out, and thy coming in: from this time forth for evermore.

PSALM cxxii.—*Lætatus sum.*

I WAS glad when they said unto me: We will go into the House of The Lord.

Our feet shall stand in thy gates: O Jerusalem!

Jerusalem is built as a city: that is at unity in itself.

For thither the tribes go up, even the tribes of The Lord: to testify unto Israel to give thanks unto The Name of The Lord.

For there is the seat of judgement: even the seat of the House of David.

O pray for the peace of Jerufalem: they fhall profper that love thee.

Peace be within thy walls: and plenteoufnefs within thy palaces.

For my brethren and companions' fakes: I will wifh thee profperity.

Yea, becaufe of The Houfe of The Lord our God: I will feek to do thee good.

Antiphons.

O Lord! raife up Thy Power and come and fave us.

When Thou waft born ineffably of a Virgin then were fulfilled The Scriptures; as the rain into a fleece Thou didft defcend to give Salvation to mankind. We praife Thee O our God!

Praife and everlafting Glory to God The Father and to The Son and to The Holy Ghoft for ever and for evermore. Amen.

Heal my foul, O Lord! and I fhall be healed; fave me and I fhall be faved, for Thou art my praife.

Chapters.

Let Thy mercies come unto me O Lord! and I fhall live.

From the beginning and before the worlds was I created, and even unto the world to come I fhall not ceafe to be; and in the holy habitation I miniftered before Him.

The Grace of Our Lord Jefus Chrift and the Love of God and the fellowfhip of the Holy Ghoft be with us all evermore.

The goodnefs and kindnefs of God our Saviour hath appeared. Not of works of righteoufnefs which we have done, but according to His mercy hath He faved us.

℟. Grace is poured forth upon Thy lips.

℣. Wherefore God hath bleffed Thee for ever.

℣. In Thy comelinefs and in Thy beauty

℟. Go on and profper, proceed and reign.

Or this,—

℟. Incline my heart O God! unto Thy teftimonies.

℣. Turn away mine eyes left they behold vanity: in Thy way quicken me.

O Lord! hear my prayer,
And let my crying come unto Thee.

Orison.

O Lord! we beseech Thee pour Thy Grace into our hearts, that we who have known the Incarnation of Christ Thy Son by the message of an Angel, by His Passion and Cross may be guided to the glory of His Resurrection Through The Same.

At SEXT.

O God! make speed, *and the rest.*

Hymn.

Creator Spirit! Power Divine! *as at Terce.*

Rector Potens, verax Deus.

Almighty Ruler! God of Truth!
Who guid'st the changing scenes of day,
With golden beams illuming Morn,
And kindling Noon with fiery ray;
O quench the baneful flames of strife,
Bid every hurtful passion cease;
Vouchsafe unto our bodies health,
And keep our hearts in perfect peace.

Most Gracious Father! grant our prayer,
And Thou Coequal Only Son!
Who with Thee, Spirit Paraclete!
Art through eternal ages One!
Amen.

Or this,—

Presepe poni pertulit.

See, in a lowly manger placed,
The Lord of Light vouchsafes to rest;
Who with His Father built the spheres,
Swathed by a Mother's care appears.

He Who dispensed His law to Earth,
The Ten great precepts uttered forth,
Our mortal nature deigns to share,
The fetters of the law to wear.

Glory to Thee, O Lord! be paid,
Born of the wondrous Mother maid!
Father and Holy Ghost shall be
Now and throughout eternity.
Amen.

Psalm cxxiii.—*Ad Te levavi.*

Unto Thee lift I up mine eyes: O Thou that dwellest in The Heavens!

Behold even as the eyes of servants look unto the hand of their masters, and as the eyes of a maiden unto the hand of her mistress: even so our eyes wait upon The Lord our God until He have mercy upon us.

Have mercy upon us O Lord! have mercy upon us: for we are utterly despised.

Our ſoul is filled with the ſcornful reproof of the wealthy: and with the deſpitefulneſs of the proud.

Psalm cxxiv.—*Niſi quia Dominus.*

If The Lord Himſelf had not been on our ſide, now may Iſrael ſay: if The Lord Himſelf had not been on our ſide when men roſe up againſt us,

They had ſwallowed us up quick: when they were ſo wrathfully diſpleaſed at us.

Yea, the waters had drowned us: and the ſtream had gone over our ſoul.

The deep waters of the proud: had gone even over our ſoul.

But praiſed be The Lord: who hath not given us over for a prey unto their teeth.

Our ſoul is eſcaped even as a bird out of the ſnare of the fowler: the ſnare is broken and we are delivered.

Our help ſtandeth in The Name of The Lord: Who hath made Heaven and Earth.

Psalm cxxv.—*Qui confidunt.*

They that put their truſt in The Lord ſhall be even as the mount Syon: which may not be removed, but ſtandeth faſt for ever.

The hills ſtand about Jeruſalem: even ſo ſtandeth The Lord round about His people, from this time forth for evermore.

For the rod of the ungodly cometh not into the lot of the righteous: leſt the righteous put their hand unto wickedneſs.

Do well, O Lord!: unto thoſe that are good and true of heart.

As for ſuch as turn back unto their own wickedneſs: the Lord ſhall lead them forth with the evil-doers; but peace ſhall be upon Iſrael.

Antiphons.

Glory and Praiſe reſound from the voice of all men to The Father and Son ſole begotten, and to The Holy Ghoſt likewiſe re-echo, Praiſe Everlaſting.

By Thine Advent deliver us, O Lord!

The Buſh which Moſes ſaw unconſumed, we acknowledge thine ever preſerved and laudable Virginity. Mother of God intercede for us!

The Angel of The Lord announced to Mary and ſhe

conceived of The Holy Ghoſt. Alleluya!

Chapters.

And ſo I was eſtabliſhed in Syon, and in the Holy City in like manner I reſted, and in Jeruſalem was my power.

Prove all things; hold faſt that which is good; abſtain from all appearance of evil.

There are Three that bear record in Heaven, The Father, The Word, and The Holy Ghoſt, and theſe Three are One.

℟. In Thy comelineſs and in Thy beauty

℣. Go on and proſper, proceed and reign.

℣. God ſhall help her with His countenance.

℟. God is in the midſt of her, ſhe ſhall not be moved.

Or this,—

℟. I will bleſs The Lord at all times.

℣. His praiſe ſhall be ever in my mouth.

℣. The Lord is my Shepherd, therefore can I lack nothing.

℟. In a green paſture there hath He placed me.

O Lord! hear my prayer,
And let my crying come unto Thee.

Oriſon.

O Lord! we beſeech Thee ſtabliſh in our hearts the Sacraments of the True Faith; that we may ſteadfaſtly confeſs Him to be True God and Man, Who was conceived and born of the Virgin Mary, and by the Power of His Saving Incarnation may attain to eternal joys Through The Same.

ℂ *At NONE.*

O God! make ſpeed, *and the reſt.*

Hymn.

Creator Spirit! Power Divine! *as at Terce.*

Or,—

Rerum Deus tenax vigor.

O God! of all the ſtrength and ſtay,
Who doſt Thyſelf unmoved abide,
And all the changing ſcenes of Day
In their ordained ſucceſſion guide;

Thy light upon our evening pour;
So may our life no ſunſet ſee,
But death to us an holy door
Of everlaſting Glory be.

O Father! we theſe gifts intreat,
And Thou Coequal Only Son!
Who with Thee, Spirit Paraclete!
Reign through eternal ages One!
Amen.

Or,—

Hora nona quæ canimus.

Jeſu! receive the hymns we ſing,
At this Ninth Hour to Thee our King;
Which Thy moſt ſacred Death hath made
To mortals ever conſecrate.

This Hour from out Thy wounded ſide
Welled forth the Church's noble tide;
O to The holy thief do Thou
By Thy ſweet grace unite us now!

Grant this, Thou God in Trinity!
One and co-equal Deity!
To Whom Praiſe, Virtue, Glory be,
Now and throughout Eternity.
Amen.

PSALM cxxvi.—*In convertendo.*

WHEN The Lord turned again the captivity of Syon: then were we like unto them that dream;

Then was our mouth filled with laughter: and our tongue with joy.

Then ſaid they among the heathen: The Lord hath done great things for them.

Yea, the Lord hath done great things for us already: whereof we rejoice.

Turn our captivity, O Lord!: as the rivers in the ſouth.

They that ſow in tears: ſhall reap in joy.

He that now goeth on his way weeping, and bearing forth good ſeed: ſhall doubtleſs come again with joy, and bring his ſheaves with him.

PSALM cxxvii.—*Niſi Dominus.*

EXCEPT The Lord build the houſe: their labour is but loſt that build it.

Except The Lord keep the city: the watchman waketh but in vain.

It is but loſt labour that ye haſte to riſe up early and ſo late take reſt and eat the bread of carefulneſs: for ſo He giveth His beloved ſleep.

Lo! children and the fruit of the womb: are an heritage and gift that cometh of The Lord.

Like as the arrows in the hand of the giant: even ſo are the young children.

Happy is the man that hath his quiver full of them: they ſhall not be aſhamed when they ſpeak with their enemies in the gate.

Psalm cxxviii.—*Beati omnes.*

Blessed are all they that fear The Lord : and walk in His ways.

For thou ſhalt eat the labours of thine hands : O well is Thee and happy ſhalt thou be !

Thy wife ſhall be as the fruitful vine : upon the walls of thine houſe.

Thy children like the olive branches : round about thy table.

Lo ! thus ſhall the man be bleſſed : that feareth The Lord.

The Lord from out of Syon ſhall ſo bleſs thee : that thou ſhalt ſee Jeruſalem in proſperity all thy life long.

Yea, thou ſhalt ſee thy children's children : and peace upon Iſrael.

Antiphons.

The Root of Jeſſe hath ſprouted forth ; there hath ariſen a Star from Jacob. A Virgin hath brought forth a Saviour. We praiſe Thee, O our God !

Come, O Lord ! and tarry not ; forgive the offences of Thy people Iſrael.

Hail ! Thou that art highly favoured, bleſſed art Thou among women and bleſſed is the fruit of thy womb—Jeſus. Alleluya !

From Whom are all things ; through Whom are all things ; in Whom are all things ; to Him be glory for evermore.

According to Thy word give me underſtanding, O Lord !

Chapters.

And I took root in an honourable people and in the portion of My God His inheritance ; and mine abode is in the full aſſembly of Saints.

A Virgin by a Word conceived, a Virgin ſhe remained, a Virgin ſhe brought forth The King of all Kings.

One Lord, One Faith, One Baptiſm, One God and Father of all ; Who is above all and through all and in us all.

Bear ye one another's burthen and ſo ſhall ye fulfil the law of Chriſt.

℟. Beautiful art thou and ſweet,

℣. In thy delights O holy Mother of God !

℣. God choſe her and predeſtined her.

℟. And cauſed her to dwell in His tabernacle.

Or this,—

℟. Redeem me, O Lord! and have mercy upon me.

℣. For my foot hath ftood in the right way; in the Churches I will blefs Thee, O Lord!

℣. O Lord God of Hofts! convert us.

℟. And fhow us Thy countenance and we fhall be faved.

O Lord! hear my prayer.

And let my crying come unto Thee.

Orifon.

O Lord Jefu Chrift! Son of The living God! Who didft defcend from Heaven to Earth, from the bofom of The Father into the womb of the Virgin; and upon The Tree of the Crofs didft fuffer Five Wounds and fhed forth Thy precious Blood for the remiffion of my fins; I humbly befeech Thee, that in the Day of Judgment, placed at Thy Right Hand I may be found worthy to hear from Thee thofe moft fweet words: Come ye bleffed of my Father, inherit the kingdom prepared for you! Who with The Same Father in the Unity of The Holy Ghoft liveft and reigneft. Amen.

Psalm cxxx.—*De profundis.*

Out of the deep have I called unto Thee, O Lord! Lord! hear my voice.

O let Thine ears confider well: the voice of my complaint.

If Thou Lord! wilt be extreme to mark what is done amifs: O Lord! who may abide it?

For there is mercy with Thee: therefore fhalt Thou be feared.

I look for The Lord; my foul doth wait for Him: in His word is my truft.

My foul fleeth unto the Lord: before the morning watch, I fay, before the morning watch.

O Ifrael! truft in The Lord, for with The Lord there is mercy: and with Him is plenteous redemption.

And He fhall redeem Ifrael from all his fins.

Glory be to The Father.

Abfolve I befeech Thee, O Lord! the fouls of Thy fervants and handmaidens, our relations, our neighbours, our friends, our benefactors, as well as of all the faithful departed, from all the chains of their sins: that in the Glory of the Resurrection they may be raised up to life and breath amongst Thy Saints and Elect, Through Christ our Lord. Amen.

Hymn at None.

Stabat Mater dolorosa.

Lo! The Mother standeth fearful
By The Cross, forlorn and tearful,
Where her dying Offspring hung;
And the piercing sword, deep driven,
Hath aghast and sorrow riven
All her soul with anguish wrung.

O! how sad and sore distressèd
Was that Mother ever blessèd
Of The Sole-begotten One!
How she grievèd so bereavèd
When she all the pangs perceivèd
Of her meek and Royal Son!

Who could e'er refrain from weeping
That had seen Christ's Mother keeping
Vigil, in that Hour of woe?
Who upon the grief amazing
Of that Son and Mother gazing,
Must not sympathy bestow?

For His people's sins in anguish
She beheld her Jesus languish,
And His limbs the scourges tear;
Her sweet Son, from judgement taken,
Dying and of all forsaken
Yield to God His Spirit there.

Ah, Mother! Fount of kind affection!
May I feel thy deep affliction,
With thee all His woes deplore;
With the love of Jesus burning
Let my bosom share thy yearning
To bewail Him, and adore.

Deeply in my heart indented
Be the stripes, which then tormented
Him, Thy Holy Crucified;
All the Wounds thy Child which covered,
And the pains for me He suffered,
Let my heart with thee divide.

May I with thee weep sincerely,
With thee whilst I live most dearly
For The Crucified condole;
By The Cross myself to station,
And partake thy lamentation,
Is the longing of my soul.

Virgin! among Virgins peerless!
Mourn no longer, sad and cheerless;
Be it mine those griefs to share;
By His death my life to fashion,
All the sorrows of His Passion,
And The Cross with thee to bear!

With His Wounds so penetrated,
With The Cross in spirit sated,
With the love which He has borne
Kindling and enflamed, O yield me
Virgin! all thine aid to shield me
In the awful Judgement Morn.

May The Guardian Cross direct me,
And the Death of Christ protect me,
And his nurturing Grace control;
So when flesh in death shall perish,
He with glory decked shall cherish
In His Paradise my soul! Amen.

℣. The sword of very grief pierced through thy soul.

℟. That the thoughts of many hearts might be revealed.

Orison.

O Lord Jesu Christ! we salute and venerate Thy Cross and Passion, and humbly implore Thy clemency; that Thou Who didst condescend to be born of The Virgin Mary wouldest vouchsafe to pity and spare us sinners, Who livest and reignest. Amen.

ℭ *At Vespers.*

O God! make speed, *and the rest.*

Psalms.—cxxii., *Lætatus sum*, I was glad *(as at Terce)*; cxxiii., *Ad Te levavi*, Unto Thee lift I up; cxxiv., *Nisi quia Dominus*, If The Lord; cxxv., *Qui confidunt*, They that put their trust *(as at Sext)*; cxxvi., *In convertendo*, When The Lord turned *(as at None)*.

Psalm cx.—*Dixit Dominus.*

The Lord said unto my Lord: Sit Thou on My Right Hand until I make Thine enemies Thy footstool.

The Lord shall send the rod of Thy power out of Syon: be Thou Ruler; even in the midst among Thine enemies.

In the day of Thy Power shall the people offer Thee freewill offerings with an holy worship: the dew of Thy Birth is of the womb of the morning.

The Lord sware and will not repent: Thou art a Priest for ever after the order of Melchisedec.

The Lord upon Thy right hand: shall wound even kings in the day of His wrath.

He shall judge among the heathen; He shall fill the places with the dead bodies: and smite in sunder the heads over divers countries.

He shall drink of the brook in the way: therefore shall He lift up his head.

Psalm cxi.—*Confitebor Tibi.*

I will give thanks unto The Lord with my whole heart: secretly among the faithful, and in the congregation.

The works of The Lord are great: sought out of all them that have pleasure therein.

His work is worthy to be praised and had in honour: and His righteousness endureth for ever.

The merciful and gracious Lord hath ſo done His marvellous works : that they ought to be had in remembrance.

He hath given meat unto them that fear Him : He ſhall ever be mindful of His covenant.

He hath ſhewed His people the power of His works : that He may give them the heritage of the heathen.

The works of His hands are verity and judgement : all His commandments are true.

They ſtand faſt for ever and ever : and are done in truth and equity.

He ſent redemption unto His people : He hath commanded His covenant for ever; holy and reverend is His Name.

The fear of The Lord is the beginning of wiſdom : a good underſtanding have all they that do thereafter ; the praiſe of it endureth for ever.

Psalm cxii.—*Beatus vir.*

Blessed is the man that feareth The Lord : he hath great delight in His commandments.

His ſeed ſhall be mighty upon earth : the generation of the faithful ſhall be bleſſed.

Riches and plenteouſneſs ſhall be in his houſe : and his righteouſneſs endureth for ever.

Unto the godly there ariſeth up light in the darkneſs : he is merciful, loving, and righteous.

A good man is merciful, and lendeth : and will guide his words with diſcretion.

For he ſhall never be moved : and the righteous ſhall be had in everlaſting remembrance.

He will not be afraid of any evil tidings : for his heart ſtandeth faſt, and believeth in The Lord.

His heart is eſtabliſhed, and will not ſhrink : until he ſee his deſire upon his enemies.

He hath diſperſed abroad and given to the poor : and his righteouſneſs remaineth for ever ; his horn ſhall be exalted with honour.

The ungodly ſhall ſee it, and it ſhall grieve him : he ſhall gnaſh with his teeth, and conſume away ; the deſire of the ungodly ſhall periſh.

Psalm cxxxii.—*Memento, Domine.*

Lord ! remember David : and all his trouble ;

How he ſware unto The Lord : and vowed a vow unto The Almighty God of Jacob ;

I will not come within the tabernacle of mine houſe : nor climb up into my bed ;

I will not ſuffer mine eyes to ſleep, nor mine eye-lids to ſlumber : neither the temples of my head to take any reſt ;

Until I find out a place for the temple of The Lord : an habitation for the mighty God of Jacob.

Lo ! we heard of the ſame at Ephrata : and found it in the wood.

We will go into His tabernacle : and fall low on our knees before His footſtool.

Ariſe, O Lord ! into Thy reſting-place : Thou, and the Ark of Thy ſtrength.

Let Thy prieſts be clothed with righteouſneſs : and let Thy Saints ſing with joyfulneſs.

For Thy ſervant David's ſake : turn not away the preſence of Thine Anointed.

The Lord hath made a faithful oath unto David : and He ſhall not ſhrink from it ;

Of the fruit of thy body : ſhall I ſet upon thy ſeat.

If thy children will keep My covenant, and My teſtimonies that I ſhall learn them : their children alſo ſhall ſit upon thy ſeat for evermore.

For The Lord hath choſen Syon to be an habitation for Himſelf : He hath longed for her.

This ſhall be my reſt for ever : here will I dwell, for I have a delight therein.

I will bleſs her victuals with increaſe : and will ſatisfy her poor with bread.

I will deck her prieſts with health : and her Saints ſhall rejoice and ſing.

There ſhall I make the horn of David to flouriſh : I have ordained a lantern for Mine Anointed.

As for his enemies, I ſhall clothe them with ſhame : but upon himſelf ſhall his crown flouriſh.

Psalm cxvi.—*Credidi.*

I believed, and therefore will I ſpeak ; but I was ſore troubled : I ſaid in my haſte, All men are liars.

What reward ſhall I give unto The Lord : for all the benefits that He hath done unto me ?

I will receive the Cup of

ſalvation : and call upon The Name of The Lord.

I will pay my vows now in the preſence of all His people : right dear in the ſight of The Lord is the death of His Saints.

Behold, O Lord ! how that I am Thy ſervant : I am Thy ſervant, and the ſon of Thine handmaid ; Thou haſt broken my bonds in ſunder.

I will offer to Thee the ſacrifice of thankſgiving : and will call upon The Name of The Lord.

I will pay my vows unto The Lord in the ſight of all His people : in the courts of The Lord's Houſe, even in the midſt of thee, O Jeruſalem! Praiſe The Lord.

Glory be to The Father.

Antiphons.

THE Prophets foretold that The Saviour ſhould be born of The Virgin Mary.

Sit Thou on My Right Hand, ſaid The Lord unto my Lord.

Faithful are all His Commandments ; they are ſtabliſhed for ever and ever.

Let The Name of The Lord be bleſſed for evermore.

Chapters.

BEHOLD ! a Virgin ſhall conceive and bring forth a Son, and His Name ſhall be called Emmanuel ; butter and honey ſhall He eat, that He may know how to refuſe the evil and chooſe the good.

Rejoice in The Lord alway ; again I ſay Rejoice. Let your moderation be known unto all men ; The Lord is at hand.

Bleſſed be God, even The Father of our Lord Jeſus Chriſt, The Father of mercies, and The God of all conſolation, Who comforteth us in all our tribulation.

The Blood of Chriſt, Who through the Eternal Spirit offered Himſelf without ſpot to God, ſhall purge your conſcience from dead works, to ſerve The Living God.

Chriſt being raiſed from the dead, dieth no more ; Death hath no more dominion over Him ; for in that He died He died unto ſin once, but in that He liveth He liveth unto God. Likewiſe reckon ye alſo yourſelves to be dead indeed unto ſin but alive unto God, Through Jeſus Chriſt our Lord.

The Lord is in His Holy Temple, The Lord's ſeat is in Heaven.

Jeſus ſaid, I will pray The Father and He ſhall give you another Comforter that He may abide with you for ever, even The Spirit of Truth.

The Grace of our Lord Jeſus Chriſt, and the Love of God, and the fellowſhip of The Holy Ghoſt be with us all evermore.

I beheld and Lo! a great multitude which no man could number, of all nations and kindreds and people and tongues, ſtood before the Throne, and before The Lamb, clothed in white robes, and palms in their hands; and cried with a loud voice ſaying, Salvation to our God Which ſitteth upon the Throne and unto The Lamb.

Hymn.

Ave Maris Stella.

HAIL! Star of ocean, Mary!
God's fair Mother were ye;
Virgin thou! immortal!
Heaven's own happy portal!

When that bliſsful Ave
Gabriel's meſſage gave thee,
Peace was ſtabliſhed ever,
Reverſed the name of Eva;

Guilt was looſed in kindneſs,
Light ſhone o'er our blindness,
All our ſickneſs curing,
And all good aſſuring.

A Son's love diſplaying,
He will hear thy praying,
Who for us deigned ſurely
To be thine Offspring purely.

Virgin all excelling!
Meek beyond all telling!
Aſk Him chaſte and tender
All our hearts to render;

Thus our life protecting,
And our way directing,
Till the ſight of Jeſus
E'er with thee ſhall pleaſe us.

Praiſe to God The Father,
To The Son all Honour;
And to The Holy Spirit,
Three, yet One! all merit.
Amen.

℣. Grace is poured forth upon thy lips,

℟. Wherefore God hath bleſſed thee for ever.

For the Summer.

O Lux! Beata Trinitas!

O LIGHT! Thou Trinity Moſt Bleſt!
Chief Unity, Supreme and Beſt!
E'en as the fiery Sun departs
Outpour Thy beams upon our hearts.

Thee with our hymns at dawn we praiſe,
To Thee our evening prayer we raiſe;
And Thou our glorious theme ſhall be
Ador'd through all eternity!

Now darkneſs veils the earth; do Thou
A night of quiet reſt beſtow;
When morning breaks, from Heaven Thy Throne
On us moſt graciouſly look down.

O Chriſt! the chains of ſin unbind,
From all defilement cleanſe the mind;
From guilt that's paſt my ſoul relieve,
And all my evil deeds forgive.

I pray Thee hear thy ſuppliant's call;
O help me Saviour! ere I fall;
Chriſt Jeſu! King of boundleſs might!
Shield me from every ill this night.
Amen.

Lucis Creator optime.

Creator of the Light Supreme!
Bright Parent of the morning beam!
Who when the Day-Spring had its birth
Didſt lay the pillars of the earth;

Who blending morn with evening grey,
Haſt in Thy wiſdom named them Day;
Now o'er the earth night's ſhadows fall,
O hearken to Thy ſuppliant's call;

Let not my ſoul by ſin oppreſſed
Loſe Thy reward of endleſs reſt;
Nor e'er, with earthly lures beſet,
Thee and Eternity forget.

O may my cry to Heaven aſcend;
Give me the life that hath no end;
From peril all my path ſecure,
And make my life devout and pure.

Moſt gracious Father! hear my prayer,
Co-equal Only Son! give ear;
Who with Thee, Spirit Paraclete!
Reign throughout ages infinite.
Amen.

Antiphons.

Fear not Mary! thou haſt found favour with The Lord; Behold! thou ſhalt conceive and bring forth a Son. Alleluya.

The Virgin Mother, unknown by man, brought forth without pain The Saviour of the worlds. She only of Virgins filled with Grace from Heaven, nurtured The Very King of Angels at her breaſt.

Psalm.—*Magnificat.*

My ſoul doth magnify The Lord: and my ſpirit hath rejoiced in God my Saviour.

For He hath regarded: the lowlineſs of His hand-maiden.

For behold, from henceforth: all generations ſhall call me bleſſed.

For He that is mighty hath magnified me: and Holy is His Name.

And His mercy is on them that fear Him: throughout all generations.

He hath ſhewed ſtrength with His arm: He hath ſcattered the proud in the imagination of their hearts.

He hath put down the mighty from their ſeat: and hath exalted the humble and meek.

He hath filled the hungry with good things : and the rich He hath ſent empty away.

He remembering his mercy hath holpen His ſervant Iſrael : as he promiſed to our forefathers, Abraham and his ſeed for ever.

Glory be to The Father.

O Lord! hear my prayer;

And let my ſupplication come unto Thee.

℣. There ſhall come forth a Rod from the ſtem of Jeſſe;

℟. And a Flower from his root ſhall grow up.

Oriſon.

O God! we beſeech Thee, grant us Thine help, that we who with due reverence and praiſe venerate the memory of the Incarnation, Nativity, Paſſion, Reſurrection, and Aſcenſion of Thy Son, our Lord Jeſus Chriſt, and of the coming of The Holy Ghoſt, may through the Grace of The Same Holy Ghoſt riſe again from the death of the ſoul, and ever hereafter live in Thee a life of holineſs, Through The Same our Lord Jeſus Chriſt. Amen.

Antiphon.

The gate of Paradiſe through Eve to all men was cloſed, and through Mary Virgin again was thrown open. Alleluya.

℣. Beautiful is His form before the ſons of men.

℟. Full of Grace are Thy lips.

God! Who by the fruitful Virginity of The Bleſſed Mary didſt beſtow the gifts of eternal Salvation upon mankind; Grant we beſeech Thee that we may perceive that ſhe intercedes for us, through whom we have been found worthy to obtain The Author of Life our Lord Jeſus Chriſt Thy Son, Who with Thee. Amen.

O Lord! we beſeech Thee pour Thy grace into our minds; that we who have known the Incarnation of Chriſt Thy Son by the Meſſage of an Angel, by His Paſſion and Croſs may be guided to the Glory of His Reſurrection through The Same our Lord Jeſus Chriſt Thy Son, Who with Thee liveth and reigneth in The Unity of The Same Spirit God, world without end. Amen.

Of The Holy Ghost.

Antiphon.

The Spirit of The Lord fulfilled the orb of the world, and that which pervadeth all things inspired the knowledge of tongues.

℣. Send forth Thy Spirit, and they shall be created.

℟. And Thou shalt renew the face of the earth.

Orison.

O God! to Whom every heart lieth open, every will speaketh, and from Whom no secret is hid; purify the thoughts of our hearts by the infusion of Thy Holy Spirit, that we may be enabled perfectly to love Thee and meetly to praise Thee, Through Christ our Lord. Amen.

Of the Holy Cross.

Antiphon.

The Holy Cross He endured Who vanquished Hell. He is girded with might, He rose again the Third Day. Alleluya.

℣. Tell ye among the nations

℟. That The Lord hath reigned from the Tree.

Orison.

God! Who for our sakes didst will Thy Son to undergo the suffering of The Cross that Thou mightest expel from us the power of the enemy; grant to us Thy servants that we may ever live in the joys of His Resurrection, Through The Same Jesus Christ our Lord. Amen.

Or this,—

Antiphon.

We adore Thee O Christ and we bless Thee, for by Thy Cross Thou hast redeemed the world.

℣. Let all the Earth worship Thee O God! and praise Thee,

℟. And sing psalms unto Thy Name.

Orison.

God! Who didst ascend Thy Holy Cross and enlighten the darkness of the world, do Thou vouchsafe to enlighten our hearts and bodies O Saviour of the World! Who livest and reignest with God The Father in the Unity of The Holy Ghost God world without end. Amen.

S. John the Baptist.

Thou Child! shalt be call-' a Prophet of The Highest

Thou ſhalt go before the Face of The Lord to prepare His ways; to give knowledge of Salvation for the remiſſion of ſins.

℣. There was a man ſent from God

℟. Whoſe name was John.

God! Who haſt made this Day honourable unto us by the birth of the bleſſed S. John Baptiſt; grant unto Thy people the grace of ſpiritual joy, and direct the hearts of all Thy faithful ones into the way of eternal Salvation, Through.

S. Peter and S. Paul.

Thy friends are exceeding honourable O God! their princedom is very greatly ſtrengthened.

℣. Their ſound is gone out into all lands,

℟. And their words unto the ends of the world.

God! Who didſt conſecrate this Day by the martyrdom of Thine Apoſtles Peter and Paul, grant unto Thy Church, which received from them the rudiments of The Faith, to follow their precepts in all things, Through.

God! Who didſt looſe the bleſſed Peter from his chains and cauſed him to depart in ſafety; abſolve us we beſeech Thee from the bands of our ſins, and of Thy goodneſs ward off all dangers from us. Through.

S. Mary Magdalene.

O most ſurpaſſing love of Mary Magdalene! who departed not from the ſepulchre of The Lord; to whom Jeſus ſaid, Mary! touch me not, for I am not yet aſcended to My Father!

℣. Mary choſe the better part

℟. Which ſhall not be taken away from her.

O Lord! we humbly beſeech Thy Mercy, that we who celebrate the moſt holy memory of the bleſſed Mary Magdalene, and call to mind the excellence of her devotion, may with her from Thine everlaſting mercy obtain the pardon of our ſins, and be made partakers of eternal Glory. Amen.

S. Laurence Martyr.

The bleſſed Laurence, placed upon the grate, forgot not God; caſt upon the fire, he confeſſed Chriſt.

℣. He prayed and ſaid

℟. O Lord Jeſus Chriſt! have pity upon me Thy ſervant.

Grant, we beſeech Thee, Almighty God, that with due fervour of faith we may remember the triumph of Laurence Thy bleſſed Martyr, who regarded not the flames which conſumed him on earth; ſo that with him we may ſhine forth in the everlaſting light of Heaven, Through.

For other Saints ſee Lauds, ſupra.

For Saints Days.

These are The Saints that are without fault before The Throne of God, and they are not parted from Him; they drank of the Cup of The Lord, and are made the friends of God; wherefore they are crowned and have received palms.

℣. They have waſhed their robes and made them white in the Blood of The Lamb.

℟. With Glory and Honour haſt Thou crowned them, O Lord!

O Lord our God! multiply upon us Thy Grace, that we may celebrate with gladneſs the glorious memory of Thy Saints, and joyfully follow them in all holy living, Through.

Almighty and everlaſting God, Who didſt kindle the heart of Thy Holy Apoſtle [Evangeliſt, Martyr, Confeſſor] with the flame of Thy Love, and didſt ſend him to preach the Goſpel to all the earth, endue our minds likewiſe, we beſeech Thee, with the virtues of Faith and Charity, that ſo we may profit by the example of him in remembrance of whom we this day rejoice, Through.

Of All Saints.

In the celeſtial Kingdom is the habitation of The Saints. Alleluya. And everlaſting is their reſt. Alleluya.

℣. The voice of joy and exaltation

℟. Is in the dwellings of the righteous.

Grant, we beſeech Thee, Almighty God! that in the Reſurrection of our Lord Jeſus Chriſt with All His Saints we may in very deed receive our portion, Who with Thee liveth and reigneth. Amen

Or this,—

O HOW glorious is the Kingdom in which with Christ rejoice All His Saints! clothed in white robes they follow The Lamb whithersoever He goeth.

℣. Rejoice in The Lord and be glad O ye righteous!

℟. And be joyful all ye that are upright of heart.

We beseech Thee, O Lord! favourably regard our infirmities, and for the intercessions of All Thy Saints turn from us all those evils which we justly deserve, Through Christ our Lord. Amen.

For Peace.

GIVE Peace in our days, O Lord! because there is none other that fighteth for us except Thou our God.

℣. O Lord! let there be Peace in Thy strength.

℟. And abundance in Thy towers.

O God! of Whom are all holy desires, all right counsels, and all just works, give unto Thy servants that Peace which the world cannot give; that both our hearts may be set to obey Thy commandments, and we being freed from the fear of our enemies, may pass our time in quietness, under Thy protection, Through our Lord Jesus Christ Thy Son, Who with Thee. Amen.

ℭ *At COMPLINE.*

CONVERT us, O God! our Salvation!

And turn away Thine anger from us.

O God! make speed to save me.

O Lord! make haste to help me.

Glory be to The Father.

As it was in the beginning.

Alleluya.

PSALM xiii.—*Usque quo, Domine.*

How long wilt Thou forget me, O Lord! for ever: how long wilt Thou hide Thy Face from me?

How long shall I seek counsel in my soul, and be so vexed in my heart: how long shall mine enemies triumph over me?

Consider and hear me, O Lord my God!: lighten mine eyes that I sleep not in death.

Lest mine enemy say, I have prevailed against him: for if I be cast down, they that trouble me will rejoice at it.

But my truſt is in Thy mercy : and my heart is joyful in Thy ſalvation.

I will ſing of The Lord, becauſe He hath dealt ſo lovingly with me : yea, I will praiſe The Name of The Lord Moſt Higheſt.

Psalm xliii.—*Judica me, Deus.*

Give ſentence with me, O God! and defend my cauſe againſt the ungodly people : O deliver me from the deceitful and wicked man.

For Thou art The God of my ſtrength, why haſt Thou put me from Thee : and why go I ſo heavily, while the enemy oppreſſeth me?

O ſend out Thy Light and Thy Truth, that they may lead me : and bring me unto Thy holy hill, and to Thy dwelling.

And that I may go unto the Altar of God, even unto The God of my joy and gladneſs : and upon the harp will I give thanks unto Thee, O God, my God!

Why art thou ſo heavy, O my ſoul : and why art thou ſo diſquieted within me?

O put thy truſt in God : for I will yet give Him thanks, which is the help of my countenance, and my God.

Psalm cxxix.—*Sæpe expugnaverunt.*

Many a time have they fought againſt me from my youth up : may Iſrael now ſay.

Yea, many a time have they vexed me from my youth up : but they have. not prevailed againſt me.

The plowers plowed upon my back : and made long furrows.

But the righteous Lord : hath hewn the ſnares of the ungodly in pieces.

Let them be confounded and turned backward : as many as have evil will at Sion.

Let them be even as the graſs growing upon the houſetops : which withereth afore it be plucked up;

Whereof the mower filleth not his hand : neither he that bindeth up the ſheaves his boſom.

So that they who go by ſay not ſo much as, The Lord proſper you : we wiſh you good luck in The Name of The Lord.

Psalm cxxxi.—*Domine, non est.*

Lord! I am not high-minded : I have no proud looks.

I do not exercise myself in great matters : which are too high for me.

But I refrain my soul, and keep it low, like as a child that is weaned from his mother : yea, my soul is even as a weaned child.

O Israel! trust in The Lord : from this time forth for evermore.

Psalm iv.—*Cum invocarem.*

Hear me when I call, O God of my righteousness!: Thou hast set me at liberty when I was in trouble; have mercy upon me, and hearken unto my prayer.

O ye sons of men, how long will ye blaspheme mine honour : and have such pleasure in vanity, and seek after leasing?

Know this also, that The Lord hath chosen to himself the man that is godly : when I call upon The Lord He will hear me.

Stand in awe, and sin not : commune with your own heart, and in your chamber, and be still.

Offer the sacrifice of righteousness : and put your trust in The Lord.

There be many that say : Who will shew us any good?

Lord! lift Thou up : the light of Thy Countenance upon us.

Thou hast put gladness in my heart : since the time that their corn, and wine, and oil, increased.

I will lay me down in peace, and take my rest : for it is Thou, Lord! only, that makest me dwell in safety.

Psalm xxxi.—*In te, Domine, speravi.*

In Thee, O Lord! have I put my trust : let me never be put to confusion, deliver me in Thy righteousness.

Bow down Thine ear to me : make haste to deliver me.

And be Thou my strong rock, and house of defence : that Thou mayest save me.

For Thou art my strong rock, and my castle : be Thou also my Guide, and lead me for Thy Name's sake.

Draw me out of the net, that they have laid privily for me : for Thou art my strength.

Into Thy hands I commend

my ſpirit : for Thou haſt redeemed me, O Lord! Thou God of Truth.

PSALM xci.—*Qui habitat.*

WHOSO dwelleth under the defence of The Moſt High : ſhall abide under the ſhadow of The Almighty.

I will ſay unto The Lord, Thou art my hope, and my ſtrong hold : my God, in Him will I truſt.

For He ſhall deliver thee from the ſnare of the hunter : and from the noiſome peſtilence.

He ſhall defend Thee under His wings, and thou ſhalt be ſafe under His feathers : His faithfulneſs and truth ſhall be Thy ſhield and buckler.

Thou ſhalt not be afraid for any terror by night : nor for the arrow that flieth by day;

For the peſtilence that walketh in darkneſs : nor for the ſickneſs that deſtroyeth in the noon-day.

A thouſand ſhall fall beſide thee, and ten thouſand at thy right hand : but it ſhall not come nigh thee.

Yea, with thine eyes ſhalt thou behold : and ſee the reward of the ungodly.

For Thou, Lord! art my hope : Thou haſt ſet Thine houſe of defence very high.

There ſhall be no evil happen unto thee : neither ſhall any plague come nigh thy dwelling.

For He ſhall give His angels charge over thee : to keep thee in all thy ways.

They ſhall bear thee in their hands : that thou hurt not thy foot againſt a ſtone.

Thou ſhalt go upon the lion and adder : the young lion and dragon ſhalt thou tread under thy feet.

Becauſe he hath ſet his love upon Me, therefore will I deliver him : I will ſet him up, becauſe he hath known My Name.

He ſhall call upon Me, and I will hear him : yea, I am with him in trouble; I will deliver him, and bring him to honour.

With long life will I ſatisfy him : and ſhew him My Salvation.

Antiphons.

BLESSED is ſhe that believed, for there ſhall be a performance of thoſe things which were told her of The Lord.

The Lord being born, Angel-choirs ſang forth, ſaying, Salvation to our God ſitting on the Throne, and to The Lamb.

There is ſhewn forth upon us the light of Thy Countenance O Lord! Thou haſt given joy to my heart.

Have mercy upon me, O Lord! and hearken unto my prayer.

Alleluya! The Lord hath riſen. Alleluya! as He ſaid unto us, Alleluya!

Chapters.

LIKE as cinnamon and aromatic balm I gave a ſweet odour; as choſen myrrh I yielded the ſweetneſs of perfume.

The Day of The Lord cometh as a thief in the night; be ye therefore ready, for in an hour that ye know not The Son of Man ſhall come.

In peace in The Very Same
I will ſleep and take my reſt.

When I give ſleep to mine eyes, and ſlumber to mine eyelids.

I will ſleep and take my reſt.

Glory be to The Father.

Into Thine hands, O God! I commend my ſpirit,

For Thou haſt redeemed me, O Lord! Thou God of Truth!

Hymn.

O quam glorifica luce coruſcas.

O WITH what glorious luſtre reſplendent [deſcendant,
Shineſt thou, David's own royal
Mary ſweet Virgin! who loftily dwelleſt, [celleſt.
And in God's favour all women ex-

Mother, yet all honour virginal bearing, [ber preparing,
For The Lord of all angels a cham-
Him in thy boſom thou chaſtely enſhrineſt, [The Divineſt;
And from thy womb cometh Chriſt

Whom all earth with veneration adoreth, [ploreth,
Every knee bowing for ever im-
From Whom we ſeek, He a gracious ear lending, [ending.
Light in our darkneſs and joy never-

Father of Lights! all theſe bleſſings beſtowing [Ghoſt flowing;
Grant, for Thy Son, from The Holy
Who as with Thee He in Glory abideth,
All things ſupremely diſpoſeth and guideth. Amen.

Jeſu noſtra Redemptio.

JESU! Redeemer! Thou Who art
Deſire and Joy of every heart;
God! Framer of the earth and ſky,
Man! when the end of Time was nigh;

What mighty love, what pitying care,
Conſtrained Thee all our ſins to bear!
A death of pain and woe to endure,
From death Thy people to ſecure.

Hell's priſons Thou, with might ſupreme,
Didſt ope Thy captives to redeem;
Triumphant Victor! ſeated high
At God's Right Hand in Majeſty.

O let that pity move Thee ſtill,
Our ſins and ſickneſſes to heal;
Forgive us, and our mental gloom
With Thy kind countenance illume.

Be Thou our only joy, O Lord!
Who art our future great reward!
In Thee may all our glorying be
Now and throughout eternity!

All Glory, Lord! to Thee be given,
Enthroned above the Stars of Heaven;
To Father and to Holy Ghoſt,
Long as Eternity ſhall laſt! Amen.

Let my evening prayer be directed unto Thee, O Lord!

Like as incenſe in Thy ſight.

Preſerve me, O Lord!

As the apple of an eye protect me under the ſhadow of Thy wings.

Psalm.—*Nunc Dimittis.*

Now letteſt Thou O Lord! Thy ſervant depart in peace: according to Thy word,

For mine eyes have ſeen: Thy Salvation;

Which Thou haſt prepared: before the face of all people;

To be a Light to lighten the Gentiles: and to be the glory of Thy people Iſrael.

Glory be to The Father.

As it was in the beginning.

Antiphons.

We praiſe thee O Mother of God! becauſe of thee was born Chriſt, The Saviour of the world!

Alleluya! The Word was made Fleſh, and dwelt among us. Alleluya!

Save us O Lord! whilſt waking, and keep us ſleeping, ſo that we may watch with Chriſt and may repoſe in peace. Amen.

Thy light O Lord! do Thou beſtow upon us; ſo that being rid of the darkneſs of our hearts we may attain to The Light, Which is Chriſt.

Lord have mercy.

Chriſt have mercy.

Lord have mercy.

Our Father.

And lead us not into temptation;

But deliver us from evil.

In peace in The Very Same,

I will ſleep and take my reſt.

I believe in God.

The Reſurrection of the fleſh;

And Life everlaſting. Amen.

Bleſs we The Father and

The Son with The Holy Ghoſt;

Let us praiſe and highly extol Him for ever.

Bleſſed art Thou O Lord! in the firmament of Heaven,

And greatly to be praiſed and Glorious and highly exalted for ever.

The Almighty and merciful Lord bleſs and preſerve us. Amen.

I will confeſs unto The Lord, for He is gracious;

And His mercy endureth for ever.

Confeſſion.

I confess to God, the bleſſed Mary, and All the Saints, I have ſinned exceedingly in thought, word, and deed, of mine own fault, of my grievous fault; I beſeech All the Saints and Elect of God to pray for me.

Almighty God have mercy upon me, and forgive me all my ſins, deliver me from all evil, preſerve and ſtrengthen me in all goodneſs, and bring me to everlaſting life. Amen.

The Almighty and merciful God grant me Abſolution and Remiſſion of all my ſins, ſpace for true penitence, amendment of life, and the grace and conſolation of The Holy Spirit. Amen.

O God! be Thou turned and Thou ſhalt quicken us;

And Thy people ſhall rejoice in Thee.

O Lord! ſhew Thy mercy upon us;

And grant us Thy ſalvation.

Vouchſafe, O Lord! in this night

To keep us without ſin.

Have mercy upon us, O Lord! have mercy upon us.

Let Thy mercy, O Lord! be upon us,

Like as we have put our truſt in Thee.

Ariſe, O Lord! help us;

And deliver us for Thy Name's ſake.

O Lord God of Hoſts! convert us;

And ſhew us Thy countenance and we ſhall be ſaved.

O Lord! hear my prayer.

And let my crying come unto Thee.

Oriſon.

Enlighten our darkneſs we beſeech Thee, O Lord God! and all the perils of this night do Thou graciouſly turn away from us; Save us, O Almighty

God! and grant us Thy perpetual light. Through our Lord. Amen.

O Lord! favourably receive my prayers; that being delivered from all adversity and error I may serve Thee in safety and freedom; and grant us Thy Peace in our time. Through our Lord Jesus Christ Thy Son, Who with Thee liveth and reigneth in The Unity of The Holy Ghost, God world without end. Amen.

May the souls of the faithful through the mercy of God rest in peace. Amen.

Bless we The Lord.

Thanks be to God. Amen.

ℭ *Here follow* THE SEVEN PENITENTIAL PSALMS

Psalm vi.—*Domine, est in furore.*

LORD! rebuke me not in Thine indignation: neither chasten me in Thy displeasure.

Have mercy upon me, O Lord! for I am weak: O Lord! heal me, for my bones are vexed.

My soul also is sore troubled: but, Lord, how long wilt Thou punish me?

Turn Thee, O Lord! and deliver my soul: O save me for Thy mercy's sake.

For in death no man remembereth Thee: and who will give Thee thanks in the pit?

I am weary of my groaning; every night wash I my bed: and water my couch with my tears.

My beauty is gone for very trouble: and worn away because of all mine enemies.

Away from me, all ye that work vanity: for The Lord hath heard the voice of my weeping.

The Lord hath heard my petition: The Lord will receive my prayer.

All mine enemies shall be confounded, and sore vexed: they shall be turned back, and put to shame suddenly.

Psalm xxxii.—*Beati, quorum.*

Blessed is he whose unrighteousness is forgiven: whose sin is covered.

Bleſſed is the man unto whom The Lord imputeth no ſin : and in whoſe ſpirit there is no guile.

For while I held my tongue : my bones conſumed away through my daily complaining.

For Thy hand is heavy upon me day and night : and my moiſture is like the drought in ſummer.

I will acknowledge my ſin unto Thee : and mine unrighteouſneſs have I not hid.

I ſaid, I will confeſs my ſins unto The Lord : and ſo Thou forgaveſt the wickedneſs of my ſin.

For this ſhall every one that is godly make his prayer unto Thee, in a time when Thou mayeſt be found : but in the great water-floods they ſhall not come nigh Him.

Thou art a place to hide me in, Thou ſhalt preſerve me from trouble : Thou ſhalt compaſs me about with ſongs of deliverance.

I will inform thee, and teach thee in the way wherein thou ſhalt go : and I will guide thee with Mine eye.

Be ye not like to horſe and mule, which have no underſtanding : whoſe mouths muſt be held with bit and bridle, leſt they fall upon thee.

Great plagues remain for the ungodly : but whoſo putteth his truſt in The Lord, mercy embraceth him on every ſide.

Be glad, O ye righteous, and rejoice in The Lord : and be joyful, all ye that are true of heart.

Psalm xxxviii.—*Domine, ne in furore.*

Put me not to rebuke, O Lord ! in Thine anger : neither chaſten me in Thy heavy diſpleaſure.

For Thine arrows ſtick faſt in me : and Thy hand preſſeth me ſore.

There is no health in my fleſh, becauſe of Thy diſpleaſure : neither is there any reſt in my bones, by reaſon of my ſin.

For my wickedneſſes are gone over my head : and are like a ſore burden, too heavy for me to bear.

My wounds ſtink, and are corrupt : through my fooliſhneſs.

I am brought into ſo great trouble and miſery : that I go mourning all the day long.

For my loins are filled with

a ſore diſeaſe: and there is no whole part in my body.

I am feeble, and ſore ſmitten: I have roared for the very diſquietneſs of my heart.

Lord, Thou knoweſt all my deſire: and my groaning is not hid from Thee.

My heart panteth, my ſtrength hath failed me: and the ſight of mine eyes is gone from me.

My lovers and my neighbours did ſtand looking upon my trouble: and my kinſmen ſtood afar off.

They alſo that ſought after my life laid ſnares for me: and they that went about to do me evil talked of wickedneſs, and imagined deceit all the day long.

As for me, I was like a deaf man, and heard not: and as one that is dumb, who doth not open his mouth.

I became even as a man that heareth not: and in whoſe mouth are no reproofs.

For in Thee, O Lord! have I put my truſt: Thou ſhalt anſwer for me, O Lord my God!

I have required that they, even mine enemies, ſhould not triumph over me: for when my foot ſlipped, they rejoiced greatly againſt me.

And I, truly, am ſet in the plague: and my heavineſs is ever in my ſight.

For I will confeſs my wickedneſs: and be ſorry for my ſin.

But mine enemies live, and are mighty: and they that hate me wrongfully are many in number.

They alſo that reward evil for good are againſt me: becauſe I follow the thing that good is.

Forſake me not, O Lord my God!: be not Thou far from me.

Haſte Thee to help me: O Lord God of my ſalvation!

Psalm li.—*Miſerere mei, Deus.*

Have mercy upon me, O God! after Thy great goodneſs: according to the multitude of Thy mercies do away mine offences.

Waſh me thoroughly from my wickedneſs: and cleanſe me from my ſin.

For I acknowledge my faults: and my ſin is ever before me.

Againſt Thee only have I ſinned, and done this evil in Thy ſight: that Thou mighteſt be juſtified in Thy ſaying, and clear when Thou art judged.

Behold, I was ſhapen in wickedneſs: and in ſin hath my mother conceived me.

But Lo! Thou requireſt truth in the inward parts: and ſhalt make me to underſtand wiſdom ſecretly.

Thou ſhalt purge me with hyſſop, and I ſhall be clean: Thou ſhalt waſh me, and I ſhall be whiter than ſnow.

Thou ſhalt make me hear of joy and gladneſs: that the bones which Thou haſt broken may rejoice.

Turn Thy face away from my ſins: and put out all my miſdeeds.

Make me a clean heart, O God!: and renew a right ſpirit within me.

Caſt me not away from Thy preſence: and take not Thy Holy Spirit from me.

O give me the comfort of Thy help again: and ſtabliſh me with Thy free Spirit.

Then ſhall I teach Thy ways unto the wicked: and ſinners ſhall be converted unto Thee.

Deliver me from blood-guiltineſs, O God! Thou that art the God of my health: and my tongue ſhall ſing of Thy righteouſneſs.

Thou ſhalt open my lips, O Lord!: and my mouth ſhall ſhew Thy praiſe.

For Thou deſireſt no ſacrifice, elſe would I give it Thee: but Thou delighteſt not in burnt-offerings.

The ſacrifice of God is a troubled ſpirit: a broken and contrite heart, O God! ſhalt Thou not deſpiſe.

O be favourable and gracious unto Syon: build Thou the walls of Jeruſalem.

Then ſhalt Thou be pleaſed with the ſacrifice of righteouſneſs, with the burnt-offerings and oblations: then ſhall they offer young bullocks upon Thine altar.

PSALM cii.—*Domine, exaudi.*

HEAR my prayer, O Lord!: and let my crying come unto Thee.

Hide not Thy face from me in the time of my trouble: incline Thine ear unto me when I call; O hear me, and that right ſoon.

For my days are conſumed away like ſmoke: and my bones are burnt up as it were a fire-brand.

My heart is ſmitten down,

and withered like graſs: ſo that I forget to eat my bread.

For the voice of my groaning: my bones will ſcarce cleave to my fleſh.

I am become like a pelican in the wilderneſs: and like an owl that is in the deſert.

I have watched, and am even as it were a ſparrow: that ſitteth alone upon the houſe-top.

Mine enemies revile me all the day long: and they that are mad upon me are ſworn together againſt me.

For I have eaten aſhes as it were bread: and mingled my drink with weeping;

And that becauſe of Thine indignation and wrath: for Thou haſt taken me up, and caſt me down.

My days are gone like a ſhadow: and I am withered like graſs.

But, Thou, O Lord! ſhalt endure for ever: and Thy remembrance throughout all generations.

Thou ſhalt ariſe, and have mercy upon Syon: for it is time that Thou have mercy upon her, yea, the time is come.

And why? Thy ſervants think upon her ſtones: and it pitieth them to ſee her in the duſt.

The heathen ſhall fear Thy Name, O Lord!: and all the kings of the earth Thy Majeſty;

When The Lord ſhall build up Syon: and when His glory ſhall appear;

When He turneth Him unto the prayer of the poor deſtitute: and deſpiſeth not their deſire.

This ſhall be written for thoſe that come after: and the people which ſhall be born ſhall praiſe The Lord.

For He hath looked down from His Sanctuary: out of the Heaven did The Lord behold the earth;

That He might hear the mournings of ſuch as are in captivity: and deliver the children appointed unto death;

That they may declare the Name of The Lord in Syon: and His worſhip at Jeruſalem;

When the people are gathered together: and the kingdoms alſo, to ſerve The Lord.

He brought down my ſtrength in my journey: and ſhortened my days.

But I ſaid, O my God! take

me not away in the midſt of mine age: as for Thy years, they endure throughout all generations.

Thou, Lord, in the beginning haſt laid the foundation of the earth: and the heavens are the work of Thy hands.

They ſhall periſh, but Thou ſhalt endure: they all ſhall wax old as doth a garment;

And as a veſture ſhalt Thou change them, and they ſhall be changed: but Thou art the ſame, and Thy years ſhall not fail.

The children of Thy ſervants ſhall continue: and their ſeed ſhall ſtand faſt in Thy ſight.

Psalm cxxx.—*De profundis.*

Out of the deep have I called unto Thee, O Lord!: Lord, hear my voice.

O let Thine ears conſider well: the voice of my complaint.

If Thou, Lord, wilt be extreme to mark what is done amiſs: O Lord! who may abide it?

For there is mercy with Thee: therefore ſhalt Thou be feared.

I look for The Lord; my ſoul doth wait for Him: in His word is my truſt.

My ſoul fleeth unto The Lord: before the morning watch, I ſay, before the morning watch.

O Iſrael, truſt in The Lord, for with The Lord there is mercy: and with Him is plenteous redemption.

And He ſhall redeem Iſrael: from all his ſins.

Psalm cxliii.—*Domine, exaudi.*

Hear my prayer, O Lord! and conſider my deſire: hearken unto me for Thy truth and righteouſneſs' ſake.

And enter not into judgement with Thy ſervant: for in Thy ſight ſhall no man living be juſtified.

For the enemy hath perſecuted my ſoul; he hath ſmitten my life down to the ground: he hath laid me in the darkneſs, as the men that have been long dead.

Therefore is my ſpirit vexed within me: and my heart within me is deſolate.

Yet do I remember the time paſt; I muſe upon all Thy works: yea, I exerciſe myſelf in the works of Thy hands.

I ſtretch forth my hands

unto Thee: my ſoul gaſpeth unto Thee as a thirſty land.

Hear me, O Lord! and that ſoon, for my ſpirit waxeth faint: hide not Thy face from me, leſt I be like unto them that go down into the pit.

O let me hear Thy loving-kindneſs betimes in the morning, for in Thee is my truſt: ſhew Thou me the way that I ſhould walk in, for I lift up my ſoul unto Thee.

Deliver me, O Lord! from mine enemies: for I flee unto Thee to hide me.

Teach me to do the thing that pleaſeth Thee, for Thou art my God: let Thy loving Spirit lead me forth into the land of righteouſneſs.

Quicken me, O Lord! for Thy Name's ſake: and for Thy righteouſneſs' ſake bring my ſoul out of trouble.

And of Thy goodneſs ſlay mine enemies: and deſtroy all them that vex my ſoul; for I am Thy ſervant.

Glory be to The Father.

As it was in the beginning.

Antiphon.

Remember not O Lord! our offences, nor the offences of our forefathers; neither take Thou vengeance of our ſins. Spare O Lord! ſpare Thy people whom Thou haſt redeemed with Thy precious Blood; be not angry with us for ever; and give not up Thine heritage to perdition; be not forgetful of us for ever. Amen.

☙ THE LITANY.

ORD! have mercy.
Chriſt! have mercy.
Lord! have mercy.
O Chriſt! Hear us.

O Father of Heaven! God! Have mercy upon us.

O Son, Redeemer of the world! God! Have mercy upon us.

O Holy Ghoſt! God! Have mercy upon us.

Holy Trinity! One God! Have mercy upon us.

Holy Mary! Pray for us.
Holy Michael! Pray for us.
Holy Gabriel! Pray for us.
Holy Raphael! Pray for us.

All ye holy Angels and Archangels of God! Pray for us.

All ye holy Orders of Blessed Spirits! Pray for us.

All ye holy Patriarchs and Prophets! Pray for us.

All ye holy Apostles and Evangelists! Pray for us.

All ye holy Disciples of The Lord and Innocents! Pray for us.

All ye holy Martyrs! Pray for us.

All ye holy Confessors! Pray for us.

All ye holy Monks and Hermits! Pray for us.

All ye holy Virgins! Pray for us.

All ye holy Widows and Continent! Pray for us.

All ye Saints of God! Pray for us.

Be favourable: Spare us O Lord!

From all evil: Deliver us O Lord!

From the snares of the Devil: Deliver us O Lord!

From everlasting damnation: Deliver us O Lord!

From the assaults of evil spirits: Deliver, &c.

From the spirit of fornication:

From the appetite of vain glory:

From all impurity of mind and body:

From the pestilence of pride:

From carnal desires:

From the persecution of the Pagans and all our enemies:

From anger and hatred and all ill will:

From the wrath to come:

From unclean thoughts:

From blindness of heart:

From lightning and tempest:

From sudden and unforeseen and eternal death.

By the Mystery of Thy Holy Incarnation:

By Thy Nativity:

By Thy Holy Circumcision:

By Thy Baptism:

By Thy Fasting:

By Thy Cross and Passion:

By Thy precious Death:

By Thy glorious Resurrection:

By Thy wonderful Ascension:

By The Grace of The Holy Ghost The Comforter: Deliver us O Lord!

In the hour of death: Succour us O Lord!

From the pains of Hell: Deliver us O Lord!

In the Day of Judgement: Deliver us O Lord!

Sinners we beseech Thee hear us!

That Thou wouldest grant us peace and concord;

We beseech Thee hear us.

That Thy mercy and goodness may alway preserve us:

We beseech Thee hear us.

That Thou wouldest vouchsafe to govern and defend Thy Holy Church: We beseech, &c.

That Thou wouldest vouchsafe to preserve our Primate, Archbishops, and Bishops, and all orders of The Church, in Thy Holy Religion:

That Thou wouldest vouchsafe to grant to our Queen and princes peace and true concord and victory:

That Thou wouldest vouchsafe to visit and comfort our habitation and all who dwell in it:

That Thou wouldest vouchsafe to preserve the congregations of all Thy Saints in Thy service:

That Thou wouldest vouchsafe to preserve all Christian people redeemed by Thy precious Blood:

That Thou wouldest render to all our benefactors everlasting benefits:

That Thou wouldest grant us remission of all our sins:

That Thou wouldest deliver our souls and the souls of our forefathers from eternal condemnation:

That Thy mercy and goodness may ever preserve us:

That Thou wouldest bestow on us seasonable weather:

That Thou wouldest vouchsafe to give and preserve the fruits of the earth:

That Thou wouldest vouchsafe to grant health of mind and of body to all our brethren and to all the faithful who are in sickness:

That Thou wouldest dispose the way of Thy servants in the prosperity of Thy Salvation:

That Thou wouldest vouchsafe to cast the eyes of Thy mercy upon us:

That Thou wouldest make reasonable the obedience of our service:

That Thou wouldest exalt our minds to heavenly desires:

That Thou wouldest vouchsafe to regard and relieve the miseries of the poor and captives:

That Thou wouldest grant to all the faithful living and departed eternal rest:

That Thou wouldest vouchsafe to bring us to everlasting joys:

That Thou wouldest vouchsafe to hearken unto us:

We beseech Thee hear us.

Son of God! we beseech Thee hear us.

Lamb of God! Who takest away the sins of the world: Spare us O Lord!

Lamb of God! Who takest away the sins of the world: Have mercy upon us.

Lamb of God! Who takest away the sins of the world: Hear us O Lord!

O Christ! hear us.

Lord! have mercy.

Christ! have mercy.

Lord! have mercy.

OUR FATHER.

Hail Mary.

And lead us not into temptation.

But deliver us from evil.

O Lord! shew Thy mercy upon us.

And grant us Thy Salvation.

O Lord! let Thy mercy come upon us.

Even Thy Salvation according to Thy word.

Be unto us O Lord! a tower of strength.

From the face of the enemy.

Be mindful of Thy congregation.

Which Thou hast possessed from the beginning.

We have sinned with our fathers.

We have done amiss and dealt wickedly.

Remember not our old sins O Lord!

Let Thy mercies speedily prevent us, for we are brought very low.

Help us O God our Salvation! and for the Glory of Thy Name deliver us.

And be merciful unto our sins for Thy Name's sake.

O Lord! deal not with us after our sins:

Neither recompense us according to our iniquities.

Let us pray for every degree of the Church.

May Thy Priests be clothed with righteousness, and let Thy Saints rejoice.

For our brethren and sisters.

O my God! Save Thy servants and handmaidens who put their trust in Thee.

Let us pray for all Christian people.

Save Thy people O Lord! and bless Thine inheritance, and govern them and lift them up even for evermore.

O Lord! Save the Queen.

And hear us in the day when we call upon Thee.

Arise O Lord! help us.

And deliver us for Thy Name's ſake.

O Lord! let there be peace in Thy ſtrength;

And abundance in Thy towers.

Let us pray for the faithful departed.

May the ſouls of Thy ſervants and handmaidens reſt in peace! Amen.

Eternal reſt grant them O Lord!

And may perpetual light ſhine upon them.

O Lord! hear my prayer.

And let my crying come unto Thee.

Oriſon.

O God! Whoſe property it is ever to have mercy and to ſpare, receive our petitions: ſo that thoſe whom the chain of their ſins doth bind, the pitifulneſs of Thy goodneſs may abſolve.

Stretch forth O Lord! unto Thy ſervants and handmaidens the Right Hand of Thy celeſtial help: that they may ſearch for Thee with their whole heart, and obtain what they worthily requeſt.

O God! the ſtrength of all them that put their truſt in Thee, favourably hearken to our ſupplications; and becauſe our mortal infirmity can without Thee do nothing: grant us the help of Thy Grace, that in fulfilling Thy Commandments we may pleaſe Thee both in will and deed.

O God! The Protector of all that truſt in Thee, without Whom nothing is ſtrong, nothing is holy, multiply upon us Thy mercy, that Thou being our Ruler, Thou our Guide, we may ſo paſs through good things temporal as not to loſe thoſe which are eternal.

O God! to Whom every heart lieth open, every will ſpeaketh, and from Whom no ſecret is hid; purify the thoughts of our hearts by the infuſion of Thy Holy Spirit: that we may be enabled perfectly to love Thee and meetly to praiſe Thee.

Almighty and everlaſting God! Who alone doeſt great wonders, ſend forth upon Thy ſervants the Biſhops, and upon all the Congregations committed to them, The Spirit of Thy ſaving Grace; and that they may pleaſe Thee in very truth pour upon them the continual dew of Thy bleſſing.

God! Who through the grace of Thy Holy Spirit dost pour the gifts of charity into the hearts of Thy faithful people: grant to Thy servants and handmaidens [our brethren and sisters], for whom we beseech Thy clemency, health both of mind and of body; that they may love Thee with their whole strength, and with entire satisfaction may perform those things which are pleasing unto Thee.

Be present O Lord! with our supplications, and dispose the way and actions of Thy servants in the prosperity of Thy Salvation: that among all the changes of our way and of this life, we may ever be protected by Thy help.

O God! of Whom are all holy desires, all right counsels, and all just works; give unto Thy servants that peace which the world cannot give; that both our hearts may be set to obey Thy Commandments and we being freed from the fear of our enemies may pass our time in quietness under Thy protection.

O Lord! we beseech Thee of Thy clemency shew us Thine unspeakable mercy, and both rid us of all our sins and mercifully deliver us from the punishments which we deserve for them.

We beseech Thee O Lord! humble the pride of our enemies, and overthrow them by the strength of Thy Right Hand.

Almighty and everlasting God! the Eternal Salvation of believers; hear us on behalf of those Thy servants for whom we implore the help of Thy compassion; that their health being restored to them they may return to Thee thanksgivings in Thy Church.

O God! The Creator and Redeemer of all the faithful; grant remission of all their sins to the souls of all the faithful departed: so that the pardon which they have ever desired by our pious supplications they may obtain.

O Lord! we beseech Thee of Thy goodness loose the chains of all our sins: and the blessed and glorious ever Virgin Mother of God, Mary, together with all Thy Saints, interceding for us, keep us Thy servants and all Catholic people in all fanctity ; and all who are connected with us by relationship, friendship, or profession, as well as all Christian people, do Thou purge from sin and enlighten with virtues ; bestow on us peace and health ; drive away pestilence ; give charity to our friends and to our enemies ; and to all the faithful living and departed, grant life and eternal rest in the land of the living. Through The Same Our Lord Jesus Christ, Who with Thee liveth and reigneth in the Unity of the Holy Ghost, God ! world without end. Amen.

END OF PART I.

THE ENCHEIRIDION.—Part II.

SPECIAL DEVOTIONS.

☙ AT CONFESSION.

This Prayer is for a ſoul falling into ſin, as well of great eſtate as of low, on account of which he or the people be puniſhed, to get grace thereof.

Oriſon of David, Hezekiah, and others.

LORD God! King of Iſrael! Who ſitteſt above the Cherubim, Thou alone art God above all the kings of the Earth: Thou haſt made Heaven and Earth. Incline Thine ear, and open Thine eyes, and behold our tribulation, and my confeſſion; and be intent unto us, O Lord! who all as ſheep have gone aſtray, who are all dying creatures; and like waters paſs away, never to return. Do Thou, O Lord! conſider, and ſuffer me not to periſh; for Thou art kind and merciful, and wouldeſt not that a ſoul ſhould periſh, but doſt repent, purpoſing that the caſtaway ſhould not utterly be deſtroyed. I have ſinned, O Lord! in theſe my doings; but I beſeech Thee, O Lord! that Thou wouldeſt put away the iniquity of Thy ſervant, for I have done fooliſhly, and now I am in a great ſtrait; but it is better for me to fall into the hands of The Lord, for His mercies are many, than into the hands of man. It is I who have ſinned; it is I who have done wickedly. Let Thy hand, I beſeech Thee, be turned away from me and from my father's houſe; impute not to me iniquity, nor remember the offences of Thy ſervant. O Lord! lay not to heart my wickedneſs; I acknowledge, I, Thy ſervant, my ſin; but be favourable unto me, and ſave me from the hand of my enemies, that all men may know that Thou art God alone, my Deliverer. Amen.

¶ *This is the Prayer of the sinful King Manasses, that shed the blood of innocents and of prophets, and did many other sins as Scripture witnesseth, more than any other that was afore him, or after following, reigning. And yet after all this, he besought God of His mercy entirely, and did penance, and had mercy.*

O Lord Almighty! God of our fathers Abraham, Isaac, and Jacob, and of their righteous seed; Who hast made Heaven and Earth with all the ornature thereof; Who hast sealed the Sea with the Word of Thy command, and shut up the deep with Thy terrible and wonderful Name, at which all men fear and tremble before the face of Thy power; the wrath of Whose threatening against sinners is intolerable, but the mercy of Thy promises is immeasurable, true and unsearchable; for Thou art The Most High Lord over all the Earth, longsuffering and very merciful, and repentest of the evils of men. Thou, O Lord! according to Thy goodness hast promised repentance and forgiveness of sins; and Thou, O God of the just! hast appointed repentance unto me who have sinned in number above the sands of the Sea. Mine iniquities are multiplied, I am bowed down with many fetters of iron, and I have no breathing time; for I have provoked thy wrath, and have done evil before Thee, I have done abominably and multiplied offences. And now I bow the knees of my heart, beseeching grace of Thee, O Lord! I have sinned and I acknowledge mine offences. I pray and intreat Thee, O Lord! forgive me and destroy me not with mine iniquities, nor reserve evil unto me for evermore; but save me, unworthy that I am, according to Thy great mercy, and I will praise Thee all the days of my life; for all the powers of the Heavens do praise Thee, and Thine is the Glory, for ever and ever. Amen.

Our Father.

Memorial of the Incarnation.

Hail! thou that art full of grace, The Lord is with thee; blessed art thou among women and blessed is the Fruit of thy womb Jesus! Amen.

¶ *Orison before a Representation of The Body of Christ.*

Maker of Heaven and Earth! King of kings and Lord of lords! Who hast made me out of nothing after Thine image and likeness, and hast redeemed me with Thine own Blood, Whom I, a sinner, am not worthy to name, nor to invoke, nor to think of in my heart; I a supplicant intreat and humbly beseech Thee that Thou wouldest mercifully look upon me Thine unworthy servant, and pity me as Thou didst pity the Chanaanitish woman, and Mary Magdalene, Who sparedst the publican a--

the thief when hanging on the Croſs. To Thee, O moſt merciful Father! I confeſs my ſins, which, if I deſired, I could not hide from Thee, O Lord! Spare me, O Chriſt! for I am humbled; much have I offended Thee, in pride, avarice, gluttony, luxury, in vain-glory, in hatred, in bitterneſs, in adultery, in theft, in falſehood, in blaſphemy, in jeſting, in laughter, in idle words, in hearing, in taſte, in touch, in thinking, ſpeaking, doing, and in all the modes in which I, a frail man and a ſinner, am capable of ſinning, of mine own fault, of mine own fault, of my very grievous fault. Wherefore I beſeech Thy clemency, Who cameſt down from Heaven for my ſalvation, Who didſt raiſe up David from his fall into ſin, ſpare me, O Lord! ſpare me, O Chriſt! who ſparedſt Peter though he denied Thee. Thou art my Creator, and my Helper, my Framer, and my Redeemer, my Governor, and my Father. O my Lord! my God, and my King! Thou art my hope, my confidence, my guide, mine aid, my conſolation, and my ſtrength, my defence, and my deliverance, my life, my ſalvation, my reſurrection; Thou art my ſupport, and my refuge, my light, and my deſire, my help, and my Patron. I intreat and beſeech Thee aſſiſt and defend me, ſtrengthen me and conſole me, confirm me and gladden me, enlighten me and viſit me. Raiſe me up who am dead, for I am Thy faſhioning and work; deſpiſe me not, O Lord! I am Thy ſervant and ſlave, unworthy and a ſinner though I be. But whatever I may be, whether good or evil, yet I am ever Thine. To whom then ſhall I flee unleſs I go to Thee? If Thou caſteſt me out, who will receive me? If Thou doſt deſpiſe me, who will regard me? Acknowledge me ſo unworthy, who fly for refuge unto Thee, vile and unclean though I be, for Thou canſt cleanſe me; if blind, Thou canſt enlighten me; if ſick, Thou canſt heal me; if dead and buried, Thou canſt again quicken me; for Thy mercy is greater than my iniquity; Thy pity is greater than my impiety. Thou canſt forgive more than I can commit, and ſpare more than I, a ſinner, can ſin. Regard not therefore, O Lord! nor be intent unto the multitude of my iniquities, but according to the multitude of Thy compaſſions have mercy upon me, and be favourable to me a moſt miſerable ſinner. Say unto my ſoul, I am Thy Salvation, Who haſt ſaid, I would not the death of a ſinner, but rather that he ſhould be converted and live. Convert me, O Lord! and be not Thou angry with me, I beſeech Thee, Moſt Gracious Father; for Thy mercy I ſupplicate: and I intreat Thee, that Thou wouldeſt bring me to a good end, to true penitence, to a pure confeſſion, and worthy amends for all my ſins. Amen.

And then begin your Confeſſion in this manner.

ℭ *The Form of Confeſſion.*

Firſt, I acknowledge myſelf guilty unto Almighty God, to all the Company of Heaven, and to you, my ghoſtly father, that, ſince the time of my laſt Confeſſion, I have offended my Lord God grievouſly: and eſpecially in the Seven deadly Sins.

Pride. I have ſinned in Pride of heart, not thinking lowly of God's gifts and talents which He hath lent me. Alſo I have ſinned in pride of dreſs; in ſtrength; in eloquence; in beauty; in proud words; whereof I cry God mercy.

Envy. Alſo I have ſinned in Envy, hearing any man more praiſed than I, or better cheriſhed than I, or if he hath more proſperity than I; and I have miſanſwered my fellow Chriſtians, and have rejoiced therein: whereof I cry God mercy.

Wrath. Alſo I have ſinned in Wrath, as in bitterneſs of heart againſt my fellow Chriſtians, whether it were in a little matter or great; and in every word or thing whereof I wiſhed to be avenged of them, and when I anſwered them with evil words, or have ſmitten them: whereof I cry God mercy.

Sloth. Alſo I have ſinned in Sloth, eſpecially in dulneſs of heart, and when I delighted myſelf with evil thoughts and imaginations of this world, and of my fleſh — not thanking God for His benefits, neither being ſorry for my ſins; not having occupied myſelf in prayers nor holy meditations for the ſtrengthening of my ſoul: whereof I cry God mercy.

Covetouſneſs. Alſo I have ſinned in Covetouſneſs, through unlawful deſires of worldly goods, in miſpending and unreaſonable keeping of them; and I have overmuch deſired wealth, and proſperity, and more worldly dignities, and riches than I had, and have repined at any tribulations, adverſity, or poverty: whereof I cry God mercy.

Gluttony. Alſo I have ſinned in Gluttony, by unreaſonable love of eating and drinking, more for fleſhly pleaſure than for bodily ſuſtenance; and I have greatly exceeded in meat and drink beyond what nature could bear; whereby I was the worſe diſpoſed to ſerve my Lord God, and the more ſtirred up to ſin, wrath, and retchleſſneſs: whereof I cry God mercy.

Luſt. Alſo I have ſinned in wantonneſs, by foul actions, by thought of filthy luſts, and uncleanneſs; ſometimes done in deed and in act: whereof I cry God mercy.

The Ten Commandments.

Alſo I have ſinned in breaking of the Ten Commandments. I have not loved my Lord God above all things, nor my neighbour as myſelf. I have been in the habit of ſwearing by my Lord God; by His Name, in vain; by His ſweet Body, and His Saints all. I have not hallowed the Feaſts of Holy Days commanded by the Church. I have not done due reverence to my father and mother, nor to my ghoſtly father, nor followed their teaching. I have ſinned in backbiting my fellow Chriſtians, in aſſailing their good name, and defiling them with my words. I have harmed my neighbours, taking their goods againſt their will by wrong. I have ſinned carnally with divers perſons, and would have done ſo more if I could have had time and place. I have borne falſe witneſs againſt my fellow Chriſtians. I have coveted to have my neighbour's wife, daughter, or ſervant, and would if I might. I have inordinately deſired the goods of my neighbours, contrary to the laws of God: whereof I cry God mercy.

ℭ *The Five Senses.*

Furthermore I have sinned in misusing my five Senses: that is to say, in the sight of mine eyes, the tasting of my mouth, the hearing of mine ears, the smelling of my nose, the touching of my hands and feet, and with other members of my body: whereof I cry God mercy.

ℭ *The Seven Works of Mercy bodily.*

Also I have sinned in not fulfilling the Seven Works of Mercy bodily, in will, strength, and deed. I have not clothed the naked; I have not given drink to the thirsty; I have not fed the hungry; I have not visited the prisoners and the sick; I have not parted with my goods to the poor; I have not harboured the harbourless; I have not buried the dead, according to the commandments of my God: whereof I cry God mercy.

ℭ *The Seven Works of Mercy ghostly.*

Also I have sinned in not fulfilling the Seven Works of Mercy spiritual. I have not given counsel to them that had need; I have not taught the ignorant; I have not discreetly corrected them that have offended; I have not comforted them that have been in heaviness; I have not forgiven them that have missaid or misdone anything against me; I have not patiently suffered them that have reproved me; I have not devoutly prayed to God for my neighbour, to give him grace to alter his sinful living, and to continue in virtue: whereof I cry God mercy.

ℭ *The Seven Gifts of The Holy Ghost.*

Also I have not used the Gifts of The Holy Ghost to the honour of God; as the gift of Understanding, the gift of Wisdom, the gift of Counsel, the gift of Knowledge, the gift of Strength, the gift of Piety, and the gift of Fear: whereof I cry God mercy.

ℭ *The Sacraments.*

Also I have not given thanks to our Lord for His Sacraments of Baptism and The Body and Blood of our Lord; neither have I praised Him for Confirmation, Penance, Wedlock, Priesthood, and Anointing: whereof, being repentant, I cry God mercy.

¶ *The Eight Beatitudes.*

Alſo I have not diſpoſed me to the Eight Beatitudes; as Poverty of Spirit, Perfect meekneſs in adverſity, Perfect meekneſs in proſperity, Deſire of right wiſdom, Perfect mercy, Cleanneſs of heart, Peace in deſire, joyful Endurance of perſecution in the cauſe of virtue: whereof I cry God mercy.

For theſe and all other ſins, known and not known, that ever I did ſince I was born unto this day, I aſk God mercy. And moſt merciful Lord God, I yield up myſelf guilty unto Thee, and I utterly commit myſelf unto Thy grace, pity, and mercy, and I pray you, my ghoſtly Father, to be between my ſin and me, that God of His mercy may forgive me for this my lowly confeſſion, that I may be delivered from my ghoſtly enemy, and obtain the endleſs bliſs which God hath bought for me, wherefore I pray.

[¶ *Oriſon of the Prieſt only.*

Be preſent, O Lord! with our ſupplications, and graciouſly hear me, who am the firſt to need Thy mercy; and alſo grant unto me, whom, not by election for mine own merit but by the gift of Thy grace, Thou haſt appointed Miniſter of this work, boldneſs in executing Thy commiſſion; and do Thou through our Miniſtry perform that which cometh only of Thy goodneſs: through Chriſt our Lord. Amen.]

Let us pray.

Oriſon of the Prieſt and of the Penitent.

O God! moſt kind Creator and merciful Reſtorer of the human race! Who, by the Blood of Thine Only Son didſt redeem man when ruined for eternity through the malice of the Devil; quicken this Thy ſervant, whom Thou deſireſt not on any account to die unto Thee; and do Thou, Who forſakeſt not the wandering, reclaim and correct him. O Lord! we beſeech Thee let the prayers and tears of this Thy ſervant move Thy compaſſion. Do Thou heal his wounds: ſtretch forth Thy ſaving hand to the proſtrate, that Thy Church be not ſpoiled of any portion of its Body, that Thy flock ſuſtain no hurt, that the enemy rejoice not over the bodies of Thy family, that the ſecond death poſſeſs not one who was born anew in the Laver of Salvation.

Wherefore, unto Thee, O Lord! we, Thy ſupplicants, prefer our prayers; unto Thee we pour forth the tears of our hearts. Spare Thou them that confeſs, that by Thy help they may ſo lament the ſins which they have committed in this mortal ſtate, that in the day of Thy fearful Judgment they may eſcape the ſentence of eternal damnation, and, O moſt gracious Father! never know the terrors of that darkneſs, the roaring of that flame; and returning from the ways of error into the path of righteouſneſs, may never more be afflicted with wounds, but poſſeſs whole and for ever what Thy grace hath beſtowed, and Thy mercy hath reſtored; through Chriſt our Lord. Amen.

Let us pray.

O Holy Lord! Almighty Father! Eternal God! Who haſt vouchſafed to heal our wounds; we, Thy humble Prieſt, and this Thy ſuppliant, beſeech and intreat Thee that Thou wouldeſt deign to incline the Ears of Thy pity to our prayers, and to be moved to repentance by his confeſſion; that Thou wouldeſt remit all his offences and forgive all his ſins. And do Thou, O Lord! beſtow on this Thy ſervant pardon inſtead of puniſhment, joy for ſorrow, life for death: that he who hath been brought to ſo great a hope of celeſtial happineſs, truſting in Thy mercy, may be enabled to attain to the good things of Thy rewards, and to peace, and to Thy heavenly gifts; through Chriſt our Lord. Amen.

[*Then let the Prieſt ſay*

Almighty God have mercy upon you, and forgive you all your ſins, deliver you from all evil, preſerve and ſtrengthen you in all goodneſs, and bring you to everlaſting life. Amen.

Then let the Prieſt abſolve him from all his ſins. It may be thus:

Our Lord Jeſus Chriſt of His great goodneſs abſolve thee; and I, by the authority of The Same God and Lord Jeſus Chriſt, and of the bleſſed Apoſtles Peter and Paul, committed to me, abſolve thee from all thoſe ſins which being contrite in heart, with thy mouth thou haſt confeſſed to me; and from all other thy ſins which if they had occurred to thy remembrance thou wouldeſt have been ready to confeſs; [and I reſtore thee to the Sacraments of the Church.] In The Name of The Father, and of The Son, and of The Holy Ghoſt. Amen.

Let us pray.

Stretch forth, O Lord! unto this Thy servant the right hand of Thy celestial help, that he may search for Thee with his whole heart and obtain what he worthily requests, through Christ our Lord. Amen.

Let the Benediction follow.

The Blessing of God The Father Almighty, and of The Son, and of The Holy Ghost, descend upon thee and abide with thee for ever. Amen.

The Lord be with you.

℟. And with thy spirit.

Let us pray.

O merciful God! O gracious God! Who according to the multitude of Thy mercies dost blot out the sins of the penitent, and by the remission of Thy pardon makest void the guilt of past transgressions, regard this Thy servant *N.* who with entire contrition of heart doth beseech for himself forgiveness of all his offences. Renew in him, most merciful Father, whatsoever hath been hurt by the assaults of the Devil, and restore to the unity of Thy Church this weak member, having received from Thee remission of his sins. Have pity, O Lord! upon his lamentations, have pity upon his tears, have pity upon his trouble and sorrows; and since he putteth not his trust in any thing but in Thy mercy, admit him to the sacrament of reconciliation, through Christ our Lord. Amen.

Let us pray.

Grant to us, Lord, we beseech Thee, that as Thou wast appeased by the prayers and confession of the ·ublican, so Thou wouldest look favourably upon this Thy servant, that abiding with tears in his confession he may speedily obtain Thy mercy, and restored to Thy holy Altar may once more be admitted to the privileges of Thy divine service, through Christ our Lord. Amen.]

¶ *AFTER CONFESSION.*

A Prayer against Temptation.

O God! Who rejectest not the sighing of the contrite, nor dost despise the grief of the sorrowful; Be present with the prayers which in meekness I offer to Thee in this my tribulation and sorrow; imploring Thee mercifully to regard me, and to grant me the wonted heed of Thy pity: that whatsoever the assaults of the devil or man work against me Thou wouldest bring to nought and destroy by the counsels of Thy mercy, so that hurt by no adversities but delivered from all tribulation and anguish, I may with comfort render thanks unto Thee in Thy Holy Church; through Christ our Lord. Amen.

Orison of S. Bernard.

O Good Jesu! O sweet Jesu! Son of the Virgin Mary, full of grace and truth! O kind Jesu! have mercy upon me according to Thy great mercy. O benign Jesu! I beseech Thee by that precious Blood which for us miserable sinners Thou didst vouchsafe to pour forth upon the Altar of the Cross, that Thou wouldest cast away all mine iniquities, and despise me not who humbly seek Thee and call upon Thy Holy Name of Jesus. This Name Jesus is a sweet Name; this Name Jesus is a saving Name: for what is Jesus but Saviour? O good Jesu! Who hast created me and redeemed me by Thy precious Blood, suffer me not to be condemned, whom Thou didst create out of nothing! O good Jesu! let not mine iniquity be my destruction, whom Thine Almighty goodness hath formed. O good Jesu! welcome what is Thine in me, abolish all that is alien from Thee. O good Jesu! have mercy upon me whilst it is the season of mercy, and destroy me not in the time of Thy fearful judgments. O good Jesu! if I a miserable sinner have of Thy true justice deserved eternal punishment for my sins, yet do I appeal in faith from Thy true justice to Thine ineffable mercy; that Thou wouldest pity me as a kind Father and a compassionate Lord, O good Jesu: for what profit is there in my blood if I go down into eternal corruption? For the dead praise not Thee, nor all they that go down into Hell. Most merciful Jesus! have pity upon me. Most sweet Jesus! deliver me. Most kind Jesus! be favourable to me a sinner. O Jesu! admit me, wretched criminal that I am, into the number of Thine elect. O Jesu! the Salvation of them that trust in Thee, have pity upon me. O sweet Jesu, the Remission of all my sins! O Jesu, Son of the Virgin Mary! pour upon me Thy grace, Wisdom, Charity, Chastity, and Humility, and moreover, in all mine adversities, holy Patience, so that I may perfectly love Thee, and make Thee my glorying and delight for ever and for evermore. Amen.

Orison.

O God! Who didst render the penitence of the blessed Mary Magdalene so pleasing and grateful to Thyself, that not only Thou forgavest her ſins, but didſt light up her heart with ſuch abundant ſweetneſs of love, that ſhe watered Thy Feet with her tears; Grant to us, we beſeech Thee, ſo worthily to weep for the evil deeds we have committed, that we may be enabled to obtain Thy holy pardon, and alſo in all our petitions may experience the grace of Thy propitiation; Who liveſt and reigneſt with God The Father, in The Unity of The Holy Ghoſt, God, world without end. Amen.

ℭ *A Prayer againſt Evil Thoughts.*

Lord God, I beſeech Thee not to be long abſent from me, but alway give heed to me and help me. Vain thoughts have riſen againſt me and many terrors have troubled me. How ſhall I paſs unhurt and how ſhall I break through them and eſcape unleſs Thou doſt aſſiſt me? Thou ſayeſt through Thy ſervant, I will go before them, and I will humble them that joy and truſt in earthly glory; I will ſhow thee My ſecrets. Do good, O Lord! as Thou haſt promiſed; dwell in me and chaſe from me all wicked and evil thoughts. My hope and my refuge! cauſe me to flee to Thee in every tribulation, to call upon Thee with inward confidence to be holpen, patiently awaiting Thy conſolation.

ℭ *A devout Prayer for the Illumination of Man's mind.*

O Thou Good Jeſu! enlighten me with the brightneſs of everlaſting light, and chaſe from my heart all manner of darkneſs; ſtabliſh the great variations of my mind which I ſuffer, break and deſtroy the burthen of the yoke wherewith I am encumbered, fight mightily for me and fray away thoſe evil beaſts my luſts and concupiſcence, whereby I am moved and tempted, that peace may be in me through Thy virtue and ſtrength, and praiſe may reſound through the whole of my ſoul. Command the winds and tempeſts of trouble and temptation and the ſea full of monſters and perils to ceaſe, and ſay to the north wind that it blow not, and there ſhall be a great tranquillity. Send out the light of Thy Truth that it may ſhine upon the earth, for

I am as the earth empty and barren until Thou illumine me. Pour out Thy grace from above, anoint my heart with Thy celeſtial grace, give unto me the tears of devotion to moiſten and diſſolve my dry ſoul, that it may bring forth good fruit, and the harveſt of good works. Raiſe up my mind, which is oppreſſed with the burden of ſin, and attach my deſires wholly to things celeſtial, ſo that having taſted the ſweetneſs of heavenly felicity, I may loathe all that is earthly. Raviſh me from the unſteadfaſt conſolation of all creatures, for nothing created may fully ſatisfy mine appetite. Join me, good Lord, unto Thyſelf by the band of inſeparable love, for Thou alone ſufficeſt to Thy lover, and without Thee all other things be vain and of no value. Amen.

Hymn.

Deus Pater Piiſſime.

O God! O Father, kind and beſt!
What we ſhould aſk of Thee ſuggeſt;
And, when Thy ſervants rightly pray,
O! ne'er Thy loving gifts delay.

A heart in penitence brought low,
And ſtreams of ſorrowing tears beſtow,
To waſh our ſinful conſcience clear
From all the guilt and ſhame we fear.

The grace of faith in us renew,
And with unfailing ſtrength endue;
So ne'er our conſtancy ſhall fail,
Though very Antichriſt aſſail.

Grant us pure wiſdom to attain,
And fervent charity to gain;
O ſureſt Heaven-deſcended ſign
Of them that pleaſe Thy will Divine!

Now Thy ſweet promiſe we believe,
How they that aſk ſhall more receive;
So may Thine own free mercy grant
All other gifts Thy ſervants want.

All Honour, Glory, Might, and Power,
Through countleſs ages evermore,
To Thee, O Father! Son, to Thee,
And Spirit Paraclete ſhall be. Amen.

ℭ AT THE HOLY COMMUNION.

Rex cedet in cœnâ turbâ cinctus duodenâ. Se tenet in manibus, Se cibat Ipse Cibus.

ℭ *Invitatory.*

Let us worship Christ, The King, The Ruler of the nations; Who to them that feed on Him giveth the fulness of His Spirit.

ℭ *Orisons before Holy Communion.*

SACRED Feast! wherein Christ is received; the memory of His Passion is brought to our remembrance; our souls are fulfilled with grace, and the pledge of eternal Glory is given unto us. Alleluya.

℣. Thou didst give them Bread from Heaven.

℟. Having in Itself every delight.

Orison.

O God! Who unto us in this wonderful Sacrament hast left a Memorial of Thy Passion; grant to us, we beseech Thee, so to venerate the sacred Mysteries of Thy Body and Blood, that we may evermore perceive in ourselves the fruit of Thy Redemption: Who livest and reignest, with God The Father, in The Unity of The Holy Ghost, God, world without end. Amen.

Our Father.

Memorial of The Incarnation.

Hail! Thou that art full of grace; The Lord is with thee; Blessed art thou among women and blessed is The Fruit of thy womb, Jesus! Amen.

ℭ *Devout Prefatory Anthems.*

Christ The Lord, a Priest for ever after the order of Melchisedek. offered Bread and Wine.

The merciful Lord giveth Food to them that fear Him, in memorial of His wonderful works.

I will receive the Cup of Salvation, and ſacrifice the Victim of praiſe.

The Lord hath prepared a Table for us againſt all them that trouble us.

The Lord maketh the borders of The Church peace. With the fatneſs of wheat and with honey out of the ſtony rock doth He ſatisfy us.

Thou haſt prepared Thy ſweetneſs, O God! for the poor, Who makeſt men to dwell of one mind in Thy Houſe.

With the Bread of Angels Thou haſt nouriſhed Thy people, and Food from Heaven haſt Thou given unto them. Alleluya.

Thou doſt bring Bread out of the earth, and Wine that maketh glad the heart of man.

O how ſweet, O Lord! is Thy Spirit, which Thou doſt diſpenſe, a very pleaſant favour to Thy children! Beſtowing delectable Bread from Heaven Thou feedeſt the hungry, and ſendeſt the rich and proud empty away.

Rich is the Bread of Chriſt, affording delight unto Kings. Alleluya.

Wiſdom hath built her an houſe; ſhe hath mingled her Wine, and diſpoſed her Table. Alleluya.

Elias ſaw at his head bread baked on the coals, and he aroſe and did eat and drink; and he went in the ſtrength of that meat, even unto the Mount of God.

A certain man made a great Supper, and ſent his ſervant at ſupper-time to bid the gueſts to come, For all things are ready. Come, eat ye my Bread and drink ye the Wine I have mingled for you. For all things are ready.

I will go in unto The Altar of God: I will receive Chriſt Who reneweth my youth.

Chriſt our Paſſover is ſacrificed for us, therefore let us keep The Feaſt; with the unleavened bread of ſincerity and truth.

This is The Bread which The Lord hath given us for food. Moſes gave you not that Bread from Heaven, but My Father giveth you The True Bread from Heaven.

The Bread which I will give is My Fleſh for the life of the world.

I am The Living Bread which came down from Heaven. If any man eat of this Bread, he ſhall live for evermore. Alleluya.

When they were at Supper Jeſus took bread and bleſſed, and brake, and gave to His diſciples, and ſaid, Take, eat; This is My Body.

Jeſus took The Cup after Supper, ſaying, This Cup is The New Teſtament in My Blood; Do This, in remembrance of me.

Whoſo eateth My Fleſh and drinketh My Blood abideth in Me and I in him.

There is no other nation ſo great which hath God ſo nigh unto them as our God is preſent with us.

As often as ye eat This Bread and drink This Cup, ye do ſhow The Lord's death till He come.

We being many are one Bread and One Body; for we are all partakers of One Bread and of One Cup.

To Him that overcometh I will give the hidden Manna and a new name. Alleluya.

℣. He gave them Bread from Heaven. Alleluya.

℟. Man doth eat Angel's food. Alleluya.

Orison.

O most merciful God! incline Thy gracious ears to our prayers, and enlighten our hearts with the grace of The Holy Spirit, that we may worthily celebrate Thy Holy Myſteries, and love Thee with an everlaſting love, through Chriſt our Lord. Amen.

Collects which may be ſaid before the Epiſtle, or at other times.

O Lord Jesu Christ! Son of The living God! Who for our redemption didſt will to be born, and to be circumciſed, to be rejected by the Jews, to be betrayed by Judas with a kiſs, to be taken, bound with chains, to be haled before Annas, Caiaphas, Herod, and Pilate, and in their preſence to be mocked, to be ſmitten with blows, buffets, ſtripes, and with the reed; to be ſpitted on in the face, to be crowned with thorns, to be accuſed moreover by falſe witneſſes, to be judged, and as an innocent lamb, bearing Thy Croſs, to be led forth as a Victim; to be pierced with nails, to be made to drink of vinegar and gall, and upon the Croſs to be condemned to a moſt ſhameful death, and to be wounded with a ſpear; Do Thou, O Lord! for theſe Thy moſt ſacred pains, deliver us from all ſin and puniſhment, and by Thy holy Croſs bring us miſerable ſinners to that place whither Thou didſt bring the thief, late in his penitence, who was crucified with Thee; Who liveſt and reigneſt, God, world without end. Amen.

O kind Lord Jesu! may all Thy ſufferings help and defend us from all tribulation and diſtreſs, from all grief and ſadneſs, from all danger and wretchedneſs, from all ſin and impurity of heart, from all offence and ill fame, from evil diſeaſes of ſoul and body, from ſudden and unforeſeen death, and from all the perſecutions of our enemies, viſible and inviſible; for we know that in whatſoever hour or day we have a memory of Thy Paſſion, we ſhall be in ſafety. Wherefore, trusting in Thine immeasurable goodness, we intreat Thee, O merciful Saviour! for Thy very benign and most holy Sufferings, that Thou wouldest protect us with Thy kind help and continual pity, and preserve us evermore from all evil; Who livest. Amen.

[ℭ *Orison of the Priest only.*

God, Who makest worthy the unworthy, and sinners to be righteous and holy, and purifiest the impure; cleanse my heart and body from all taint and defilement of sin, and make me a worthy and strenuous Minister at Thy Holy Altars; and mercifully grant that on this Altar, to which I, so unworthy, now approach, I may offer sacrifices pleasing and acceptable to Thy goodness for all my sins and offences, and for my numberless daily transgressions; for all moreover who are here present, and for every one who is connected with me by friendship or affinity, or who pursue me with hatred, or who are my adversaries; so also for washing away the sins of all Christian people; and may my vows be acceptable unto Thee, through Him Who offered Himself unto Thee, O God The Father! a Sacrifice for us, Who with Thee liveth and reigneth in The Unity of The Holy Ghost, God world without end. Amen.]

ℭ *Orison of S. Anselm.*

O Supreme High Priest and true Chief Bishop, Jesus Christ! Who didst offer Thyself to God The Father, a pure and spotless Victim upon the Altar of The Cross for us miserable sinners, and Who didst give us Thy Flesh to eat, and Thy Blood to drink, and didst ordain that Mystery in the might of The Holy Spirit, saying, "This Do, in remembrance of Me;" I intreat Thee by the Same Blood, the great price of our Salvation; I intreat Thee by that wonderful and unspeakable love wherewith Thou didst vouchsafe so to love us, miserable and unworthy, as to wash us from our sins in Thy Blood, teach me Thy unworthy servant [whom among Thine other gifts, not for any merit of mine, but of the condescension of Thy mercy alone, Thou hast vouchsafed also to call to the dignity of Priesthood, teach me, I pray Thee,] by Thy Holy Spirit to handle so great a Mystery with that reverence and honour, with that devotion and fear as I ought and as it becometh me. Make me, through Thy grace, always so to believe and understand, to conceive, and firmly to hold, to think and to speak of this wondrous Mystery, as shall please Thee and benefit my ſoul. Let Thy good Spirit enter my heart, there to be heard without utterance, and without the ſound of words ſpeak all truth. For theſe things are exceeding deep and covered with a ſacred vail. Of Thy great mercy, grant me to celebrate this Solemnity with a clean heart and pure mind. Free my heart from all defiling and unholy, from all vain and hurtful thoughts. Fence me with the holy and faithful guard and mighty protection of Thy bleſſed Angels, that the enemies of all good may fly away aſhamed. By the virtue of this vaſt Myſtery, and by the hand of Thy Holy Angel, repel from me and all Thy ſervants the hard ſpirit of pride and vain glory, of impurity and uncleanneſs, of doubting and miſtruſt. Let them be confounded that ſeek after my ſoul to deſtroy it: let them periſh that ſeek my hurt.

King of Virgins, and Lover of chaſtity and innocence, extinguiſh in my frame, by the dew of Thy heavenly bleſſing, the fuel of evil concupiſcence, that ſo one even purity of ſoul and body may abide in me. Mortify in my members the luſts of the fleſh, and all hurtful emotions, and give me true and perſevering chaſtity with Thine other gifts which pleaſe Thee in truth; ſo that I may with chaſte body and pure heart offer unto Thee the Sacrifice of Praiſe. For with what mighty contrition of heart and fountain of tears, with what reverence and awe, with what chaſtity of body and purity of ſoul, ſhould that Divine and Heavenly Sacrifice be celebrated, wherein Thy Fleſh is indeed taken, where Thy Blood is indeed drunk, wherein things loweſt and higheſt, earthly and divine, are united, where is the preſence of The Holy Angels, where Thou art in a wonderful and unſpeakable way both Sacrifice and Prieſt.

Who can worthily celebrate this Sacrifice unleſs Thou, O God! makeſt him worthy? I know, O Lord! yea truly do I know, and this do I confeſs to Thy loving kindneſs, that I am not worthy to approach ſo high a Myſtery, by reaſon of my very many ſins and numberleſs negligences; but I know, and truly with my own heart do I believe, and with my mouth confeſs, that Thou canſt make me worthy Who alone canſt make that clean which cometh from that which is unclean, and ſinners to be righteous and holy. By this Thine Almighty power I beſeech Thee, O my God! to grant that I, a ſinner, may celebrate this Sacrifice with fear and trembling, with purity of heart and ſtreams of tears, with ſpiritual gladneſs, and celeſtial joy; may my mind feel the ſweetneſs of Thy moſt bleſſed preſence, and the guardianſhip of The Holy Angels round about me.

For now, O Lord! mindful of Thy Venerable Paſſion, I approach Thine Altar, to offer Thee that Sacrifice which Thou haſt inſtituted, and commanded to be offered in remembrance of Thee for our well-being. Receive it, we beſeech Thee, O God Moſt High! for Thy Holy Church, and for the people whom Thou haſt purchaſed with Thy Blood. [And ſince Thou haſt willed that I, a ſinner, ſhould ſtand between Thee and this Thy people, although Thou canſt diſcern no good work in me, yet at leaſt reject not the office of the diſpenſation intruſted to me; let not through my unworthineſs the price of their ſalvation be waſted, for whom Thou didſt vouchſafe to be a ſaving Victim and Redemption!] We bring before Thee, O Lord! if Thou wilt graciouſly vouchſafe to behold, the tribulations of the poor, the perils of the people, the groans of priſoners, the miſeries of orphans, the neceſſities of ſtrangers, the helpleſſneſs of the weak, the depreſſions of the languiſhing, the infirmities of the aged, the aſpirations of the young, the vows of virgins, the wailing of widows.

We intreat Thee alſo, O Lord! Holy Father! for the ſouls of the faithful departed . . . that this great Sacrament of Thy love may be unto them ſalvation and health, joy and refreſhment. O Lord my God! grant them this day a great and abundant feaſt of Thee, The living God, Who cameſt down from Heaven, and gaveſt life unto the world, even of Thy holy and bleſſed Fleſh, the Lamb without ſpot, Who takeſt away the ſins of the world; even of that Flesh which was taken of the holy and glorious Virgin Mary, and conceived of The Holy Ghost, and of that Fountain of mercy which from the soldier's spear flowed from Thy most sacred Side, that therewith enlarged and sated, refreshed and comforted, they may rejoice in Thy praise and glory.

I PRAY Thy clemency, O Lord! that on the bread to be offered unto Thee may descend the fulness of Thy Benediction, and the Sanctification of Thy Divinity. May there descend also The invisible and incomprehensible Majesty of Thy Holy Spirit, as it descended of old on the sacrifices of the fathers, Which may make our oblations Thy Body and Blood. [And teach me an unworthy priest to handle so great a Mystery with purity of heart and the devotion of tears, with reverence and trembling, so that Thou mayest graciously and favourably receive the Sacrifice of my hands for the good of all, living and departed.]

I BESEECH Thee also, O Lord! by this most Sacred Mystery of Thy Body and Blood, wherewith we are daily fed, washed, and sanctified in Thy Church, and are made partakers of The One Supreme Divinity, give unto me Thy Holy Virtues, that fulfilled therewith I may approach with a good conscience unto Thy Holy Altar, so that these Holy Sacraments may be made unto me Salvation and Life; for Thou hast said with Thy Holy and Blessed Mouth, "The Bread which I will give is My Flesh, which I will give for the life of the world. I am The Living Bread Which came down from Heaven. If any man shall eat of This Bread, he shall live for ever."

O most sweet Bread! heal the palate of my heart, that I may taste the sweetness of Thy love. Heal it of all infirmities, that I may find sweetness in nothing out of Thee. O most pure Bread, having all delight and all savour, Which dost ever refresh us, and never failest, let my heart feed on Thee, and may my inmost soul be fulfilled with the sweetness of Thy savour. The Angels feed on Thee fully. Let pilgrim man feed on Thee after his measure, refreshed by this sustenance on his way.

Holy Bread! Living Bread! Pure Bread! Who camest down from Heaven, and givest life unto the world; come into my heart, and cleanse me from all defilement of flesh and spirit. Enter into my soul, heal and cleanse me within and without; be the protection and continual health of my soul and body, so that I may by a straight way arrive at Thy kingdom; where not as now in mysteries, but face to face, we shall behold Thee; when Thou shalt have delivered up the kingdom to God Thy Father, and shalt be God All in all, then shalt Thou satisfy me with Thyself by a marvellous fulness, so that I shall never hunger nor thirst any more, Who with The Same God The Father and The Holy Ghost livest and reignest for ever and ever. Amen.

¶ *Other Orisons.*

I. I BESEECH Thee, O most kind Lord Jesu Christ! that for the sake of the most blessed Virgin Mary Thy Mother, and of All Thy Saints, Thou wouldest teach me and permit me to approach this wonderful Sacrament of Thy Body and Blood with that pureness of heart and cleanness of mind, with that devotion and reverence which becometh me, and is expedient for my soul. O most gracious Lord Jesu Christ! may my heart perceive the sweetness of Thy blessed presence. Let it be the purgation of all my spiritual sloth, the washing away of all mine offences, my protection against all the numberless perils of the world. May my soul now taste how sweet The Lord is, that at the taste of Thee all carnal delights may give place. O delectable Bread! O Repast of life! O Food much to be desired! O Banquet of exceeding sweetness, refreshing all things, and never failing! The Angels and spirits of the just partake of Thee with plenteous fulness. May it please Thee, O Lord! that now my sinful soul, in this its pilgrimage, may faithfully partake of Thee, that so receiving strength from Thee, it may perform its journey through Thee, even unto Thee, without hindrance from Satan. Mortify in my members and in my heart all the incitements of the flesh, and all hurtful passions, that Thou, The King of Virgins and lover of Chastity, mayest have a peaceful abode in this my tabernacle. O Lord! Thou knowest with how many and how great disquietudes my soul is afflicted. But do Thou, O Lord! Who art the Supreme Physician, come and heal it, to Whom is committed all power and dominion through infinite ages of ages. Amen.

II. O gracious Lord Jesus Christ, I Thy sinful servant, nothing presuming on my own deserts, but trusting in Thy mercy and goodness, with fear and trembling approach to the Table of Thy most sweet Feast. For my heart and body are defiled with many sins, my mind and tongue have not been faithfully guarded. So then, O gracious God! O terrible Majesty! I, miserable that I am, being in a great strait, turn to Thee, the Fountain of mercy. To Thee I hasten to be cured, under Thy protection I flee, longing to have Thee for my Saviour, before Whom I cannot stand as my Judge. To Thee, O Lord! I show my wounds, to Thee I lay bare my shame; I know my sins, many and great, for which I fear, and I hope in Thy mercies, which are countless. Look down then on me with the eyes of Thy mercy, O Lord Jesu Christ, Eternal King! God and man! Crucified for man! Hear me who hope in Thee; have pity on me who am full of miseries and sins, Thou Who wilt never cease to pour forth the streams of mercy. Blessed be Thou, life-giving Victim, Who for me and all mankind wast offered on the Cross of suffering. Hail! Holy and precious Blood which did flow from the Wounds of my crucified Lord Jesus Christ and wash away the sins of the whole world. Remember, Lord, Thy creature which Thou hast redeemed with Thine own Blood. I repent me that I have sinned, and long to amend what I have done. Take from me, then, most merciful Father, all my iniquities and sins, that purified in mind and body I may be made worthy, worthily to taste The Holy of Holies. And grant that this sacred foretaste of Thy Body and Blood which I unworthy purpose to take, may be the remission of my sins, the perfect cleansing of my offences, the scaring away of all evil thoughts, the renewal of all good desires, the healthful effectuating of works wellpleasing unto Thee, the most firm protection of soul and body against the wiles of mine enemies. Amen.

III. O Fountain of entire mercy which dost never cease to flow! come unto me this day and enable mine ailing soul devoutly to receive Thy Flesh and drink Thy precious Blood. Not for that I am righteous, but because I am a sinner, for they that are whole need not a physician, but they that are sick. O Thou True Charity wherein is eternal felicity! O Thou only hope of my soul! Take from me mine iniquities that I may be enabled with a pure mind to enter into The Holy of Holies. My heart awaiteth Thee, fulfil the desire which Thou hast put into my heart as Thou willest. I am Thine, O Christ! O give me not over to another. May Thy right hand ever prevent me and defend me from all evil. Come, O Lord! Thou against Whom I most miserable have sinned. Remember not my sins, for which Thou hast shed forth Thy Blood. Come, O God! Who art most dear unto my soul, give unto me the Food of eternal salvation. Come, Thou immaculate Sacrifice, deliver me from eternal death. Come, Thou Physician of the sick; come, Thou Food of the hungry. Come, O Lord! and visit this my tabernacle dedicate in Thy Name; and Lo! I come with my whole heart, as is my desire unto Thee, to Whom with my whole soul I aspire, Whom with my whole affection I embrace, Whose Body and Blood, I long to receive, that Thou mayest ever abide in me now and for evermore. Send me not empty away, O most gracious Father Almighty. Amen.

IV. Lord! I am not worthy that Thou shouldest enter in under my roof, but trusting in Thy goodness I approach unto Thine Altar, to The Sacrament of The Body and Blood of Thine Only-begotten

Son, our Lord Jesus Christ; sick, to The Physician of Life; unclean, to The Fountain of Mercy; blind, to The Light of Eternal Splendour; poor, unto the Lord of Heaven and Earth; naked, to The King of Glory; a sheep, to The Shepherd; a creature, to its Creator; desolate, to The kind Comforter; miserable, to The Pitier; guilty, to The Bestower of Pardon; wicked, to The Justifier; hardened, to The Infuser of Grace; beseeching the abundance of Thy boundless mercy that Thou wouldest vouchsafe to heal mine infirmities, to wash away my defilements, to enlighten my blindness, to enrich my poverty, to clothe my nakedness, to restore the wandering, to console the forsaken, to reconcile the guilty, to grant pardon to the sinner, forgiveness to the wretched, life to the criminal, righteousness to the dead; that I may be found worthy to receive Thee, The Bread of Angels, The King of Kings, the Lord of Lords, with that chastity of body and purity of soul, with that contrition of heart and fountain of tears, with that spiritual gladness and celestial joy, with that fear and awe, that reverence and honour, that faith and humility, that purpose and love, with that devotion and thankfulness, which becometh me, and as is expedient for the health of my soul; so that it may profit me unto eternal life, and be unto me the remission of all my sins. Grant unto me, I beseech Thee, that I may receive not only The Sacrament of This The Body and Blood of The Lord, but also the Virtue of That Sacrament. O most gracious God! grant me so to receive The Body of Thine Only-begotten Son, our Lord Jesus Christ, which He took of the Virgin Mary, that I may be found worthy to be incorporated into His Mystical Body, and to be reckoned among His members. O most loving Father! grant unto me that Thy Beloved Son, Whom now I purpose to receive beneath a veil in this my pilgrimage, I may at length, with unveiled face, contemplate for ever; Who, with Thee liveth and reigneth in The Unity of The Holy Ghost, God, through infinite ages of ages. Amen.

ℭ *AT THE TIME OF CONSECRATION.*

The grace of The Holy Spirit kindle and enlighten thine heart and lips, and may the Lord accept this as a worthy Sacrifice from thine hands for our ſins and offences! Amen.

[Ave! verum Corpus natum
De Maria Virgine,
Vere paſſum immolatum
In Cruce pro homine!
Cujus latus perforatum
Unda fluit ſanguine;
Eſto nobis preguſtatum,
Mortis in examine!
O Clemens! O Pie!
O dulcis Fili Mariæ!]

Hail! True Body of the Virgin!
Spotleſs Mary's Virgin Birth!
Slain upon the Croſs and purging
By His pains the ſins of earth.

From Whoſe Side for ſinners riven,
Water flowed and mingled Blood;
May'ſt Thou, deareſt Lord! be given
In death's hour to be my Food,

Hear us, merciful and mild,
Jeſu! Mary's gracious Child.

Hail! Jeſu Chriſt, Word of the Father! Son of the Virgin, Lamb of God! Salvation of the world! Holy Sacrifice! Word in Fleſh! Fountain of Pity!

Hail! Jeſu, Praiſe of Angels, Glory of Saints, Viſion of Peace, Entire Deity, True Man, Flower and fruit of the Virgin Mother!

Hail! Jeſu Chriſt, Brightneſs of The Father, Prince of Peace, Gate of Heaven, Living Bread, Offspring of the Virgin, Veſſel of The Godhead!

Hail! Jeſu Chriſt, Light of Heaven, Ranſom of the world, Joy of our hearts, Bread of Angels, King and Spouſe of Virginity!

Hail! Jeſu Chriſt, the moſt ſweet Way, Supreme Truth, Reward of ours, Living Charity, Fountain of Love, Peace, Sweetneſs of Eternal Life!

Hail! moſt Holy and precious Body of Chriſt which ſet on the Altar of the Croſs for the ſaving of the world, I believe with my heart, I confeſs with my mouth, a True Sacrifice a Pure Sacrifice, a Holy Sacrifice, a Sacrifice unſpotted and acceptable to God, the Holy Bread of eternal life and the Cup of everlaſting ſalvation. I worſhip Thee in ſpirit and truth. O kind Jesu! Good Jesu, have mercy upon me! I pray Thee, therefore, O God, that like as I see Thee here present under the form of bread and wine, so I may be found worthy to behold Thee in the Glory of Thy Majesty, in peace and gladness for ever and ever. Amen.

In the presence of Thy most Holy Body and Blood, O Lord Jesu Christ, I commend unto Thee myself most miserable Thy servant, that by the virtue of Thy Holy Cross, and by the Mystery of Thy Holy Incarnation, Nativity, Baptism, Fasting, Passion, Death, Resurrection, Ascension, and by the coming of The Holy Ghost The Comforter, and by Thy Name Ineffable, Thou, Who art God Almighty, Alpha and Omega, The Beginning and the End, Sabaoth, Adonai, Emmanuel Which is God with us, The Way, The Truth, and The Life, our Salvation, Victory, and Resurrection, especially by the invocation of This life-giving Sacrifice of Thy Body and Blood which I invoke for my help, entangled though I be in many sins, yet created by Thee, and redeemed by Thy most precious Blood, and believing and trusting in Thee, The Only living and True God, Thou wouldest guard and defend me from all evils at all times, and deliver me from injury and snares, from captivity and bonds, from the tongues and weapons and shafts of all my enemies, visible and invisible; also that Thou wouldest vouchsafe to deliver me from all wicked works, poisonous and deadly food, from grief, shame, disease, confusion, slander, and from all offences and dangers, from all falling, ruin, hurt, detriment and hindrances of soul and of body, and from sudden and unforseen and eternal death; and wouldest deign mercifully to drive all these evils far away from me, by The Holy Mystery of Thy Passion and of our redemption, to which I do trustfully commit me for my salvation, hoping that through It I may be saved. Therefore, most merciful God, Who wouldest not the death of a sinner, but that he should be converted and live, Who hearest all that cry unto Thee, and truſt in Thee, hearken to me alſo a ſinner; and all thoſe whom Thou haſt redeemed with Thy precious Blood, recall unto Thyſelf and enlighten with the gift of Thy grace; and according to the multitude of Thy mercy have pity upon me according to Thy good will, and as Thou knoweſt, beſtow on me true health both of body and ſoul. Sinner though I be, yet I have not denied Thee: hearken unto my prayer, O kind Jeſu! and ſend me Thy grace to accompany and preſerve me from all evils, and bring me to eternal life, Thou ſhowing pity upon me, Who with The Father and The Holy Ghoſt, liveſt and reigneſt God, world without end. Amen.

O Lord Jeſu Chriſt! Who didſt take upon Thyſelf This Thy moſt ſacred Fleſh from the womb of the glorious Virgin Mary, and didſt pour forth This Thy precious Blood from Thy moſt ſacred Side for our ſalvation upon the Altar of the Croſs, and in This glorious Fleſh didſt riſe again from the dead and aſcend into Heaven, and art again to come in The Same Fleſh to judge the living and the dead, deliver us by This Thy moſt Holy Body now on Thy Altar, from all ſins and impurities of ſoul and body, and from all evils and dangers, now and for evermore.

Oriſon of S. Auguſtine.

Look upon me unhappy, God of boundleſs pity! look upon me with the regards of Thy mercy. Caſt down, I come to Thee, Almighty One! Wounded, I run to The Phyſician. Continue Thy pity and loving kindneſs, Who haſt ſo long delayed the ſword of vengeance. Blot out the number of mine offences by the multitude of Thy mercies.

Oriſon.

Soul of Chriſt, ſanctify me; Body of Chriſt, ſave me: Blood of Chriſt, inebriate me: Water from the ſide of Chriſt, waſh me: Brightneſs of the Countenance of Chriſt, enlighten me: Paſſion of Chriſt, ſtrengthen me: Bloody Sweat of the moſt noble Countenance of Chriſt, heal me; O good Jeſu, hearken unto me, in Thy Wounds hide me, let me never be ſeparated from Thee, from the malicious enemy defend me, in the hour of my death call me, and place me beſide Thee, that with Angels and ſaints I may praiſe Thee, O Lord my Saviour for evermore! Amen.

[Ave! Caro Chriſti cara
Immolata Crucis Arâ
Pro redemptis Hoſtia;
Morte Tua nos amara,
Fac redemptos luce clara
Tecum frui Gloria.

Ave! Verbum Incarnatum,
In Altari conſecratum!
Panis vivus Angelorum,
Salus et ſpes infirmorum,
Medicina peccatorum!
Salve! Corpus Jeſu Chriſti
Qui de Cœlo deſcendiſti;
Et populum redemiſti
Cum in Cruce pependiſti.]

Hail! Fleſh of Chriſt, beloved Oblation!
Sacrifice for our ſalvation!
On the Croſs a Victim ſlain.
O! by that Thy death of ſadneſs [gladneſs
Raiſe us decked in light and
With Thee glorified to reign.

Hail! Word Incarnate! Which Divineſt
Hallowed on the Altar ſhineſt;
Bread of Angels everliving!
Health and hope to mortals giving,
Antidote! all guilt relieving.
Hail! Thou Body of Chriſt Jeſus
Heaven-deſcended to releaſe us,
Thy redeemed from ruin buying
On the Croſs when nailed and dying.

O Good Jeſu, Fount of Pity! Prince of Angels! Glory of the Saints! Hope of Sinners! have mercy upon us.

Hail! Thou Light of the World, Word of the Father, Very Sacrifice, Fleſh of Life, Entire Deity, Very Man. Hail! Principle of our creation. Hail! Price of our Redemption. Hail! Viaticum of our pilgrimage. Hail! Comfort of our expectation. Hail! Health, Surety of our Salvation: Who art here ſlain and hallowed for us; help us, O our God! diſpoſe us in Thy peace, and number us among the flock of thine elect. Amen.

May Thy Blood, O Lord Jeſu Chriſt! poured forth for us, be unto me the remiſſion of all my ſins, negligencies, and ignorances, an increaſe of ſtrength, and for the perfecting of my faith, hope, and charity, and all other graces and virtues; for the guard of my life, for my adoption to eternal Glory, for the benefit of the souls of my father and mother, and of all for whom I am bound to pray.

Orison.

Hail! for evermore, most Holy and precious Flesh. Hail! for evermore, most Holy and precious Blood of our Lord Jesus Christ. Hail! Saving Victim for the salvation of mankind, offered on the Altar of the Cross. Hail! most sufficient Sacrifice. Hail! most delectable refreshment. Hail! Jesu Christ. Hail! Redeemer of the world, inestimable Glory of all the elect, Who, for us miserable sinners didst vouchsafe to take upon Thee This Flesh from the immaculate Virgin, and to shed forth This Blood from Thy Side, whilst hanging on the Cross; purify us, sanctify us, direct us in the way of eternal salvation. And, as in This Sacred Mystery is made a change in the Bread and Wine, so change us into Thyself, and conform us wholly to Thy grace. Amen.

Rhythm of S. Thomas Aquinas.

Adoro Te devote latens Deitas.

Devoutly, I adore Thee, unseen Deity!
Here beneath these dread symbols shrined in mystery;
Prostrate before Thee all my spirit sinks subdued
Lost in the contemplation of Thy Plenitude!
In Thee the sight, the touch, entirely are deceived;
Only the hearing may securely be believed.
This I believe, whate'er the Son of God declared;
Naught verily is truer than God's Very Word;
Upon the Cross was veiled the Deity alone,
But here the Manhood also is to sense unknown;
Yet both believing and confessing, at Thy Feet
What the repentant thief intreated, I intreat.
Now those Thy Wounds, like Thomas, though I cannot see,
Like him, my Lord and Saviour, I acknowledge Thee.
O make my faith in Thee for evermore increase;
Give me unfading Hope and Love that ne'er shall cease.
Divine Memorial of my kind and dying Lord!
Thou Living Bread! Who dost to man true life afford,
Grant that my soul for evermore on Thee may live
And all the eternal Savour of Thy sweetness give.
Lord Jesu! loving Pelican! Thy children's Food,

O cleanse Thou me the unclean in Thine atoning Blood!
One drop of Which a ruined universe could save
And pure from all pollution all creation lave!
Jesu! Whom here beneath a veil I dimly view,
O with one blessed gift my thirsting soul bedew;
For me within the veil do Thou prepare a place,
There to behold Thee in Thy Glory face to face.

ℂ *Before receiving.*

Hail! Saving Sacrifice for me and for all mankind offered on the Cross of suffering. Hail! noble and most precious Blood, flowing from the Side of my crucified Lord Jesus Christ, and washing away all my sins which defile me, old as well as new. Remove therefore from me, O most merciful Jesus! all the iniquities whereby I have offended, for I am exceedingly polluted with very heinous sins, so that purified in soul and body I may be worthy to approach the Holy of Holies and taste the Sacraments of Thy Body and Blood. O Thou pitier of man! I a suppliant intreat Thee that what Thou hast given to blot out the sins of mankind may not be to me an increase of my offences, but may be for my pardon and protection. O Lord! make me so to receive them into my mouth and heart, and to embrace them with the affection of faith, that by their strength I may be fashioned into the likeness of Thy Death and Resurrection by mortification of the old man and renewal to a holy life, that so I may be worthy to be incorporated with Thy Body which is the Church, and may be Thy member and Thou my Head, and may abide in Thee and Thou in me until in the Resurrection Thou dost renew this body of my humiliation and fashion it like unto Thy glorious Body, as Thou hast promised to Thine Apostle, and that in Thee I may rejoice evermore for Thy Glory. Amen.

ℂ *In receiving.*

O Lord! I am not worthy that Thou shouldest come under my roof, but say the word only and my soul shall be healed. Thou, O Lord! hast said, Whoso eateth My Flesh and drinketh My Blood abideth in me and I in him; be favorable to me a sinner, for this my taking of Thy Body and Blood, and grant that I may not receive It to my judgment or condemnation, but by the gift of Thy mercy for my salvation and the remiſſion of all my ſins.

ℭ *WHEN THOU HAST RECEIVED.*

MAY the true perception of Thy Body and Blood, O Almighty God! not be unto me for my judgment to condemnation, but be the deſired remiſſion of all my ſins both of ſoul and body, the gracious and mighty governance of my ſoul and body, and my admiſſion into life both preſent and everlaſting, through Chriſt my Lord. Amen.

O Almighty and everlaſting God! Jeſus Chriſt The Lord! be merciful unto my ſins for this my taking of Thy Body and Blood. For Thou haſt ſpoken and ſaid, "Whoſo eateth My Fleſh, and drinketh my Blood, abideth in Me, and I in him." Wherefore I ſupplicate and beſeech Thee to create in me a clean heart, and to renew a right ſpirit within me; and ſo to ſtrengthen me with Thy Chief Spirit, and to deliver me from all the ſnares of the devil and from all iniquity, that I may be found worthy to partake of Thy celeſtial joys, Who liveſt and reigneſt God world without end. Amen.

ℭ *AFTER RECEIVING.*

I GIVE thanks to Thee, O my Almighty and Merciful God! I render thanks unto Thy tremendous Majeſty. O moſt kind and Infinite Father! Who haſt vouchſafed to comfort and ſatiate me an unworthy and miſerable ſinner with the precious Body and Blood of Thy Son our Lord Jeſus Chriſt. I intreat Thee, therefore, O moſt ſweet Lord Jeſus! that this Holy Communion may not be for my judgment or condemnation, but through Thy grace and pity, be ſweetneſs and fragrance to my ſoul, my ſafeguard and ſanctity in every temptation, peace and joy in all tribulation, light and ſtrength in every word and work, my comfort and defence to the end, at my death for my deliverance and the deſtruction of the ſnares of all my enemies, and may profit for the ſalvation of my ſoul and body in eternal life; and grant that no ſtain of ſin may abide there where Sacraments ſo Holy have entered in. Amen.

OUR FATHER.

Hail! thou that art full of grace.

Or this.

I RENDER thanks to Thee, O Lord! Holy Father! Almighty Everlaſting God! Who haſt vouchſafed, not for any deſert of mine, but only out of the condeſcenſion of Thy mercy, to feed me a ſinner, Thine unworthy ſervant, with the precious Body and Blood of Thy Son, our Lord Jeſus Chriſt; and I pray that this Holy Communion may not bring guilt upon me to condemnation, but may intercede for me to my pardon and ſalvation; let it be to me an armour of faith, and a ſhield of good purpoſe; a riddance of all vices; an extermination of evil deſires and concupiſcence; an increaſe of love and patience, of humility and obedience, and of all virtues; a firm defence againſt the wiles of my enemies viſible and inviſible; a perfect quieting of all my impulſes fleſhly and ſpiritual; a firm adherence to Thee, The One True God, and a bleſſed conſummation of my end; and I pray that Thou wouldeſt vouchſafe to bring me a ſinner, to that ineffable Feaſt, where Thou, with Thy Son, and Thy Holy Spirit, art to Thy holy ones true Light, full Satiety, everlaſting Joy, Pleaſure conſummated, and perfect Happineſs; through the ſame our Lord Jeſus Chriſt. Amen.

[ℂ *Oriſon of the Prieſt only, after Celebration.*

ALMIGHTY and everlaſting God! the Preſerver of ſouls and the Redeemer of the world! vefy favourably regard me Thy ſervant proſtrate before Thy Majeſty, and moſt graciouſly accept This Sacrifice which in honour of Thy Name, I have offered for the ſaving health of the faithful living as well as departed, as alſo for all our ſins and offences. Take away Thine anger from me, ſtretch out Thine hand unto me; open unto me the gates of Paradiſe; deliver me in Thy might from all evils; and whatever guilt I have in mine own perſon incurred, do Thou forgive; and make me ſo to perſevere in Thy precepts in this world, that I may be rendered worthy to be joined to the company of Thine Elect; of Thine only gift, O my God! Whoſe bleſſed Name, Honour, and Dominion endureth for ever and ever. Amen.

Another Orison for the Priest only.

I GIVE thanks to Thee, O Lord Jesus Christ! Who didst advance me, an unclean and unworthy sinner, to the dignity of Thy Priesthood; and Who this day of the gift of Thine own exceeding bounty, and not from any merit of mine, hast vouchsafed unto me the grace of consecrating and receiving Thy Most Holy Body and Blood. Grant, I beseech Thee, of Thy most benign mercy and unspeakable goodness, and for the sake of Thy Most Holy Passion and Thy Cross, that this ineffable Sacrament of Which I, an unworthy sinner, have partaken, may not be unto me guilt for my condemnation, but may intercede for my forgiveness; and whatever I have done amiss this day at Thy Holy Altar, in sinful, unlawful, or unclean thoughts, in too little reverence, in any unworthy gesture, act, or neglect, in vain repetition of words, or distraction of mind, or in any other manner whatsoever, I implore Thy Most Holy Goodness do Thou most mercifully pardon; and vouchsafe fully to absolve me from these and all mine offences, Who with God The Father and The Holy Ghost livest and reignest God world without end. Amen.]

¶ *A very devout Orison to be said after the celebration of Holy Communion.*

I RENDER thanks to Thee, O most sweet Lord Jesus Christ! Very Light! Salvation of believers! Consolation of the sorrowful! Hope of all men! Joy of Angels! Who hast vouchsafed this day to feed me Thy servant, a guilty and miserable sinner, with Thy Most Sacred Body and Thy Blood. Wherefore I very wretched and stained as I am with numberless offences, with tears and prayers implore Thy Divine mercy and supreme clemency that this most sweet refreshment, most excellent and incomprehensible Communion, may not be for the condemnation of my soul, but may profit for my salvation and for the avoidance of all the snares and wicked deceits of the Devil, so that no iniquity may ever domineer in my heart, body, soul, or senses, but Thy clemency may bring me heavenward to the banquets of the Angels, where Thou art Very Blessedness, Cloudless Light, and Everlasting Day. Amen.

Or this,—

I GIVE thanks unto Thee, O Lord God! Almighty Father! Who hast vouchsafed to satiate me with The Body and Blood of Thy beloved Son, our Lord Jesus Christ. I beseech of Thy boundless clemency, O Almighty and merciful Lord! that this Holy Communion may not be unto me for my judgement or for my condemnation, but may be a sure pledge of faith and a shield of good purpose to guard my soul from all the snares of the enemy; to extirpate the pestilence of pride, the lust of gluttony, and petulance of speech, so that I may enter in unto that Feast where is True Light and where are the perpetual joys of the just. Moreover I beseech Thee, O Lord! that this Holy Communion may be unto me my guide and provision to the haven of eternal salvation. Let it be unto me consolation when I am afflicted, love and exceeding delight in every good purpose, patience in tribulation and anguish, medicine in sickness. By these Sacramental Mysteries which I have received, grant unto me right Faith, steadfast Hope, and perfect Charity, renunciation of the world, purity of desire, happiness of mind, ardent affection for Thee, a remembrance of and heartfelt fellowship with the Passion of Thy beloved Son; preserve my life filled with virtues in Thy praise, and in a sincere faith; and in the hour of my departure may I receive the grace of so great a Mystery with true Faith, certain Hope, and sincere Charity, that I may behold Thee without end. Amen.

These be the Feasts which are well-pleasing unto Thee, which Thou hast left to us orphans in remembrance of Thy love! O Wisdom of The Father! Offspring of the Virgin! Who hast not disdained that Thy reverend Body should be touched and received by me an unworthy sinner, what shall I worthily requite Thee for all that Thou hast bestowed upon me? For if the merits of all the world were heaped together in one they would not be in the very least comparable with Thy worth. I render thanks to Thee, O Lord Jesus Christ, Son of The living God! King of Kings, and Lord of Lords! O most kind Jesu! to the utmost of my frail ability I return thanksgiving to Thy tremendous Majesty and boundless pity, Who hast sweetly refreſhed the exceeding drought of my ſoul with Thy ſacred Body and Blood. I intreat Thee that whatever fault is found in me contrary to Thy Will may be utterly rooted out from the foundation by the Communion of This Sacrament, and my heart prepared to be a worthy dwelling-place for Thy Holy Spirit. And O moſt ſweet Jeſu! may this Sacrament of Thy Body and Blood be to my ſoul delight and pleaſure, ſalvation and ſanctity in every temptation, peace and joy in every tribulation, light and virtue in every word and work, and finally, my conſolation and defence in the hour of death. Amen.

¶ *Here begin*

THE HOURS OF THE MOST SWEET NAME OF JESUS.

Health of mind and of body grant us; Thou Wiſdom of The Father, bleſſed Jeſus! Amen.

O Lord! open Thou my lips.

And my mouth ſhall ſhew forth Thy praiſe.

O God! make ſpeed to ſave me.

O Lord! make haſte to help me.

Glory be to The Father, and to The Son, and to The Holy Ghoſt;

As it was in the beginning, is now, and ever ſhall be, world without end. Amen.

Invitatory.

The Fountain of Eternal Wiſdom let us now adore; And for The Glory of The Name of Jeſus joy devoutly evermore.

Psalm.—*Venite, exultemus.*

O come, let us ſing unto The Lord: let us heartily rejoice in God our Salvation.

And the firſt ℣. *of the Pſalm only is ſaid with*

Glory be to The Father, and to The Son, and to The Holy Ghoſt.

Hymn.

Jesus! how ſweet the thought of Thee!
True joy of heart it brings to me;
But Oh! than honey ſweeter far
The raptures of Thy preſence are.

No music is more soft and clear,
No sound more pleasant to the ear,
For thought there is no sweeter theme
Than Jesus, Son of God Supreme.

Jesus! of penitents the stay,
How good to them that ask the way;
To those that seek Thee, Oh! how kind,
But what? Oh! what? to them that find.

Eternal Wisdom! unto Thee
With God The Father Glory be;
So to The Spirit Paraclete,
Now and through ages infinite!

Psalm.

O BE joyful in God, all ye lands! sing praises unto the Honour of His Name: make His praise to be glorious.

Say unto God, O how wonderful art Thou in Thy works: through the greatness of Thy power shall thine enemies be found liars unto Thee.

For all the world shall worship Thee: sing of Thee, and praise Thy Name.

Glory be to The Father.

Antiphon.

WISDOM hath builded Her house, She hath hewn out her seven pillars, She hath subdued to Herself the nations, and upon the necks of the proud and haughty She hath trodden in her own strength.

℣. But I will rejoice in The Lord.

℟. And will be glad in God my Jesus.

OUR FATHER (*secretly*).

And lead us not into temptation;

But deliver us from evil.

O Lord! bid a blessing.

May The Wisdom of The Father repel all adversaries that may assail us. Amen.

Lesson I.

O ETERNAL Wisdom! Brightness of The Glory, and Image of The Substance of The Father! Who didst create the universe out of nothing, and that Thou mightest restore mankind to his lost happiness, didst descend unto this vale of tears, and by Thy most sweet converse shew to him the way for his return; Who as the Satisfaction for all men didst will like an innocent lamb to be offered up to The Father upon The Cross; by Thy most precious Death open my heart, that with the eyes of a most entire faith I may ever behold Thee The

King of Kings and Lord of Lords. Set me as a prophet in Thy Wounds, as a wise man in Thy Prints of The Nails, so that hereafter I may find profit in Thee alone, in The Book of Thy Love, and in Thy Death, that I may depart from all things in this life; so that I may be no longer myself, but that Thou in me and I in Thee may eternally abide in an indissoluble bond of love! But Thou, O Lord, have mercy upon me.

Thanks be to God.

℟. Send forth, O Lord, Wisdom from the Throne of Thy Majesty. That She may be with me and labour with me, that I may at all times know what is acceptable in Thy sight.

℣. Give me, O Lord! Wisdom that sitteth by Thy Throne.

That She may be with me and labour with me, that I may at all times know what is acceptable in Thy sight.

O Lord! bid a blessing.

The Eternal Wisdom vouchsafe to enlighten our souls and our bodies. Amen.

Lesson II.

O my Jesu! the most Sweet Wisdom, and most happy Word of The Father! the End and the Beginning of all being! I intreat Thee regard me with the eyes of Thy favour; for I am but dust and flesh; and it is not of him that runneth, nor of him that willeth, but of God Who sheweth mercy. Call to remembrance, I beseech Thee, Thy most bitter Passion, which for me, an unworthy sinner, Thou didst endure. And that goodwill which hath been by Thee begun do Thou preserve in me. O Thou my Mercy! forsake me not! O Thou my Refuge! depart not from me! O my Deliverer! make speed to save me; and bury me, dead to this world, in the sepulchre along with Thee, and hide me from all the assaults of mine enemies; that neither life nor death or any event of fortune may separate me from Thee, but may Thy love, stronger than death itself, abide with me for ever! But Thou, O Lord, have mercy upon me.

Thanks be to God.

℟. Give me, O Lord! Wiſdom that ſitteth by Thy Throne, and reject me not from among Thy children. For I am Thy ſervant and the ſon of Thine handmaid!

℣. Send Her forth from the Throne of Thy Majeſty, that She may be with me and may labour with me.

For I am Thy ſervant and the ſon of Thine handmaid!

O Lord! bid a bleſſing.

With the gifts of wiſdom and underſtanding may The Holy Ghoſt ever fulfil us. Amen.

Leſſon III.

O MY Refuge and my Deliverer! by that boundleſs love which prompted Thee to endure ſor me, a miſerable ſinner, a moſt bitter Death on The Croſs of Suffering, mercifully pardon the ſins which I, an impure ſinner, have committed, and from thoſe which I may commit, and from all perils do Thou kindly keep me in the Wound of Thy Side. Direct my ſteps over the billows of this liſe to a holy end, and grant that I may attain even to behold Thy Glory. But Thou, O Lord! have mercy upon me!

Thanks be to God.

℟. I loved Wiſdom above health and all beauty, and I choſe to have Her inſtead of light. All good things together came to me with Her.

℣. I ſaid unto Wiſdom, Thou art my ſiſter, and I called Prudence my friend.

All good things together came to me with Her.

Glory be to The Father, and to The Son, and to The Holy Ghoſt.

I loved Wiſdom above health and all beauty, and choſe to have Her inſtead of light. All good things together came to me with Her.

Canticle.

THEE GOD we praiſe: Thee The Lord we confeſs. *(And the reſt, ante, p. 61.)*

ℭ *BEFORE LAUDS.*

HEALTH of mind and of body grant us; Thou Wiſdom of The Father, bleſſed Jeſus!

OUR FATHER.

Hail, Mary!

ℂ *AT LAUDS.*

O God! make ſpeed.
Glory be to The Father.
Alleluya.

Pſalm.

O praise The Lord, all ye heathen: praiſe Him, all ye nations.

For His merciful kindneſs is ever more and more towards us: and the Truth of The Lord endureth for ever. Praiſe The Lord.

Glory be to The Father.

Antiphon.

Wisdom crieth aloud in the Heavens. If any man loveth Wiſdom, let him turn unto Me and he will find Her, and when he ſhall have found Her, bleſſed ſhall he be if he lay hold on Her.

Chapter.

Wisdom viii., 2.

I loved Her and ſought Her out from my youth, and I deſired to make Her my ſpouſe, and I was a lover of Her beauty.

Thanks be to God.

Hymn.

Jesus! Thou King of wondrous ſtate!
Supreme, triumphant Potentate!
Sweetneſs that may not be expreſſed!
And altogether lovelieſt!

No tongue can worthily relate,
No writing duly celebrate,
Experience only can believe
What 'tis in Jeſus' love to live.

With Jeſus' endleſs love poſſeſſed,
What ceaſeleſs longings fill my breaſt!
Jeſus! with flowing honey riſe,
Perennial Fruit of endleſs life,

Eternal Wiſdom! unto Thee
With God The Father glory be;
So to The Spirit Paraclete,
Now and through ages infinite!
Amen.

℣. Wiſdom reſteth in His heart.

℟. And prudence in the diſcourſe of His mouth.

Psalm.—*Benedictus.*

Blessed be The Lord God of Iſrael *(ante, p. 70)*.

Antiphon.

O Wisdom! Who didſt proceed from the mouth of The Moſt High, reaching from one end to another, mightily and ſweetly ordering all things, come and teach me the way of underſtanding.

Orison.

God! Who by Wisdom coeternal with Thee, didst form man out of nothing, and when perished didst mercifully create him anew; grant, we beseech Thee, that The Same Wisdom inspiring our minds we may love Thee with our whole souls, and run after Thee with our whole hearts. Through our Lord Jesus Christ. Amen.

ℭ *AT PRIME.*

Health of mind and of body grant us; Thou Wisdom of The Father, blessed Jesus! Amen.

O God make speed.

Glory be to The Father.

Hymn.

The Love of Jesus, full of bliss,
And rich with holy fragrance is;
A thousand fold its joys excel
All that the tongue of man can tell.

Jesus! Whom Angel-hosts revere,
A dulcet strain to every ear,
As honey to the taste Thou art,
And heavenly nectar to the heart.

Good Jesus! grant me here below
The riches of Thy love to know;
Then in Thy blissful presence place
To see Thy Glory face to face.

Eternal Wisdom! unto Thee
With God The Father glory be;
So to The Spirit Paraclete,
Now and through ages infinite!
Amen.

Psalm.

O let me hear Thy loving-kindness betimes in the morning: for in Thee is my trust.

Shew me the way that I should walk in: for I lift up my soul unto Thee.

Deliver me, O Lord! from mine enemies, for I flee unto Thee to hide me: teach me to do the thing that pleaseth Thee; for Thou art my God.

Glory be to The Father.

Antiphon.

I love them that love Me, and they that seek Me early shall find me.

Chapter.

Wisdom vanquisheth evil, reaching from one end even to another; mightily and sweetly ordering all things.

Thanks be to God.

℟. Jesu Christ! Son of The living God! have mercy upon us.

℣. Thou Who wast born of The Virgin Mary, have mercy upon us.

Glory be to The Father.

Jesu Christ! Son of The living God! have mercy upon us.

℣. Arise, O Lord! help us.
℟. And deliver us for Thy Holy Name's sake.
O Lord Jesu! hear my prayer,
And let my crying come unto Thee.

Orison.

O Lord! we beseech Thee let the splendour of Eternal Wisdom enlighten our hearts, so that being rid of the darkness of this world we may attain to the land of eternal Brightness. Through Christ our Lord. Amen.

ℂ *At Terce.*

Health of mind and of body grant us; Thou Wisdom of The Father, blessed Jesu! Amen.
O God make speed.
Glory be to The Father.

Hymn.

Jesus! what solace to the heart
Doth Thy refreshing Love impart!
Need without surfeit it fulfils,
New hunger and desire instils.

Who taste Thee ever long for more,
Who drink, thirst for Thee as before;
For nought can their affection move
But Jesus, Whom alone they love.

A thousand times I long for Thee,
When, Jesu! wilt Thou visit me?
When glad me with Thy presence blest?
And make me of Thyself possessed?

Eternal Wisdom! unto Thee
With God The Father glory be;
So to The Spirit Paraclete,
Now and through ages infinite!
Amen.

Psalm.

Let Thy loving Spirit lead me forth unto the land of righteousness: Quicken me, O Lord! for Thy Name's sake.
For Thy righteousness' sake bring my soul out of trouble: and of Thy goodness slay mine enemies.
And destroy all them that vex my soul: for I am Thy servant.
Glory be to The Father.

Antiphon.

My son, desire Wisdom; keep righteousness, and God will give Her to thee.

Chapter.

Wisdom viii., 2.

I loved Her and sought Her out from my youth, and I desired to make Her my spouse, and I was a lover of Her beauty.
Thanks be to God.

℟. I will rejoice in The Lord.

℣. And I will exult in God my Jesus.

I will rejoice in The Lord.

Glory be to The Father.

℣. Blessed be The Name of The Lord.

℟. From this time forth, now and even for evermore.

Orison.

God! Who by Wisdom co-eternal with Thee, didst form man out of nothing, and when perished didst mercifully create him anew; grant, we beseech Thee, that The Same Wisdom inspiring our minds, we may love Thee with our whole souls, and run after Thee with our whole hearts, through Christ our Lord. Amen.

ℭ *AT SEXT.*

Health of mind and of body grant us; Thou Wisdom of The Father, blessed Jesus! Amen.

O God make speed.

Glory be to The Father.

Hymn.

Jesu! Supreme Benignity!
Of hearts Divine Felicity!
Of Goodness The Infinity!
Constrain me with Thy Charity!

How good in Jesus' love to rest,
To seek naught else of Him possessed;
To die to all that is mine own,
That I may live to Him alone!

Jesu! to me so passing dear,
Hope of my fainting spirit here,
For Thee these wistful tears arise,
For Thee mine inmost bosom cries.

Eternal Wisdom! unto Thee
With God The Father glory be;
And to The Spirit Paraclete,
Now and through ages infinite!
Amen.

Psalm.

Our soul hath patiently tarried for The Lord: for He is our help and our shield.

For our heart shall rejoice in Him: and we have hoped in His Holy Name.

Let Thy merciful kindness, O Lord! be upon us: like as we do put our trust in Thee.

Glory be to The Father.

Antiphon.

The Lord possessed Me in the beginning of His ways, before He made anything; from the first saith The Lord.

Chapter.

Wisdom vii., 26.

For She is the Brightness of The everlasting Light, the unspotted Mirror of The Power of God, and The Image of His Goodness.

Thanks be to God.

℟. Blessed be The Name of The Lord.

℣. From this time forth, now and even for evermore.

Blessed be The Name of The Lord.

Glory be to The Father.

℣. From the rising of the sun even unto the going down thereof.

℟. Praised be The Name of The Lord.

Orison.

Hearken unto us, O Almighty and merciful God! and make the light of Thy Wisdom to shine upon our minds. Through our Lord Jesus Christ, Thy Son, Who with Thee liveth and reigneth in The Unity of The Holy Ghost God world without end. Amen.

Our Father.

ℂ *At None.*

Health of mind and of body grant us; Thou Wisdom of The Father, blessed Jesus!

O God make speed.

Glory be to The Father.

Hymn.

Where'er on earth my home may be,
May Jesus e'er abide with me;
What joy when Him I find at last!
What transport when I hold Him fast!
Then are His kind embraces mine,
Than cups of nectar more divine;
Then with Christ's sacred friendship blest,
Here would I fain no longer rest;
E'en now I view the wished-for goal,
I reach the longings of my soul;
The love of Christ my heart inspires,
And all my kindling bosom fires.

Eternal Wisdom! unto Thee
With God The Father glory be;
And to The Spirit Paraclete,
Now and through ages infinite!
Amen.

Psalm.

Create in me a clean heart, O God: and renew a right spirit within me.

Cast me not away from Thy presence: and take not Thy Holy Spirit from me.

Restore to me the joy of Thy salvation: and stablish me with Thy Chief Spirit.

Glory be to The Father.

Antiphon.

As yet the Abysses were not when I was brought forth; when He prepared the Heavens, I was present with Him, disposing all things.

Chapter.

Wisdom vii., 29.

For Wisdom is more beautiful than the sun, and above all the order of the stars; ✝

ing compared with the light, She is found before it.

Thanks be to God.

℟. From the riſing of the ſun even to the going down thereof.

Praiſed be The Name of The Lord.

Even to the going down thereof.

Glory be to The Father.

From the riſing of the ſun even to the going down thereof.

℣. Wiſdom reſteth in His heart.

℟. And prudence in the diſcourſe of His mouth.

Oriſon.

O Lord! we beſeech Thee, pour into our hearts the light of Thy Wiſdom, that we may truly know Thee, and faithfully love Thee. Through Chriſt our Lord. Amen.

Our Father. Hail, Mary.

ℭ *At Vespers.*

Health of mind and of body grant us; Thou Wiſdom of The Father, bleſſed Jeſus!

O God make ſpeed.

Glory be to The Father.

Psalm cx.

The Lord hath ſent redemption unto His people: He hath commanded his covenant for ever.

Holy and reverend is His Name: the fear of The Lord is the beginning of Wiſdom.

A good underſtanding have all they that do thereafter: The praiſe of It endureth for ever and ever.

Glory be to The Father.

Antiphon.

All Wiſdom is from The Lord our God. With Him She ever was and ſhall be evermore.

Chapter.

Wisdom viii., 2.

I loved Her and ſought Her out from my youth, and I deſired to make Her my ſpouſe, and I was a lover of Her beauty.

Thanks be to God.

Hymn.

Jesu! Thou Sun ſerene and calm,
More fragrant than the ſcented balm,
Than ſweetneſs' very ſelf more ſweet,
In peerleſs excellence complete;
Delight and charm of every heart,
Sum of all lovelineſs Thou art!
Jeſu! let all my glorying be,
O Saviour of the world, in Thee.

Jesu! Thou source of clemency!
Thou hope of all felicity!
O Fount of grace and pure delight!
In Whom all joys of heart unite!

Eternal Wisdom! unto Thee
With God The Father glory be;
And to The Spirit Paraclete,
Now and through ages infinite!
Amen.

℣. But I will rejoice in The Lord.

℟. And be glad in God my Jesus.

PSALM.—*Magnificat.*

MY soul doth magnify The Lord (*ante, p.* 103).

Antiphon.

O ORIENT Brightness of Eternal Light and Sun of Righteousness! Come and enlighten them that sit in darkness and in the shadow of death.

Orison.

GOD! Who by Wisdom co-eternal with Thee didst form man out of nothing, and when perished didst mercifully create him anew; grant, we beseech Thee, that The Same Wisdom inspiring our minds, we may love Thee with our whole souls, and run after Thee with our whole hearts; Through The Same One Lord Jesus Christ. Amen.

OUR FATHER. Hail, Mary.

ℂ *AT COMPLINE.*

HEALTH of mind and of body grant us; Thou Wisdom of The Father, blessed Jesus!

Convert us, O God our Salvation!

And turn away Thine Anger from us.

O God make speed.

Glory be to The Father.

Psalm.

ENLIGHTEN mine eyes, that I sleep not in death: lest mine enemy say I have prevailed against him.

They that trouble me will rejoice if I be moved: but I have put my sure trust in Thy mercy.

My heart is joyful in Thy salvation; I will sing of The Lord because He hath dealt so lovingly with me: Yea, I will praise The Name of The Lord Most Highest.

Glory be to The Father.

Antiphon.

I DWELL in the Highest, and my Throne is in the pillar of the cloud.

Chapter.

WISDOM viii., 7.

WISDOM teacheth temperance and prudence, justice and

fortitude, which are ſuch things as men can have nothing more profitable in their life.

Thanks be to God.

℟. In peace in the Very Same I will ſleep and take my reſt.

℣. When I give ſleep to mine eyes and ſlumber to mine eyelids.

I will ſleep and take my reſt.

Glory be to The Father.

In peace in the Very Same I will ſleep and take my reſt.

Hymn.

Jesus in peace o'er His domains,
Paſt all our underſtanding reigns;
To Him my longing ſoul aſpires,
And haſtes to enjoy her fond deſires.

The Heavenly Hoſts to Thee their lays
Attune, in turn to chant Thy praiſe;
For Jeſus on Creation ſmiles,
And God with mortals reconciles.

Jeſus hath gained His Father's throne,
Heaven's kingdom taken for His own.
My raviſhed heart hath paſſed away
With Jeſus to the realms of day!

Eternal Wiſdom! unto Thee
With God The Father glory be;
And to The Spirit Paraclete,
Now and through ages infinite!
Amen.

℣. His Name is great in Iſrael.

℟. At Salem is His tabernacle; and His dwelling in Syon.

Psalm.—*Nunc Dimittis.*

Now letteſt Thou O Lord! Thy ſervant depart (*ante, p.* 113).

Antiphon.

O King! Glorious among Thy Saints, Who art ever to be praiſed, and yet art ineffable, Thou O Lord! art in us, and we are called by Thy Holy Name; forſake us not O Lord our God, that in the Day of Judgement Thou mayeſt vouchſafe to place us among Thy Saints and Elect, O King moſt bleſſed!

℣. The Name of The Lord be bleſſed.

℟. From this time forth, now and for evermore.

Oriſon.

O Lord! we beſeech Thee mercifully regard our frailty, and of Thy goodneſs pour into our hearts the ſavour of Thine Eternal Wiſdom; That having taſted Its ſweetneſs which floweth with honey, we may be enabled to deſpiſe all earthly things, and continually with fervent affection to adhere to Thee, The Chiefeſt Good.

Through our Lord Jesus Christ Thy Son, Who with Thee liveth and reigneth in The Unity of The Holy Ghost God world without end. Amen.

Bless we The Lord.

Thanks be to God.

The Eternal Wisdom bless and keep our hearts and bodies. Amen.

Orison.

God! Who hast made The Most Glorious Name of Jesus Thine Only Begotten Son, wonderful in exceeding sweetness of affection to Thy faithful people, and tremendous and terrible to evil spirits; grant, we beseech Thee, that all who devoutly venerate This Thy Name upon earth may in this life receive the sweetness of Thy consolation, and in that which is to come obtain eternal joys and never ending gladness in Heaven, through The Same Jesus Christ our Lord. Amen.

¶ *Here begin*

THE HOURS OF CHRIST'S PASSION

O Lord! open Thou my lips. *(And the rest, ante, p. 163.)*

Glory be to The Father.

Praise to Thee, O Lord! we sing;

Of Glory The Eternal King.

Invitatory.

O come, let us worship Our King, Christ, Lord, The Crucified!

O come, let us worship God; let us bewail ourselves, and kneel before Him, Who for us became man, and was made subject to nature and to the law.

O come, let us worship Our King, Christ, Lord, The Crucified!

Him wearied with hunger, thirst, heat, cold, tempest, rain, watchings, fastings, labours, straits, griefs, and other infirmities, which belong to us, but are unseemly to our God

O come, let us worship.

Him Who vouchsafed to be baptized, was tempted, rejected, betrayed; Who washed the feet of His disciples, trembled in His agony, prayed long and earneſtly, poured forth His ſweat as drops of blood upon the earth, The true King, The Lord, The Crucified

O come, let us worſhip.

Him Who was ſeized, haled forth, thruſt out, bound, brought before Annas, Caiaphas, Pilate, Herod, accuſed, judged, condemned, clothed in white, ſpit upon, Whoſe Face was covered, Who was bruiſed with buffetings, ſmiting, ſcourging, and with the reed

O come, let us worſhip.

Him ſtripped of His garments, mocked with a ſcarlet robe, with a Crown of Thorns, reeden Sceptre, and with deriſive worſhip and homage, Our King, The Lord, The Crucified

O come, let us worſhip.

Glory be to The Father, and to The Son, and to The Holy Ghoſt;

As it was in the beginning, is now, and ever ſhall be, world without end. Amen.

O come, let us worſhip Our King, Chriſt, Lord, The Crucified!

Hymn.

The Sacred Paſſion of The Lord
Health unto dying man reſtored!
Be It the ſolace of our grief,
Our hearts' deſire and ſweet relief.

Henceforth be in our memory borne
The Agony, the biting Scorn,
The Thorny Crown, the Hour of Fear,
The Nails, the Croſs, the piercing Spear;

And thoſe moſt ſacred Stripes of woe,
To which all gratitude we owe;
The Vinegar, the Gall, the Reed,
Death's very Bitterneſs indeed.

May theſe our contrite ſpirits ſate,
And with Thy love inebriate;
All grace and holineſs inſtil,
And with the fruits of glory fill.

We Thee, The Crucified, adore,
And from our inmoſt hearts implore,
Unto the ſainted Choirs above
Unite us in Thy Heaven of love.

All laud and honour be to Chriſt,
Who, ſold, betrayed, and ſacrificed,
For us His people life to gain,
Died guiltleſs on the Croſs of pain.

Pſalm.

Why do the heathen ſo furiouſly rage together: and why do the people imagine a vain thing?

The wicked, even mine enemies and my foes: came upon me to eat up My fleſh.

They that are mine enemies, and would deſtroy Me guiltleſs, are mighty: I paid them the things that I never took.

They have ſharpened their tongues like a ſerpent: the poiſon of aſps is under their lips.

My heart is diſquieted within Me: and the fear of death is fallen upon Me.

Glory be to The Father.

Antiphon.

My heart is broken in the midſt of Me: I may tell all My bones.

℣. I have forſaken Mine habitation: I have divided Mine inheritance.

℟. I have given the Soul of My Beloved into the hands of mine enemies.

Lord! have mercy.

Chriſt! have mercy.

Lord! have mercy.

OUR FATHER. (*ſecretly.*)

And lead us not into temptation;

But deliver us from evil.

O Lord! bid a bleſſing.

Benediction.

MAY JESUS CHRIST, through His Moſt Holy Paſſion,

Beſtow upon us Grace and Benediction. Amen.

Leſſon I.—Iſaiah liii.

THERE is no form nor comelineſs in Him; and when we ſhall ſee Him, there is no beauty that we ſhould deſire Him: He is deſpiſed and rejected of men; a Man of ſorrows and acquainted with grief. We hid as it were our faces from Him. He was deſpiſed and we eſteemed Him not. Surely He hath borne our griefs and carried our ſorrows; we eſteemed Him ſtricken, ſmitten of God, and afflicted. But Thou, O Lord! have mercy upon us.

℟. In the Mount of Olivet I prayed to My Father; "Father! if it be poſſible, let this cup paſs from Me. The Spirit indeed is willing, but the fleſh is weak."

℣. Neverthelefs, not as I will, but as Thou wilt.

℟. The Spirit indeed is willing, but the fleſh is weak.

O Lord! bid a bleſſing.

Benediction.

THE Glorious Paſſion of Jeſus Chriſt

Bring us to the joys of Paradiſe.

Leſſon II.

BUT He was wounded for our tranſgreſſions, He was bruiſed for our iniquities; the chaſtiſement of our peace was upon Him, and with His ſtripes we are healed. All we, like ſheep, have gone aſtray, we have turned aſide every one into his own way, and The Lord hath laid on Him the iniquity of us all. But Thou, O Lord!

℟. Thou art ſad, My Soul, even unto death.

℣. Abide ye here, and watch with Me; now ſhall ye ſee the multitude which hath compaſſed Me;

Ye take to flight, and I go to be ſlain for you.

℣. Behold, the Hour draweth nigh, and The Son of Man is delivered into the hands of ſinners.

℟. Ye take to flight, and I go to be ſlain for you.

O Lord! bid a bleſſing.

Benediction.

THROUGH His Croſs may The Son of God be unto us gracious and propitious. Amen.

Leſſon III.

HE was oppreſſed and He was afflicted, yet He opened not His mouth. He is brought as a lamb to the ſlaughter, and as a ſheep before her ſhearers is dumb, ſo He opened not His mouth. He was taken ·m priſon and from judgement; and who ſhall declare His generation? for He was cut off out of the land of the living; ſor the tranſgreſſion of my people was He ſtricken. And He made His grave with the wicked, and with the rich in His death, becauſe He hath done no violence, neither was any deceit in His mouth. Yet it pleaſed The Lord to bruiſe Him; He hath put Him to grief. When thou ſhalt make His Soul an Offering for ſin, He ſhall ſee His ſeed, He ſhall prolong His days, and the pleaſure of The Lord ſhall proſper in His hand. He ſhall ſee of the travail of His Soul, and ſhall be ſatisfied: by His knowledge ſhall My Righteous Servant juſtify many; for He ſhall bear their iniquities. Therefore will I divide Him a portion with the great, and He ſhall divide the ſpoil with the ſtrong; becauſe He hath poured out His Soul unto death, and He was numbered with the tranſgreſſors. But Thou, O Lord!

℟. O all ye that paſs by in the way! behold and ſee if there be any ſorrow like unto My Sorrow.

℣. Behold, all ye people, and ſee My Sorrow;

If there be any ſorrow like unto My Sorrow.

Glory be to The Father.

O all ye that paſs by in the way! behold and ſee if there be any ſorrow like unto My Sorrow.

Canticle.

Thee, God, we praiſe: Thee, Jeſus, we confeſs: The King of Kings, and Lord of Lords.

Thee, Crucified and Glorious, we do worſhip: our ſweet and beloved Redeemer.

Who haſt waſhed us with the ſprinkling of Thy Blood.

Thou art worthy: O Lord Jeſus Chriſt! our God;

To receive praiſe, bleſſing: Glory and Honour.

Let all fleſh rejoice in Thee: and every living being glorify Thy Name!

Let every face be humbled at Thy feet.

Let every creature rejoice before Thee, and give Thee praiſe, and extol Thee:

Bleſs and Glorify Thee for ever and ever!

℣. Falſe witneſſes did riſe up againſt Me.

℟. They laid to my charge things that I knew not.

¶ *At Lauds.*

O God! make ſpeed. *(And the reſt.)*

Glory be to The Father.

Praiſe to Thee, O Lord. *(And the reſt.)*

Pſalm.

Lord, how are they increaſed that trouble Me: many are they that riſe up againſt Me.

They gape upon Me with their mouths: and, as it were, a ramping and a roaring lion.

I looked upon My right hand: and ſaw that there was no man that would know Me.

My lovers and My neighbours: did ſtand looking upon My trouble.

My kinſmen ſtood afar off: and they did violence that ſought after My Soul.

Glory be to The Father.

Antiphon.

My ſpirit is vexed within Me, and My heart within Me is deſolate.

Chapter.—Heb. xii., 3.

Consider Him that endured ſuch contradiction of ſinners againſt Himſelf: that ye be not wearied and faint in your minds.

Thanks be to God.

Hymn.

Christ, our Leader and Redeemer
By His own Crofs, from foes and ſhame,
Brethren! pouring ſtrains adoring,
With Heaven ſalute ye with acclaim.

By the deep woe of Thy Death-throe,
By all the Blood which Thou haſt ſhed,
By Thine Unction, to compunction
O Jeſus! may our hearts be led.

By thoſe bliſsful ſcars diſtreſsful,
Spittings, ſcourgings, ſtripes and pains;
Endleſs pleaſure, without meaſure,
Chriſt for our thankful ſouls obtains.

Sad and tender our hearts render,
With thoſe Thy gory Wounds and [Tears,
Therein laving us and ſaving
Thou Framer of the ſtarry ſpheres!

To the faſhion of Thy Paſſion,
Saviour! our contrite hearts in-[cline;
Faithful giving, ever living
Joys Supernal and Divine.

All Laud and Honour be to Chriſt,
Who ſold, betray'd, and ſacrific'd,
For us His people life to gain,
Died guiltleſs on the Croſs of pain. Amen.

℣. He gave His Cheek to the ſmiters.

℟. He ſhall be filled with reproach.

Canticle of Zechariah, at the firſt dawn. Benedictus.

Blessed be The Lord God *(ante, p. 70)*.

Antiphon.

O Glorious Mother of God! ever Virgin Mary! who waſt eſteemed worthy to bear The Lord of all things, and, Only Virgin, to nouriſh at thy breaſt The King of Angels; Of thy kindneſs mayeſt thou remember us; and ſo beſeech Chriſt on our behalf, that, aſſiſted by thy prayers, we may be enabled to attain to the Heavenly Kingdom.

God ſpared not His own Son, but delivered Him up for us all!

O Lord! hear my prayer.

And let my crying come unto Thee.

Oriſon.

O Lord Jesu Christ! Son of The living God! Who at this Matin Hour didſt will to be born, to be betrayed, taken, beaten with ſtripes, buffeted, and ſpit upon for the ſalvation of mankind; make us, we beſeech Thee, joyfully and patiently to endure injuries and reproaches for the Glory of Thy Name; and ſo continually to keep in remembrance the memory of Thy Moſt Sacred Paſſion, that we may be enabled happily to attain to the Glory and fellowſhip of Thy Reſurrection, Who liveſt and reigneſt with The Father and The Holy Ghoſt God world without end. Amen.

ℭ *AT PRIME.*

O God! make ſpeed. (*And the reſt.*)

Praiſe to Thee. (*And the reſt.*)

Hymn.

Thou Who, though veiled Thy glorious Face,
Waſt yet The Sun of Righteouſneſs!
Though mocked by bowing knees in ſcorn,
And with relentleſs ſcourges torn;

We ſeek Thee in adoring prayer!
O guard us with Thy favouring care!
And in Thy loving clemency
Bring us to Glory and to Thee!

All Laud and Honour be to Chriſt,
Who, ſold, betray'd, and ſacrific'd,
For us His people life to gain,
Died guiltleſs on the Croſs of pain.
Amen.

Pſalm.

The kings of the earth ſtood up, and the rulers took counſel together: againſt The Lord and againſt His Chriſt.

Many dogs are come about Me: and the counſel of the wicked layeth ſiege againſt Me.

They alſo that ſought after My life laid ſnares for Me: and they that went about to do Me evil talked of wickedneſs, and imagined deceit all the day long.

As for Me, I was like a deaf man and heard not: and like one that is dumb who doth not open his mouth.

Glory be to The Father.

Antiphon.

The Lord was led as a ſheep to the ſlaughter, and as a dumb man He opened not His mouth.

Chapter.—Iſaiah liii.

He was brought as a ſheep to the ſlaughter, and as a lamb before her ſhearers is dumb, ſo He opened not His mouth.

Thanks be to God.

℟. The Spirit of our mouth, Chriſt The Lord,

℣. Was taken for our iniquities.

Chriſt The Lord.

Glory be to The Father.

The Spirit of our mouth, Chriſt The Lord.

Lord! have mercy.

Chriſt! have mercy.

Lord! have mercy.

Our Father. (*And the reſt.*)

And lead us not into temptation: but deliver us from evil.

℣. The Word was made flesh.

℟. And dwelt among us.

I BELIEVE IN GOD.

The Resurrection of the flesh, and Life eternal. Amen.

℣. For the joy set before Him He endured the Cross.

℟. Despising all the shame.

Orison.

O LORD JESU CHRIST! Son of The living God! Who in the First Hour of the day wast brought before Pilate; Who, the Judge of all Judges, didst yet endure the severest doom; We most devoutly beseech Thee that Thou in Thy judging wouldest be lenient to us miserable sinners; that in the last eternal judgment we be not condemned to punishment, but may rather attain to the fellowship of Thy faithful ones in Heavenly places, Who livest and reignest God, world without end. Amen.

My Hope. Jesus Maria!

AT TERCE.

O GOD! make speed. (*And the rest.*)

Hymn.

THOU, Who at this First Hour of dread,
To cruel punishment wast led,
O Christ, whose suffering shoulders bore
The Cross, that we might grieve no more!

A heart, e'en so to love Thee, give,
That we a holy life may live,
And win eternal rest above,
In Heavenly homes of joy and love.

All Laud and Honour be to Christ,
Who, sold, betray'd, and sacrific'd,
For us His people life to gain,
Died guiltless on the Cross of pain! Amen.

Psalm.

BUT I am a Worm and no man: a very scorn of men, and the outcast of the people.

All the day long have I been punished, and chastened every morning.

Thou hast known My reproof: and My shame and My dishonour.

For My loins are filled with sore disease: and there is no whole part in My body.

They are despised who pitied Me: with the flatterers were busy mockers, who gnashed upon Me with their teeth.

Glory be to The Father.

Antiphon.

I WAS daily with you in the Temple, teaching, and ye took me not; and Lo, ye have scourged Me, and led Me out to be crucified.

Chapter.—2 Peter ii., 21.

CHRIST ſuffered for us, leaving us an example that we ſhould follow His ſteps; Who did no ſin, neither was guile found in His mouth.

Thanks be to God.

℟. For the joy that was ſet before Him He endured the Croſs.

℣. And He opened not His mouth.

He endured the Croſs.

Glory be to The Father.

He endured the Croſs.

℣. He was offered up, for He willed it.

℟. And He opened not His mouth.

Oriſon.

O LORD JESU CHRIST! Son of The living God! Who at the Third Hour of the day waſt led forth to the pain of the Croſs, for the Salvation of the world: we humbly beſeech Thee that by the virtue of Thy moſt ſacred Paſſion, Thou wouldeſt blot out all our ſins, and mercifully bring us to the Glory of Thy Bleſſedneſs, Who liveſt and reigneſt God, world without end. Amen.

My Hope. Jeſus Maria!

ℭ *AT SEXT.*

O GOD! make ſpeed. (*And the reſt.*)

Hymn.

THE Croſs for us The Saviour bore;
Thereon ſuſpended, thirſting ſore;
Jeſus, Whoſe ſacred Hands and Feet
The Nails remorſeleſs penetrate.

Honour and Beniſon betide
The Son of God! The Crucified!
Who by His Agony and pain
From exile brought us home again!

All Laud and Honour be to Chriſt,
Who, ſold, betray'd, and ſacrific'd,
For us His people life to gain,
Died guiltleſs on the Croſs of pain.
Amen.

Pſalm.

As for Me, I am poor and in miſery: from My youth up Thy terrors have I ſuffered with a troubled mind.

They ſtand ſtaring and looking upon Me: they part My garments among them, and caſt lots upon My veſture.

All that ſee Me laugh Me to ſcorn: they ſhoot out their lips and ſhake their heads.

I am poured out like water: and all My bones are out of joint.

Glory be to The Father.

Antiphon.

THEY placed over His Head His accuſation written "Jeof Nazareth, The King of the Jews."

Chapter.—Phil. ii., 8.

He humbled Himſelf, and became obedient unto Death, even the death of The Croſs.

Thanks be to God.

℟. He was offered up,
Becauſe He willed it.

℣. And He opened not His mouth,
Becauſe He willed it.
Glory be to The Father.
He was offered up,
Becauſe He willed it.

℣. He gave up His Soul unto death.

℟. And He was numbered with the tranſgreſſors.

Oriſon.

O Lord Jesu Christ! Son of The living God! Who at the Sixth Hour of the day in Golgotha with great tumult didſt aſcend The Croſs of Suffering, whereon, thirſting for our Salvation, Thou didſt permit Gall and Vinegar to be given Thee to drink; We Thy ſuppliants beſeech Thee that kindling and inflaming our hearts Thou wouldeſt make us to thirſt for the Cup of Thy Paſſion, and continually to find delight in Thee Only, our crucified Lord, Who liveſt and reigneſt God world without end. Amen.

My Hope. Jeſus Maria!

AT NONE.

O God! make ſpeed. (*And the reſt.*)

Hymn.

Now may Chriſt's bliſsful Paſſion ever
Our ſouls from guilt and ſhame deliver,
So through its might to us be given
Eternal joys prepared in Heaven.

All Glory be to Him our King,
Who on the Croſs of Suffering
With thrilling cry breathed forth His Soul,
And made a loſt creation whole.

All Laud and Honour be to Chriſt,
Who, ſold, betray'd, and ſacrific'd,
For us His people life to gain,
Died guiltleſs on the Croſs of pain!
Amen.

Pſalm.

My God! My God! look upon Me; why haſt Thou forſaken Me?: and art ſo far from My health, and from the words of My complaint.

I was afflicted and ſore ſmitten: I roared for the very diſquietneſs of My heart.

I looked for ſome one to have pity on Me, but there was no man: neither found I any to comfort Me.

They gave Me Gall to eat: and when I was thirsty they gave Me Vinegar to drink.

Into Thine Hands I commend My Spirit: for Thou hast redeemed Me, O Lord! Thou God of Truth!

Glory be to The Father.

Antiphon.

But Jesus, when He had received the Vinegar, said, "It is finished," and bowing The Head He gave up The Ghost.

Chapter.—1 Peter iii., 18.

Christ hath once suffered for sins, The Just for the unjust, that He might bring us to God; being put to death in the Flesh, but quickened by the Spirit.

Thanks be to God.

℟. He gave up His Soul unto Death.

℣. And He was numbered with the transgressors.

His Soul unto Death.

Glory be to The Father.

He gave up His Soul unto Death.

℣. Surely He hath borne our griefs.

℟. And He hath carried our sorrows.

Orison.

O Lord Jesu Christ! Son of The living God! Who at the Ninth Hour of the day with Hands extended upon The Cross, and bowing The Head, didst deliver up Thy Spirit to God The Father, and with the key of Thy Death didst most meritoriously unlock the gate of Paradise; Grant to us Thy suppliants, that in the hour of our death Thou wouldest mercifully cause our souls to attain unto Thee, Who art the True Paradise, Who livest and reignest God world without end. Amen.

My Hope. Jesus Maria!

ℭ *At Vespers.*

O God! make speed. (*And the rest.*)

Psalm.

What profit is there in My blood: when I go down to the pit?

For My life is waxen old with heaviness: and My years with mournings.

My strength faileth Me because of iniquity: and My bones are consumed.

My strength is dried up like a potsherd, and My tongue cleaveth to My gums: and

Thou hast brought Me unto the dust of Death.

They that did see Me without conveyed themselves from Me: I am clean forgotten as a dead man out of mind.

Glory be to The Father.

Antiphon.

They shall mourn for Him as for an Only begotten Son; For The Lord without sin hath been slain.

Chapter.—John iii., 16.

So God loved the world, that He gave His Only begotten Son, to the end that whosoever believeth in Him should not perish, but have everlasting life.

Thanks be to God.

Hymn.

Thou didst languish in Death's anguish,
Sin's galling chains in sunder [break;
Peace securing, it enduring,
O Jesus! Crown of Virgin's make!

Ah! they scourge Thee, and they urge Thee
To drink that bitter cup of gall;
Us relieving from sins grieving
Thee, King Eternal, Lord of all!

On us, weeping, here, and keeping
Memorial of Thy dying woe;
Consolation and Salvation,
Jesus! our Ransomer, bestow.

On the bitter Cross's Altar.
Rich streams of blood from Thee flow'd down;
King benignest! Thou Who shinest,
His Consort, on Thy Father's Throne.

Blood of Jesus! To release us
Thou didst compel the Fiend to fly;
Henceforth make us glad partakers
Of the slain Lamb's repast on high!

All Laud and Honour be to Christ,
Who, sold, betray'd, and sacrific'd,
For us His people life to gain,
Died guiltless on the Cross of Pain.
Amen.

℣. The chastisement of our peace was upon Him.

℟. And by His stripes we are healed.

Canticle. Magnificat.

My soul doth magnify The Lord (*ante, p.* 103).

Antiphon.

O great work of mercy! Death then died; when upon the Tree Life died.

℣. O Lord! hear my prayer.

℟. And let my crying come unto Thee.

Orison.

O Lord Jesu Christ! Son of The living God! Who at the Vesper Hour of the day, being now made subject unto death, didst will to be taken down from the Cross, and (as it is piously believed) to be received into the arms of Thy Mother; mercifully grant that we, casting away the burthens of our sins, may be enabled to attain even unto the presence of Thy Divine Majesty, Who livest and reignest God, world without end. Amen.

ℂ *At Compline.*

Convert us, O God our Salvation!

And turn away Thine anger from us.

O God! make speed. (*And the rest.*)

Psalm.

Thou hast put away Mine acquaintance out of My sight; Thou hast made Me to be abhorred of them.

I am counted as one of them that go down into the pit: I am become even as a man that hath no strength; free among the dead.

Like unto them that are wounded and lie in the grave: who are out of remembrance, and are cut away from Thy Hand.

Thou hast laid Me in the lowest pit: in a place of darkness, and in the deep.

Thine indignation lieth hard upon Me: and Thou hast vexed Me with all Thy storms.

Glory be to The Father.

Antiphon.

My Flesh shall rest in peace.

Chapter.

Christ hath suffered in the Flesh; arm yourselves therefore with the same mind.

Thanks be to God.

℣. It behoved Christ to suffer,

℟. And to enter into His Glory.

Christ to suffer.

Glory be to The Father.

It behoved Christ to suffer.

Hymn.

Thou sinless King! Who, stark and dead,
Within the rocky tomb wast laid,
O grant us there with Thee to rest,
With all Thy living graces blest.

In mercy succour us, O Lord!
And, by Thy saving Blood restor'd,
O bring us to that blissful shore,
Where light and joy last evermore!

All Laud and Honour be to Christ,
Who, sold, betray'd, and sacrific'd,
For us His people life to gain,
Died guiltless on the Cross of Pain.
Amen.

℣. He died for our sins.

℟. And rose again for our justification.

The Song of Symeon.

Now lettest Thou, O Lord (*ante, p.* 113).

Antiphon.

SAVE us, O Christ our Saviour! for we adore Thy most Holy Passion, that by It we being defended from all the assaults of our enemies may ever please Thee, and rest in peace. Amen.

Lord! have mercy.
Christ! have mercy.
Lord! have mercy.

OUR FATHER.

And lead us not into temptation, but deliver us from evil. Amen.

℣. In peace in the Very Same

℟. I will sleep and take my rest.

I BELIEVE IN GOD. The Resurrection of the flesh, and life eternal. Amen.

℣. Christ for us became obedient unto death.

℟. Even the Death of the Cross.

O Lord! hear my prayer.

And let my crying come unto Thee.

Orison.

O LORD JESU CHRIST! Son of The Living God! Who at the Hour of Compline rested in the Sepulchre, and wast bewailed and lamented by Thy most gentle Mother, and by the other women; make us, we beseech Thee, to abound in the sorrows of Thy Passion, and with entire devotion of heart to bewail that same Passion, and to keep it ever as it were fresh in the ardent affection of our hearts, Who livest and reignest God, world without end. Amen.

Orison.

I BESEECH Thee, O most beloved Lord Jesus Christ! by that exceeding love wherewith Thou didst love mankind when Thou, The King of Heaven, wast hanging on the Altar of the Cross with Divine charity, with a most compassionate Soul, in a most sad condition, with troubled senses, with pierced Heart, with stricken Members, with scourged Body, with gory Wounds, with flowing streams of Blood, with out-stretched Arms, with transfixed Feet, with swollen veins, with wailing Mouth, with hoarse voice, with ghastly Face, with deadly paleness, with tearful Eyes, with swimming brain, with burning love, with moaning throat, with parching thirſt, with bitter taſte of vinegar and gall, with bowing Head, with approaching death, with the dividing of Thy moſt tender Body and Divine Soul, with Thy rent Side, the ſource of the living fountain; by that love I intreat Thee, O moſt pitiful ſweeteſt Lord Jeſus Chriſt, wherewith Thy burning heart was then divided, that Thou wouldeſt be to me forgiving of the multitude of mine offences, and favourable to my deſire in all good things; and that for Thy moſt bountiful mercy's ſake Thou wouldeſt vouchſafe to grant me a good and holy ending to my life, and, moreover, a glorious and joyful reſurrection; Who liveſt and reigneſt God, world without end Amen.

℣. God ſpared not His own Son:

℟. But delivered Him up for us all.

Let us pray.

Almighty and Everlaſting God, Who of Thine exceeding charity haſt willed Thine Only Son to be for us Incarnate, Born, to Suffer, to be Scourged, Crucified, and to Die; grant to us we beſeech Thee, that for thoſe moſt ſacred and innumerable Wounds which He endured for us, and by His moſt precious Blood, we may be purified from all our ſins, errors, and negligences; ſo that we may be made a Temple of The Holy Ghoſt, acceptable to Thee our Lord God, and partakers of the heavenly country, through The Same our Lord Jeſus Chriſt Thy Son, Who, with Thee liveth and reigneth, in The Unity of The Holy Ghoſt, God, world without end. Amen.

¶ MEDITATIONS AND DEVOTIONS ON THE MOST HOLY PASSION OF CHRIST.

¶ *The Paſſion of our Lord Jeſus Chriſt according to John* xviii.

The Lord Jesus went forth over the brook Cedron, where was a garden, into which He entered, and His diſciples. And Judas alſo, which betrayed Him, knew the place, for ofttimes Jesus resorted thither with His disciples. Judas therefore, when he had received a band of men from the chief priests and Pharisees, cometh thither with lanterns, and torches, and weapons. Jesus therefore, knowing all things that should come upon Him, went forth and said unto them, Whom seek ye? They answered Him, Jesus of Nazareth. And Judas also, which betrayed Him, stood with them. As soon then as Jesus had said unto them, I am He, they went backward, and fell to the ground. Then asked He them again, Whom seek ye? And they said, Jesus of Nazareth. Jesus answered, I have told you that I am He; if therefore ye seek Me, let these go their way, that the saying might be fulfilled which he spake, "Of them which Thou gavest me, I have lost none." Then Simon Peter, having a sword, drew it, and smote the High Priest's servant, and cut off his right ear. The servant's name was Malchus. Then said Jesus unto Peter, Put up thy sword into the sheath; the cup which My Father hath given me, shall I not drink it? Then the band and the Captain and the Officers of the Jews took Jesus and bound Him, and led Him away to Annas first, for he was father-in-law to Caiaphas, which was the High Priest that same year. Now Caiaphas was he who had given counsel to the Jews that it was expedient that one man should die for the people. But Simon Peter followed Jesus, and another disciple; that disciple was known unto the High Priest, and went in with Jesus into the palace of the High Priest. But Peter stood at the door without. Then went out that other disciple which was known unto the High Priest, and spake unto her that kept the door, and brought in Peter; then said the damsel that kept the door unto Peter, Art not thou also one of this man's disciples? He said, I am not. And the servants and officers stood there, who had made a fire of coals, for it was cold, and they warmed themselves, and Peter was standing with them and warming himself. The High Priest then asked Jesus of His disciples and of His doctrine. Jesus answered him, I spake openly to the world, I ever taught in the synagogue and in the temple whither the Jews always resort, and in secret have I said nothing. Why askest thou Me? ask them which heard Me what I have said unto them; behold, they know what I said. And when He had thus spoken, one of the officers which stood by struck Jesus with the palm of his hand, saying, Answerest Thou the High Priest so? Jesus answered him, If I have spoken evil, bear witness of the evil, but if well, why smitest thou Me? Now Annas had sent Him bound to Caiaphas, the High Priest. And Simon Peter stood and warmed himself. They said therefore unto him, Art not thou also one of His disciples? He denied it, and said, I am not. One of the servants of the High Priest, being kinsman to him whose ear Peter cut off, saith, Did I not see thee in the garden with Him? Peter then denied again, and immediately the cock crew. Then led they Jesus from Caiaphas unto the hall of judgement, and it was early, and they themselves went not into the judgement hall, lest they should be defiled, but that they might eat the Passover. Pilate then went out unto them, and said, What accusation bring ye against this man? They answered and said unto him, If He were not a malefactor, we would not have delivered Him up unto thee. Then Pilate said unto them, Take ye Him and judge Him according to your law. The Jews therefore said unto him, It is not lawful for us to put any man to death, that the saying of Jesus might be fulfilled, which He spake, signifying what death He should die. Then entered Pilate into the judgement hall again, and called Jesus, and said unto Him, Art Thou the King of the Jews? Jesus answered him, Sayest thou this thing of thyself, or did others tell it thee of Me? Pilate answered, Am I a Jew? Thine own nation and the chief priests have delivered Thee unto me: what hast Thou done? Jesus answered, My kingdom is not of this world: if My kingdom were of this world, then would My servants fight, that I should not be delivered to the Jews;

but now is My kingdom not from hence. Pilate therefore ſaid unto Him, Art Thou a King then? Jeſus anſwered, Thou ſayeſt that I am a King; to this end was I born, and for this cauſe came I into the world, that I ſhould bear witneſs unto the truth; everyone that is of the truth heareth My voice. Pilate ſaid unto Him, What is truth? And when he had ſaid this, he went out again unto the Jews, and ſaith unto them, I find in Him no fault at all. But ye have a cuſtom that I ſhould releaſe unto you One at the Paſſover; will ye therefore that I releaſe unto you The King of the Jews? Then cried they all again, ſaying, Not this man, but Barabbas. Now Barabbas was a robber. Then Pilate therefore took Jeſus and ſcourged Him, and the ſoldiers platted a Crown of Thorns, and put it on His Head, and they put on Him a Purple Robe, and ſaid, Hail! King of the Jews; and they ſmote Him with their hands. Pilate therefore went forth again, and ſaith unto them, Behold, I bring Him forth unto you, that ye may know that I find no fault in Him. Then came Jeſus forth, wearing the Crown of Thorns and the Purple Robe; and Pilate ſaith unto them, Behold The Man! When the chief prieſts therefore and officers ſaw Him, they cried out, ſaying, Crucify Him, crucify Him. Pilate ſaith unto them, Take ye Him, and crucify Him; for I find no fault in Him. The Jews anſwered him, We have a law, and by our law He ought to die, becauſe He made Himſelf The Son of God. When Pilate therefore heard that ſaying, he was the more afraid; and he went again into the judgement hall, and ſaith unto Jeſus, Whence art Thou? But Jeſus gave him no anſwer. Then ſaith Pilate unto Him, Speakeſt Thou not unto me? Knoweſt Thou not that I have power to crucify Thee, and have power to releaſe Thee? Jeſus anſwered, Thou couldeſt have no power at all againſt Me, except it were given thee from above; therefore, he that delivered Me unto thee hath the greater ſin. And from thenceforth Pilate ſought to releaſe Him; but the Jews cried out, ſaying, If thou let this man go, thou art not Cæſar's friend; whoſoever maketh himſelf a King ſpeaketh againſt Cæſar. When Pilate therefore heard that ſaying, he brought Jeſus forth, and ſate down in the judgement ſeat, in a place that is called The Pavement, but in the Hebrew, Gabbatha. And it was the Preparation of the Paſſover, and about the Sixth Hour; and he ſaith unto the Jews, Behold your King! But they cried out, "Away with Him! Away with Him! Crucify Him!" Pilate ſaith unto them, "Shall I crucify your King?" The chief prieſts anſwered, "We have no King but Cæſar." Then delivered he Him therefore unto them to be crucified. And they took Jeſus, and led Him away, and He bearing His Croſs went forth into a place called the Place of a Skull, which is called in the Hebrew, Golgotha; where they crucified Him, and two other with Him, on either ſide one, and Jeſus in the midſt. And Pilate wrote a title, and put it on the Croſs. And the writing was "Jeſus of Nazareth, the King of the Jews." This title then read many of the Jews, for the place where Jeſus was crucified was nigh to the city; and it was written in Hebrew, and Greek, and Latin. Then ſaid the chief prieſts of the Jews to Pilate, "Write not the King of the Jews, but that He ſaid, I am the King of the Jews." Pilate anſwered, "What I have written, I have written." Then the ſoldiers, when they had crucified Jeſus, took His garments, and made four parts, to every ſoldier a part, and alſo His coat. Now the Coat was without ſeam, woven from the top throughout. They ſaid therefore among themſelves, Let us not rend it, but caſt lots for it, whoſe it ſhall be; that the Scripture might be fulfilled, which ſaith, "They parted My raiment among them, and for My veſture did they caſt lots." Theſe things therefore the ſoldiers did. Now there ſtood by the Croſs of Jeſus His mother and His mother's ſiſter, Mary, the wife of Cleophas, and Mary Magdalene. When Jeſus therefore ſaw His mother and the diſciple ſtanding by, whom He loved, He ſaith unto His mother, "Woman, behold thy Son." Then ſaith He to the diſciple, "Behold thy mother!" And from that hour that diſciple took her unto his own home. After this, Jeſus, knowing that all things were now accompliſhed, that the Scripture might be fulfilled, ſaith, "I thirſt." Now there was ſet a veſſel full of vinegar, and they filled a ſpunge with vinegar, and put it upon hyſſop, and put it to His mouth. When Jeſus therefore had received the vinegar, He ſaid, "It is finiſhed!" and He bowed His head, and gave up The Ghoſt. The Jews therefore, becauſe it was the Preparation, that the bodies ſhould not remain upon the Croſs on the Sabbath Day (for that Sabbath Day was an High Day), beſought Pilate that their legs might be broken, and that they might be taken away. Then came the ſoldiers, and brake the legs of the firſt, and of the other which was crucified with him. But when they came to Jeſus, and ſaw that He was dead already, they brake not His legs. But one of the ſoldiers with a ſpear pierced His Side, and forthwith came thereout Blood and Water. And he that ſaw it bare record, and his record is true, and he knoweth that he ſaith true, that ye might believe. For theſe things were done, that the Scripture ſhould be fulfilled, "A bone of Him ſhall not be broken." And again another Scripture ſaith, "They ſhall look on Him Whom they have pierced." And after this Joſeph of Arimathea, being a diſciple of Jeſus, but ſecretly, for fear of the Jews, beſought Pilate that he might take away the Body of Jeſus; and Pilate gave him leave. And there came alſo Nicodemus, which at the firſt came to Jeſus by night, and brought a mixture of myrrh and aloes about an hundred pound weight. Then they took the Body of Jeſus, and wound it in linen clothes, with the ſpices, as the manner of the Jews is to bury. Now in the place where He was crucified there was a garden, and in the garden a new ſepulchre, wherein was never man yet laid. There laid they Jeſus therefore, becauſe of the Jews' Preparation Day.

Thanks be to God.

℣. Thou Who didſt ſuffer for us.

℞. O Lord! have mercy upon us.

Lord! hear my prayer.

And let my crying come unto Thee.

Orison.

O God! Who for us sinners didst place Thy Hands, and Thy Feet, and Thy whole Body upon the Tree of the Cross, and didst endure The Crown of Thorns set upon Thy Head in dishonour of Thy most sacred Person, Who didst upon that Cross suffer Five Wounds for the sake of us sinners, and hast redeemed us by Thy Sacred Blood; grant unto us, O Lord! we beseech Thee, this day and every day the practice of Penitence, Abstinence, Patience, Humility, Chastity, Light, Sense, Understanding, true Knowledge, right Faith, firm Hope, perfect Charity, and a pure Conscience, even unto the end, and remission of all our sins. Through Thyself, O Jesus Christ! Saviour of the world! Who livest and reignest with The Father and The Holy Ghost, God, world without end. Amen.

A Psalm of the Passion of Christ.

Orison of Christ hanging on The Cross, and description of His Passion, that by continual meditation thereon we may acquire Patience.

Psalm xxii.—*Deus, Deus meus.*

My God! my God! look upon Me; why hast Thou forsaken Me: and art so far from My health, and from the words of My complaint?

O my God! I cry in the day-time, but Thou hearest not: and in the night-season also I take no rest.

And Thou continuest Holy: O thou worship of Israel!

Our fathers hoped in Thee: they trusted in Thee, and Thou didst deliver them.

They called upon Thee, and were holpen: they put their trust in Thee, and were not confounded.

But as for Me, I am a Worm, and no man: a very scorn of men, and the out-cast of the people.

All they that see Me laugh Me to scorn: they shoot out their lips, and shake their heads, saying,

He trusted in God, that He

would deliver Him: let Him deliver Him, if He will have Him.

But Thou art He that took me out of my mother's womb: Thou wast my hope, when I hanged yet upon My mother's breasts.

I have been left unto Thee ever since I was born: Thou art My God even from My mother's womb.

O go not from Me, for trouble is hard at hand: and there is none to help Me.

Many oxen are come about Me: fat bulls of Basan close Me in on every side.

They gape upon Me with their mouths: as it were a ramping and a roaring lion.

I am poured out like water, and all My bones are out of joint: My Heart also in the midst of My Body is even like melting wax.

My strength is dried up like a potsherd, and My tongue cleaveth to My gums: and Thou shalt bring Me into the dust of death.

For many dogs are come about Me: and the council of the wicked layeth siege against Me.

They pierced My Hands and my Feet; I may tell all my Bones: they stand staring and looking upon Me.

They part My garments among them: and cast lots upon My vesture.

But be not Thou far from Me, O Lord!: Thou art My succour, haste Thee to help Me.

Deliver My Soul from the sword: My Darling from the power of the dog.

Save Me from the lion's mouth: Thou hast heard Me also from among the horns of the unicorns.

I will declare Thy Name unto My brethren: in the midst of the congregation will I praise Thee.

O praise the Lord, ye that fear Him: magnify Him, all ye of the seed of Jacob, and fear Him, all ye seed of Israel;

For He hath not despised, nor abhorred, the low estate of the poor: He hath not hid his face from Him, but when He called unto Him he heard Him.

My praise is of Thee in the great congregation: my vows will I perform in the sight of them that fear Him.

The poor shall eat, and be satisfied: they that seek after

The Lord ſhall praiſe him; your heart ſhall live for ever.

All the ends of the world ſhall remember themſelves, and be turned unto The Lord: and all the kindreds of the nations ſhall worſhip before Him.

For the kingdom is The Lord's: and He is the Governour among the people.

All ſuch as be fat upon earth: have eaten, and worſhipped.

All they that go down into the duſt ſhall kneel before Him: and no man hath quickened his own ſoul.

My ſeed ſhall ſerve Him: they ſhall be counted unto The Lord for a generation.

They ſhall come, and the heavens ſhall declare His righteouſneſs: unto a people that ſhall be born, whom The Lord hath made.

¶ *A devout Oriſon to our Lord and Saviour Jeſus Chriſt, which may be ſaid at any time.*

O Lord Jesus Christ! I intreat Thee by That moſt Holy Fleſh which Thou didſt take upon Thee of the immaculate Virgin Mary, and by that holy womb in which for nine months Thou didſt vouchſafe to dwell, and by all the graces and mercies of Thy miracles which Thou didſt ever perform for the healing of mankind; and by Thy Selling, Betrayal, and Apprehenſion, Thy Bonds, Scourgings, and Accuſation, by Thy Crown of Thorns, by Thy Sceptre, by Thy ſacred Thirſt and Hunger, by the trial and triumph of Thy Paſſion, by Thy Croſs, and the holy humility of Thy Death and Burial, by The Five Wounds of Thy Body, by Thy moſt Holy Blood, by thoſe conſecrated Nails fixed in Thy ſacred Body, and by thoſe Thy Footſteps when Thou didſt walk to Thy Holy Croſs, and didſt hang thereon though guiltleſs, and by Thy precious Blood which Thou haſt ſprinkled upon us, and by Thy moſt ſacred Tears, and by Thy moſt Holy Croſs and Winding-ſheet, and by that Comfort wherewith Thou didſt will that Thou ſhouldeſt be comforted in Thine anguiſh, and by all Thy Diſtreſſes, and by that Thy Holy Faſt, by Thy precious Death and Reſurrection, Thy wonderful Aſcenſion, and by The Coming of The Holy Ghoſt

The Comforter, and for the intercessions of Thy most gentle Mother, and of All Thy Saints, hearken unto me Thy servant, and fulfil all my desire for good, and deliver me from all my sins, past, present, and future, and from all the assaults of mine enemies, visible and invisible, bodily and spiritual, from unforeseen and sudden death, and from all evil. Grant to me, O Lord! space of life and the grace of living well, so that before the day of my departure, I may be worthy to possess contrition of heart, a pure confession, and true penitence; and when Thou shalt bid my soul journey from this world, grant me happily to receive Thy most sacred and precious Body for meat, and Thy most Holy Blood for drink, and an Heavenly Unction, and deliver me in the hour of my death from the power of the Devil, and from all distress, and place me in the bosom of Abraham Thy friend, and may I be worthy to dwell with Thee for evermore, Who with The Father and The Holy Ghost, livest and reignest God world without end. Amen.

¶ *Here follow certain most devout Orisons, and first of all the Prayer of S. Ambrose on each of the particulars of the Passion of our Lord.*

O Lord Jesu Christ! Son of the living God! Creator and restorer of mankind! we offer Thee thanks, unworthy indeed, yet as we trust devout and acceptable to Thee, Who for us most miserable didst descend from Heaven, and take upon Thee Flesh of the most blessed Virgin Mary, and didst vouchsafe to be born of her, wast wrapped in swathing bands, laid in the manger, fed with milk at the breast, circumcised in the flesh, manifested to the Wise Men of the East, and by them worshipped, presented in the Temple, driven into Egypt, restored to Thine own country in subjection to Thy parents, baptized by John, attenuated by a forty days fast, thrice tempted by the devil, wearied with travail, worn by watching, hunger, and thirst, exhausted by preaching, moved to tears by Thy compassions, yet by the Jews rejected, and by them many times injured. When Thy Passion was at hand, Thou wast pleased as a true Man to be afflicted and ſorrowful, to fear, as well as to be weary; and with bended knees to fall down upon Thy Face in prayer; in Thine Agony to ſhed drops of Blood for ſweat. Finally, Thou waſt betrayed by Judas, by him traitorouſly kiſſed, and by the wicked Jews taken by violence, bound with thongs, like a robber, alone verily, and forſaken by Thy diſciples, who fled for fear; led forth to the High Prieſt Annas, and there buffeted by the hand; ſent by him to Caiaphas, there bound and greatly mocked; arraigned before the council of the judges, accuſed by falſe witneſſes, condemned to a moſt ignominious death, defiled in Thy Face with ſpitting, haraſſed with revilings, diſtreſſed by reproaches, lacerated with ſtripes, again ſmitten by the hand, in manifold ways blaſphemed, put in bonds by Pilate, delivered up to death, continually threatened, ſent by Pilate to Herod, there alſo treated as a criminal, by Herod and his army ſet at naught, clothed in a white robe, ſent back to Pilate, at the command of Pilate tied naked to a pillar, grievouſly ſcourged even to blood, by the ſame condemned to death, given up to the ſoldiers to be crucified, by whom He was again ſtripped, clothed with a purple robe, crowned with the Crown of Thorns, decked with the reed as for a ſceptre, ſaluted in ſcorn by the bowing of the knee, called King of the Jews, a third time buffeted with the palms of their hands, His Face again covered with ſpitting, ſtruck on the Head with the reed, ſtripped of His purple robe, laden with the wood of the Croſs, led forth to the place of His ſuffering, there made to drink of wine mingled with myrrh, a third time ſtripped of his own garments, at laſt ſtretched upon the Croſs, His Hands and Feet faſtened thereto with nails, and ſo crucified between thieves, and numbered with the tranſgreſſors; by the paſſers by and them that ſtood near, cruelly blaſphemed as He hung on the Croſs, crying out "My God, My God, why haſt Thou forſaken Me?" made to drink of vinegar when thirſty, bowing His Head in death, pierced with a lance by a ſoldier in His Side, whence flowed out Blood and Water:

When the even was come, taken down from the Croſs, laid in the ſepulchre, buried by Joſeph; ariſing on the third day, Thou didſt appear to Thy friends; on the fortieth Thou didſt aſcend into Heaven, and ſitting on the Right Hand of The Father, didſt ſend forth the promiſed Comforter to Thy diſciples. Finally, Thou ſhalt come to judgement, to reward every one for his merits, good or evil. Thou, O Lord Jeſus! by theſe Thy moſt ſacred Pains, and by Thy moſt precious Death, and by Thy precious Blood poured forth for us ſinners, and by all thoſe other before-mentioned Sufferings of Thine; moreover, by Thine ineffable mercy, and for the prayers and merits of the moſt bleſſed Virgin Mary, and of all Thy Saints, deliver me, an unclean ſinner, my parents, my brothers and ſiſters, my friends and mine enemies, and all who are poor, tempted, and deſolate, captive, ſick, and all others for whom I am bound to pray, and all Chriſtian people who are in tribulation and difficulties, from the ſnares of the devil, and from all the chains of their ſins; and free and ſave us from all harm in ſoul and body, and ever keep us from the ſame. Diſpoſe evermore all our thoughts and actions ſo that they may be wholly acceptable unto Thee. Fill us with Thy Holy Grace and Peace, and with all Virtues; and grant that we may perſevere therein unto death. Vouchſafe unto us a good end to our life, and redeem Thou ſuch of us who are now living from all pains after our death, and ſuch as are already dead, and all the faithful departed; and mercifully enable us all to attain to the everlaſting Glory of Thy celeſtial Kingdom, Who with The Father and The Holy Ghoſt liveſt and reigneſt God world without end. Amen.

Our Father.

Hail, Mary!

Another very devout Oriſon on each particular of the Paſſion of Jeſus Chriſt.

Hail, Jesu! Brightneſs of Thy Father's Glory, Very Bloſſom of very Virginity! promiſed to Patriarchs, predicted by prophets, deſired of the righteous, awaited for the ſalvation of all men, Who waſt announced to the Virgin Mary by Gabriel the Archangel, conceived by The Holy Ghoſt; Very God, yet born a Man, wrapped in ſwaddling clothes, laid in a manger, revealed to ſhepherds, worſhipped by the Magi, circumciſed after the law, preſented in the Temple, baptized by John, tempted by the enemy, glorious with miracles, welcomed with palm branches by the multitudes, ſupping with Thy diſciples, and delivering to them Thy moſt bleſſed Body and Blood; by Judas betrayed and ſold, bathed in a bloody ſweat, taken by Thine enemies, ſpeedily abandoned by all Thy friends, bound with cruel thongs, brought before Annas and Caiaphas, Thy Face covered, torn with ſtripes, defiled with ſpitting, overwhelmed with revilings, brought before Pilate, by Herod deſpiſed and mocked, crucified by the tongues of the Jews, long time ſcourged, derided in a purple robe, crowned with thorns, carrying Thy Croſs like a thief, driven away to death with blows and buffetings, a ſpectacle of reproach, ſtripped naked, faſtened with cruel nails to the Croſs, racked in every limb, numbered with the tranſgreſſors, deſpiſed and blaſphemed, eſteemed the very outcaſt of mankind, and as it were a leper, invoking Thy Father, praying for Thy perſecutors, promiſing Paradiſe to the thief, providing a ſon for Thy Mother, crying out for thirſt, teſtifying that Thy work of love was finiſhed, given gall to drink, growing pale with death, commending Thy Spirit to Thy Father, giving up the Ghoſt with a loud cry, pierced by the lance, taken down from the Croſs, by Thy friends bewailed and buried, riſing again from death and aſcending victorious into Heaven, and ſending down The Holy Ghoſt The Comforter upon His Spouſe in teſtimony of His perfect love! Wherefore I, the leaſt of Thy members, redeemed by Thy Blood, and deſiring the ſalvation of all, do embrace Thee, and thus in that love of Thine which conſtrained Thee to endure each and all of them, do kiſs each and all of Thy Wounds, beſeeching Thee to place Thy Self as a very beauteous bundle of myrrh within the boſom of my ſoul!

O Lord Jesu Christ! Who for the salvation of mankind wast pleased to endure Thy Five Wounds, grant, we beseech Thee, that through reverence for those Thy Wounds I may be worthy to be absolved from all my sins, and to finish this my present life by a prosperous end, and never to be separated from the contemplation of Thy most sweet Vision, Who livest and reignest with God The Father in the Unity of The Holy Ghost, God, world without end. Amen.

Orison of the Venerable Beda.

This Prayer made the worshipful S. Beda of the Seven last Sayings which our Lord Jesus Christ spake hanging on the Cross.

O Lord Jesu Christ! Who on the last day of Thy life, hanging on the Cross, didst utter Seven Sayings, that we might ever have those Seven most holy Sayings in remembrance; I intreat Thee by the virtue of those Seven Sayings to forgive me all that I have done or sinned in the seven deadly Sins, or what proceedeth from them; that is, Pride, Avarice, Luxury, Envy, Gluttony, Anger, Sloth; and forasmuch as Thou didst say, "Father, forgive them that crucify Me," cause me for the love of Thee to pardon all them that do evil to me. And forasmuch as Thou didst say to the thief, "To-day shalt thou be with Me in Paradise," cause me so to live that in the hour of death Thou mayest say to me, "To-day shalt thou be with Me in Heaven." And since Thou didst say to Thy Mother, "Woman, behold thy son," and then didst tell Thy disciple to "Behold thy Mother," grant that Thy love and Thy charity may unite me to the fellowship of Thy Mother. O Lord Jesus Christ! as Thou didst exclaim, "Eli, Eli, lama sabacthani?" that is, "My God, My God, why hast Thou forsaken Me?" so in time of my affliction and tribulation, O my Father! pity me a sinner, and help me, O my King and my God! for Thou hast redeemed me with Thine own Blood. And as Thou didst cry out, "I thirst!" as it were for the release of the holy souls who were awaiting Thy Coming, grant that I may evermore thirst for and love Thee, the Fountain of Eternal Light, with the entire desire and affection of my heart. And as Thou didst exclaim, "Father, into Thine hands I commend My Spirit!" grant that in the hour of my death I may be able perfectly and freely to say unto Thee, "Father, into Thine hands I commend my spirit." Receive me when I come unto Thee, Who hast set the bounds of my life; and like as Thou didst declare "It is finished," signifying thereby that the griefs and labours which Thou didst come to undertake for us miserable, were now ended, grant that I may be worthy to hear that most sweet Voice of Thine, "Come, My friend and My beloved, I have already laid up treasure for thee; come, that with Me thou mayest sit, and with My holy Angels, and in My kingdom, feast, rejoice, and abide throughout infinite ages of ages." Amen.

ℭ THE XV. OOS. IN ENGLISH.

ℭ *These be the xv. Oos. the which the holy Virgin S. Bridget was wont to say daily before the Holy Rood in S. Paul's Church at Rome.*

O Lord Jesu Christ! Eternal sweetness of them that love Thee! in joyfulness exceeding all gladness, and all desire; The Saviour and lover of all truly penitent sinners, Who hast testified that Thy delight is to dwell with the children of men, wherefore Thou didst become Man in the end of time; remember all the foretaste and deep anguish which in Thy human Body Thou didst sustain on the eve of Thy most healing Passion, from eternal time pre-ordained in the Divine heart. Remember the sadness and bitterness which, Thou being witness, Thou hadst in Thy Soul, when in the Last Supper Thou didst deliver to Thy disciples Thy Body and Blood, didst wash their feet, and sweetly comforting them didst foretell Thine approaching Passion. Remember all Thy trembling anguish and grief, which Thou enduredst in Thy tender Body before The Passion of The Cross, when, after Thy thrice-repeated prayer and Bloody Sweat, Thou wast betrayed by Thy disciple, led away captive by the chosen people, accused by false witnesses, judged by three judges unjustly, in the elect City, at the Paschal time, in the flower of Thy bodily youth, condemned though guiltleſs, ſtripped of Thine own garments, and clothed with a ſtrange veſture, buffeted, Thy Face and Eyes veiled, bruiſed with buffetings, bound to a pillar, ſcourged, crowned with thorns, ſmitten with the reed on Thy Head, and rent with numberleſs other injuries! Grant me, I intreat Thee, for the memory of theſe Thy Sufferings before Thy Crucifixion, ere my death, true contrition, a pure confeſſion, and worthy amends, and remiſſion of all my ſins. Amen.

OUR FATHER.

Hail, Mary!

Oriſon II.

O JESU! Very glory of Angels! Paradiſe of delights! call to remembrance the dread and horror which Thou didſt endure when all Thine enemies like ferocious lions ſtood around Thee, and with buffetings, and ſpittings, and lacerations, and other unheard-of tortures, afflicted Thee. And by all thoſe injurious words, dreadful blows, and moſt agonizing torments, O Lord Jeſu Chriſt! and by the pains wherewith all Thine enemies afflicted Thee, I beſeech Thee to deliver me from all my foes, viſible and inviſible, and grant me, under the ſhadow of Thy wings, to find the ſhelter of eternal ſalvation. Amen.

OUR FATHER.

Hail, Mary!

Oriſon III.

O JESU! Framer of the worlds! Whom no meaſurement can mete within any true bound, Who comprehendeſt the earth within the hollow of Thine Hand, remember that moſt bitter grief which Thou didſt endure when with blunted nails the Jews firſt moſt cruelly faſtened Thy moſt ſweet Hands to the Croſs, and pierced Thy moſt delicate and ſacred Feet! And when Thou waſt not obſequious to their will, heaped ſorrow upon ſorrow in Thy Wounds, and then cruelly dragged and ſtretched Thee on the length and breadth of Thy Croſs, ſo that the joints of Thy Limbs were looſed; I intreat Thee by the remembrance of this moſt ſacred and bitter Sorrow of the Croſs, that Thou wouldeſt grant unto me Thy fear and Thy love!

OUR FATHER.
Hail, Mary!

Orison IV.

O JESU! Heavenly Physician! call to remembrance the faintness, the agony, the sorrow, which, uplifted on the Cross of suffering, Thou didst endure in all Thy lacerated limbs, of which none remained aright in their place; so that no sorrow could be found like unto Thy Sorrow, for from the sole of the foot even to the crown of the head there was no soundness in Thee—yet then, as if forgetting all Thy pains, Thou didst pray to Thy Father for Thine enemies, saying, "Father, forgive them, for they know not what they do." For the tokens of that Thy pitifulness, and for the remembrance of that Thy Sorrow, grant that this the memory of Thy most bitter Passion may be to me the full remission of all my sins! Amen.

OUR FATHER.
Hail, Mary!

Orison V.

O JESU! Mirror of Divine Charity! be mindful of the terror and mourning which were Thine, when, naked and miserable Thou wast hanging on the Cross; and all Thine enemies and acquaintances stood over against Thee, and Thou didst find none to comfort Thee but Thy beloved Mother only, in bitterness of soul most faithfully standing by Thee; whom Thou didst commend to Thy beloved disciple, saying, "Woman, behold thy son," and "Behold thy Mother." I beseech Thee, kind Jesu, by the Sword of Grief, which then passed through her soul, that Thou wouldest sympathize with me in my troubles and afflictions, whether corporal or spiritual, and grant me consolation in all time of my tribulation. Amen.

OUR FATHER.
Hail, Mary!

Orison VI.

O JESU! King beloved and Friend entirely to be desired! remember that mourning which was Thine, when in the mirror of Thy most serene Majesty, Thou didst behold the predestination of Thine Elect, to be saved by the merits of Thy Passion, and the reprobation of the wicked into the multitude of the damned; and by the depth of that Pity whereby Thou didſt then commiſerate loſt and deſpairing ſinners, and eſpecially which Thou didſt ſhew to the Thief on the Croſs ſaying, "This day ſhalt thou be with me in Paradiſe," I beſeech Thee kind Jeſu Chriſt! that Thou wouldeſt grant me Thy mercy in the hour of my death.

OUR FATHER.

Hail, Mary!

Oriſon VII.

O JESU! Exhauſtleſs Fount of pity! Who from the inmoſt affection of Thy Love on the Croſs didſt ſay, "I thirſt," that is, for the ſalvation of mankind; ſtir up, we beſeech Thee, our deſires to every perfect work, and thoroughly quench and extinguiſh in us the thirſt of carnal concupiſcence, and the heat of worldly delights! Amen.

OUR FATHER.

Hail, Mary!

Oriſon VIII.

O JESU! Sweetneſs to all hearts! and boundleſs Suavity of ſouls! by the bitterneſs of that Vinegar and Gall, which for us Thou didſt endure, and didſt taſte in the hour of Thy death; grant unto us worthily to receive Thy Body and Blood, to the healing and comfort of our ſouls. Amen.

OUR FATHER.

Hail, Mary!

Oriſon IX.

O JESU! King of Might! Thou jubilation of the ſoul! call to mind that ſorrow and anguiſh which Thou didſt ſuffer, when by reaſon of the bitterneſs of death, and the inſults of the Jews, with a loud voice Thou didſt cry out that Thou waſt forſaken by God Thy Father, ſaying, "My God! My God! why haſt Thou forſaken Me?" By that anguiſh I intreat Thee, that in the anguiſh of my death Thou wouldeſt never forſake me, O our God!

OUR FATHER.

Hail, Mary!

Oriſon X.

O JESU! Alpha and Omega! the Way, the Life, and the Strength of all men; call to Thy remembrance that from the crown of Thy Head to the ſole of Thy Foot, Thou waſt plunged in the flood of Thy

Passion on our behalf. Because of the breadth and vastness of Thy Wounds, teach me, who am but too deeply plunged in sin, with true charity to keep Thy commandment, which is exceeding broad. Amen.

OUR FATHER.

Hail, Mary!

Orison XI.

O JESU! Abyss of unfathomable mercy! I beseech Thee by the depth of those Thy Wounds which pierced Thy Flesh and the very marrow of Thy Bones and Vitals, that Thou wouldest draw me forth, who am overwhelmed with sins, and hide me within the doors of Thy Wounds from the face of Thine anger, O Lord! until Thy wrath pass away! Amen.

OUR FATHER.

Hail, Mary!

Orison XII.

O JESU! Mirror of truth! Ensign of unity! and Bond of love! call to mind Thy numberless Wounds, wherewith from the crown of Thy Head even to the sole of Thy Feet Thou wast wounded, and by impious Jews maimed and imbrued in Thine own most Holy Blood! What intensity of sorrow Thou didst endure in Thy virgin Flesh, for our sakes! O kind Jesu! what more couldest Thou do than Thou hast done? Write, I intreat Thee, O kind Jesu! all Thy Wounds in my heart with Thy most precious Blood, that in them I may read Thy Griefs and Love, that I may persevere in giving of thanks continually even to my life's end. Amen.

OUR FATHER.

Hail, Mary!

Orison XIII.

O JESU! Most mighty Lion! King immortal and most invincible! remember the sorrow which Thou didst endure, when all the powers of Thy Heart and Body fainted, and, bowing Thine Head, Thou saidst, "It is finished." For that anguish and sorrow have mercy upon me when my soul at my last end, in the departure of my spirit, shall be disquieted and troubled. Amen.

OUR FATHER.

Hail, Mary!

Orison XIV.

O JESU! Only Begotten! Brightness of Thy Father Most High! and the Image of His

Subſtance, call to remembrance that earneſt intreaty wherewith Thou didſt commend Thy Spirit to Thy Father, ſaying, "Father, into Thine Hands I commend my Spirit;" and with Body rent, and Heart broken, and the bowels of Thy mercy laid open for our healing, didſt with a loud cry, expire! By this Thy precious Death I intreat Thee, O King of Saints! ſtrengthen me to reſiſt the Devil, the World, and the fleſh; and dying unto the fleſh may I live unto Thee; and in the laſt hour of my departure do Thou receive my ſpirit, returning again as it were an exile and a ſtranger unto Thee. Amen.

OUR FATHER.

Hail, Mary!

Oriſon XV.

O JESU! True and faithful Vine! Remember the overflowing and abounding effuſion of Thy Blood, which Thou, as from a rich cluſter of grapes, didſt plentifully pour forth, when upon the Croſs Thou didſt tread the wine-preſs alone, and pierced with the ſoldier's ſpear, didſt for us ſhed forth Blood and Water from Thy Side, ſo that but little and few drops remained in Thee! and at laſt, like a bundle of myrrh, waſt ſuſpended aloft, and Thy tender fleſh changed colour, and the moiſture of Thy vitals was dried up, and the marrow of Thy bones became emaciate! With This Thy moſt bitter Paſſion, and This the pouring out of Thy moſt precious Blood, O Sweet Jeſu! wound my heart, that the tears of penitence and love may be to me for meat day and night; and convert me wholly unto Thee, that my heart may be ever a manſion for Thee, and my converſation may be pleaſing and acceptable in Thy ſight, and that the cloſe of my days may be ſo praiſeworthy, that after this life be ended, I may be found worthy of praiſing Thee, with all Thy Saints, for ever and ever. Amen.

OUR FATHER.

Hail, Mary!

I BELIEVE IN GOD.

Oriſons of S. Gregory of the Croſs.

I ADORE Thee, O Lord Jeſus Chriſt! hanging upon the Croſs, and bearing the Crown of Thorns upon Thine Head! I beſeech Thee, O Lord Jeſus Chriſt! that Thy Croſs may deliver me from the avenging Angel. Amen.

I ADORE Thee, O Lord Jeſus Chriſt! wounded upon the Croſs, and made to drink of Vinegar and Gall! I beſeech Thee, O Lord Jeſus Chriſt! that Thy Wounds may be the healing of my ſoul. Amen.

I ADORE Thee, O Lord Jeſus Chriſt! laid in the ſepulchre, embalmed with myrrh and ſpices! I intreat Thee, O Lord Jeſus Chriſt! that Thy Death may be my life. Amen.

I ADORE Thee, O Lord Jeſus Chriſt! deſcending into Hell, and liberating Thy captives! I beſeech Thee that I may never enter therein. Amen.

I ADORE Thee, O Lord Jeſus Chriſt! riſing again from the dead, aſcending into Heaven, and ſitting on The Right Hand of The Father! I beſeech Thee have mercy upon me. Amen.

O LORD JESU CHRIST! The Good Shepherd! preſerve the righteous, juſtify the ſinner, have mercy upon all the faithful, and be favourable unto me a moſt miſerable ſinner. Amen.

O LORD JESU CHRIST! I intreat Thee by that very exceeding bitterneſs of Thy Paſſion which for me Thou didſt endure upon The Croſs, eſpecially when Thy moſt excellent Soul departed from Thy moſt ſacred Body, have mercy upon my ſoul in its departure. Amen.

OUR FATHER.

Hail, Mary!

I BELIEVE IN GOD.

And lead us not into temptation, but deliver us from evil.

℣. We adore Thee, O Chriſt! and we bleſs Thee.

℟. For by Thy Holy Croſs Thou haſt redeemed the world.

O moſt gracious Lord Jeſu Chriſt! regard me a miſerable ſinner with thoſe eyes of mercy wherewith Thou didſt regard Peter in the court, Mary Magdalene at the feaſt, and the thief upon the Croſs of Suffering; and grant that with bleſſed Peter I may worthily weep for my ſins, ſo that with Mary Magdalene I may perfectly love Thee, and with the holy thief may behold Thee eternally in the Paradiſe of Heaven, Who with God The Father liveſt and reigneſt in The Unity of The Holy

Ghoſt world without end. Amen.

ORISONS OF THE CROSS.

OUR FATHER.

O THOU Gracious Crucified One! Redeemer of all Thy people; Who for the ſalvation of mankind didſt ſuffer death at the hands of wicked men; for Thy Holy Name's ſake, and for the merits and interceſſions of Thy moſt bleſſed Mother Mary, and of All Thy Saints, be favourable to me a ſinner and hearken to the prayers of Thy ſervant according to the multitude of Thy mercy! Amen.

O LORD JESU CHRIST! Who didſt will that Thy glorious Head, venerated of Angels and men, ſhould be diſhonoured by a Crown of Thorns, that Thy Blood might flow from thence for the redemption of the world; for Thy Holy Name's ſake, and for the merits and interceſſions of Thy moſt bleſſed Mother Mary, and of All Thy Saints, forgive me a ſinner all the ſin which I may have done amiſs through the ſenſes of my head. O Lord! have mercy upon me a ſinner. Amen.

O LORD JESU CHRIST! Who didſt will Thy glorious Hands to be pierced with nails upon the Croſs, that Thy Blood might thence flow out for the redemption of the world; for Thy Holy Name's ſake, and for the merits aud interceſſions of Thy moſt bleſſed Mother Mary, and of All Thy Saints, forgive me a ſinner whatever I have done amiſs in unhallowed touch or in unlawful acts. O Lord! have mercy upon me a ſinner. Amen.

O LORD JESU CHRIST! Who didſt will Thy precious Side to be pierced by the ſpear of a ſoldier, that Blood and Water might thence flow out for the redemption of the world; for Thy Holy Name's ſake, and for the merits and interceſſions of Thy moſt bleſſed Mother Mary, and of All Thy Saints, forgive me a ſinner whatever I have done amiſs through unlawful thoughts or luſtful deſires. O Lord! have mercy upon me a ſinner. Amen.

O LORD JESU CHRIST! Who didſt will Thy precious Feet to be pierced with nails upon the Croſs, that Blood might thence flow out for the redemption of the world; for Thy Holy

Name's ſake, and for the merits and interceſſions of Thy moſt bleſſed Mother Mary, and of All Thy Saints, forgive me a ſinner whatever I have done amiſs through the means of my feet. O Lord! have mercy upon me a ſinner. Amen.

O Lord Jesu Christ! Who didſt will Thy whole Body to be extended upon the Croſs, ſo that all Thy Bones might be numbered; for Thy Holy Name's ſake, and for the merits and interceſſions of Thy moſt bleſſed Mother Mary, and of All Thy Saints, forgive me a ſinner whatever I have done amiſs by the inſtrumentality of any of my members. O Lord! have mercy upon me a ſinner. Amen.

℣. We worſhip Thee, O Chriſt! and we bleſs Thee.

℟. Who by Thy Holy Croſs haſt redeemed the world.

Let us pray.

O God! Who for the redemption of the world didſt will to be born therein, by the Jews to be rejected, and by Judas to be betrayed with a kiſs, to be bound with chains, and to be led as an innocent lamb to the ſlaughter, to be brought before Pilate, accuſed by falſe witneſſes, lacerated with ſtripes, to be vexed with revilings, and ſpat upon, to be crowned with thorns, lifted up upon the Croſs, wounded by a ſpear, and numbered among the tranſgreſſors; moreover, to be pierced with ſharp nails, and made to drink of vinegar and gall: do Thou, O Lord! through theſe moſt holy Pains of Thine, deliver my ſoul from the pains of hell, and by Thy Holy Croſs ſave me and keep me, and bring me forth, a miſerable ſinner, into that place whither Thou didſt bring the thief who was crucified with Thee, Who with The Father and The Holy Ghoſt liveſt and reigneſt God world without end. Amen.

Our Father.

Hail, Mary!

I Believe in God.

¶ *Of the Holy Croſs.*

The Croſs ✠ of Chriſt be with me; it is The Croſs ✠ that I ever adore; The Croſs ✠ of Chriſt is true ſalvation; The Croſs ✠ of Chriſt exceedeth all joys; The Croſs ✠ of Chriſt looſeth the chains of death; The Croſs ✠ of Chriſt is invincible in arms; The

Croſs ✠ of Chriſt is a ſtandard immoveable. May The Croſs of Chriſt be to me the path of virtue, and very virtue's ſelf. By The Divine Croſs I will ſet forward on my way. The Croſs of Chriſt procureth all good. The Croſs of Chriſt turns to flight all evil. The Croſs of Chriſt hath taken away eternal pains. O Croſs of Chriſt! preſerve me; be over me, before me, and behind me; for the ancient enemy flieth whenever he ſeeth Thee. O Height of The Croſs, which no other height ever obtained, and Depth to which no other depth ever deſcended; and Breadth of The Croſs, to which no other breadth ever comprehended, deliver me, Thy ſervant, from all the wiles of the devil, and from all the evil thoughts which may haunt me. Satan! begone from me, that I may know thee not; and as thou art cut off from Heaven, ſo may The Holy Spirit cut thee off from me. And as thou art a ſtranger to all felicity, ſo be thou ſtrange unto me. And as thou never deſireſt God, ſo mayeſt thou never deſire to come to me. Avaunt! thou Evil One! Avaunt from me, by the Sign of The Holy Croſs ✠. Behold The Croſs of the Lord! Begone, ye adverſaries. The Lion of the Tribe of Judah hath conquered. The Root of David. Alleluya! The Benediction of God The Father Almighty, The Son, and Holy Spirit, ✠, with The Croſs of Chriſt, deſcend from above, and abide with me for ever. Amen.

Oriſon.

Sanctify me, O Lord Jeſu Chriſt! with the Sign of Thy Holy Croſs, that It may be to me a ſhelter againſt the cruel darts of my enemies, viſible and inviſible. Defend me, O Jeſus Chriſt! Good Shepherd! this day and at all times, from all hurtful paſſions, from all diſtreſs and tribulation, from all evil vices, paſt, preſent, and future, by the Sign of Thy Holy Croſs, and by that ineſtimable Ranſom, with which Thou didſt mercifully redeem us, Who liveſt and reigneſt God world without end. Amen.

Our Father. *(ſecretly.)*

Hail, Mary!

And lead us not into temptation, but deliver us from evil.

℣. We adore the Sign of the Croſs.

℟. Through which we have received the Sacrament of our ſalvation.

Oriſon.

Sanctify, I beſeech Thee, O Lord! me, Thy ſervant, by the Sign of The Holy Croſs, that it may become a defence againſt the fierce darts of all my enemies, and preſerve me through That Holy and precious Death, and by That righteous Blood wherewith Thou didſt redeem me, Who with The Father and The Holy Ghoſt liveſt and reigneſt God for evermore. Amen.

Another Oriſon to The Lord.

O Lord Jesu Christ! be with me, that Thou mayeſt be my defence; within me, that Thou mayeſt refreſh me; about me, that Thou mayeſt preſerve me; and before me, that Thou mayeſt guard me; under me, that Thou mayeſt lift me up; above me, that Thou mayeſt bleſs me with Thine outſtretched Right Hand. O Single and yet Trine God! preſerve me for ever. Amen.

Holy Michael! be to me for mail!

Holy Gabriel! be to me a helmet!

Holy Raphael! be to me a ſhield!

Holy Uriel! be to me a champion!

Holy Cherubim! be to me my health!

Holy Seraphim! be to me truth!

All ye Holy Angels and Archangels! guard, protect, and defend me, and bring me at laſt to everlaſting life. Amen.

O most ſweet Jeſu! inſpire my heart with Thy moſt ſacred love, with contempt for the world, hatred of ſin, deſire for the Heavenly Country, and perſeverance and penitence, which may no evil deſires hinder, until Thy compaſſion bring them to perfect effect. Amen.

Hymn of The Holy Croſs.

Hail! Thou Monarch of Confeſſors!
King of Saints! Hope of tranſgreſſors!
Crucified as an offender;
Very Man, yet God of Splendour,
With tottering knees, with Soul oppreſſed.
Oh! how poor and bare they made Thee,
When upon the Croſs they laid Thee!

All a jeſt, and a deriſion;
Yet of Thine own free permiſſion,
With Members tortured and diſtreſſed.

Jeſus! Hail! Who life haſt given,
And in that dread combat ſtriven;
Whoſe dear Limbs by force extended
Were upon the Tree ſuſpended,
All agoniſed in ſad unreſt.

On that Croſs, deſpiſed and bleeding,
Racked and pierced, for mortals pleading,
Let me near Thee take my ſtation;
Fill me with Thy conſolation,
O grant my longing heart's requeſt!

Firſt with pure and deep affection
May I fly to Thy protection;
By no toil or foes affrighted,
Saved and cleanſed, with Thee united,
Fold me in Thine embraces bleſt!
Amen.

ℭ OF THE FIVE WOUNDS.

Here follow five moſt devout Oriſons to the Five Wounds of our Lord Jeſus Chriſt, to be ſaid before the Crucifix on bended knees.

Laud, Honour, Glory, and giving of thanks be to Thee for The Moſt Sacred Wound of Thy Right Hand! O Lord Jeſu Chriſt! by This Sacred Wound forgive me all the ſins which in any of my five ſenſes I have ever committed againſt Thee, all the tranſgreſſions which I have ever been guilty of towards Thee, in thought, word, work, in neglect of Thy ſervice, in wicked pleaſure, either ſleeping or waking, willingly or ignorantly; and through Thy moſt revered Paſſion grant that I may ever worthily cheriſh in remembrance Thy moſt gracious Death, and Thy moſt ſacred Wounds, and Thou being the giver may preſent gratefully my mortified body unto Thee. Amen.

Laud, Honour, Glory, and giving of thanks be to Thee for The Moſt Sacred Wound of Thy Left Hand! O moſt ſweet Jeſu! by This Sacred Wound have mercy upon me! and whatſoever in me diſpleaſeth Thee, vouchſafe to change it. Grant me victory over all my wicked enemies, and through Thy ſtrength may I be enabled to overcome them; and by Thy moſt bitter Death deliver me from all dangers of this preſent life, and of that which is to come; and make me worthy to obtain Thy

Grace in Thy Kingdom! Amen.

Laud, Honour, Glory, and giving of thanks be to Thee for The Moſt Sacred Wound of Thy Right Foot! O Jeſu! Who floweſt with honey, by This Thy Sacred Wound grant me to do worthy penance for my ſins, and through Thy moſt gracious Death I humbly beſeech Thee to keep me Thy ſervant by day and by night in Thy will; and deliver me from all adverſity of ſoul and body, and in that tremendous Day receive my ſoul into Thy faith and mercy, and bring it to joys everlaſting. Amen.

Laud, Honour, Glory, and giving of thanks be to Thee for The Moſt Sacred Wound of Thy Left Foot! O moſt kind Jeſu! by This Sacred Wound grant me pardon and full forgiveneſs for my ſins, ſo that through Thy ſuccour I may be worthy to eſcape Thine avenging judgement; and by Thy moſt holy Death I intreat Thee, moſt gracious Lord Jeſu Chriſt! that before the day of my departure I may deſerve worthily to receive The Sacrament of Thy moſt ſweet Body and Blood with true contrition of heart, deep heart-ſearching confeſſion of my ſins, perfect penitence, and purity of mind and body, and with Thy Heavenly Unction to attain eternal ſalvation! Amen.

Laud, Honour, Glory, and giving of thanks be to Thee for The Moſt Sacred Wound of Thy Side! O moſt benignant Jeſu! by This conſecrated Wound, and becauſe of the moſt holy plenteouſneſs of Thy mercy which Thou haſt ſhewn to me by the piercing of Thy Side, I intreat Thee, moſt gracious Jeſu! that as in Baptiſm Thou haſt cleanſed me from original ſin, ſo by Thy moſt precious Blood Which throughout the whole world is offered up in ſacrifice and received, Thou wouldeſt waſh me from all evils, paſt, preſent, and future, and by Thy moſt holy Death grant me a right faith, a firm hope, and perfect charity, that I may love Thee with my whole heart, and with my whole ſtrength. Strengthen me in good works, and give me a firm perſeverance in Thy holy ſervice, that I may be able entirely to pleaſe Thee both here and evermore! Amen.

Hymn.

Hail! O sweetest Head of Jesus,
Wreathed with thorn, Whose torture frees us;
Grant Thou that no evil doing
Lure us to eternal ruin!

Hail! Right Hand, Which, pierced in anguish,
With that throbbing Wound doth languish;
At that Right Hand place us ever,
Whom Thy Passion doth deliver!

Hail! Left Palm of Jesus; hail Thee!
See, with cruel hands they nail Thee!
From all ill and woe deliver
Us, frail progeny of Eva.

Hail! dear Side, spear-rent and bleeding;
Hail! sweet streams from thence proceeding;
Through this life O may they speed us,
And to Life eternal lead us!

Hail! Wound Which Thy Right Foot paineth,
But each contrite heart sustaineth;
Oft as It Thou kindly viewest,
Thou our hope of life renewest.

Hail! Wound through Thy Left Sole stricken,
Which doth souls in virtue quicken;
Guard us, Thy protection granting,
From all foes our steps supplanting.

Hail! dear Flesh, Which soldiers, baring,
Are with ruthless scourges tearing;
Ne'er from life, by Thee protected,
Be Thy chosen Flock rejected.

By The Death Which Thou our Lover,
Jesus! on the Cross didst suffer,
May we rise to Light eternal,
Where Thou reign'st in joys supernal.
Amen.

℣. He was wounded for our iniquities.

℟. And bruised for our offences.

Let us pray.

Grant, we beseech Thee, Almighty God, that the Most Holy Wounds of Thy very sweet Son, our Lord Jesus Christ, may be imprinted on our hearts, may appear conspicuous in them to enlighten our minds, and may render us ever fervent in Thy love. Through The Same our Lord Jesus Christ, Who liveth and reigneth with Thee in The Unity of The Holy Ghost God for evermore. Amen.

O Lord Jesu Christ! pierce my heart with Thy Holy Wounds, and inebriate my soul with Thy Most Sacred Blood, so that whithersoever I turn I may see Thee crucified, and upon whatsoever I look it may appear dyed with Thy Most Sacred Blood; so that being intent wholly upon Thee, I may be enabled to behold nothing beside Thee, Who livest and reignest God world without end. Amen.

Hymn.

All hail to Thee! my blessed Saviour's kind and wounded Side,
Whence flowed of Water and of Blood the rich and mingled tide;
To us sad sinners be it e'er the solace of our grief,
Heal all the sores of guilt, and give our ghostly woes relief.
All hail! that large and teeming Wound Thy blissful Side within;
O wash the nations from their guilt, and make them pure therein;
So from the second death of Hell shall all Thy Flock be free,
And in the Vision of our God our hearts rejoice in Thee! Amen.

Hail, benign Jesu! full of grace! Mercy is with Thee. Blessed be Thy Passion, Death, and Thy Wounds. Blessed be the Blood of Thy Wounds. O Lord! have mercy upon me a sinner! O most sweet Lord, grant me a heart pure, contrite, patient, and humble; a body chaste, obedient, stable, and ever occupied in doing Thee service. Amen.

¶ OF THE MEMBERS OF CHRIST.

Orison.

I salute Thee, Head of our Lord and Saviour Jesus Christ! by all Powers to be feared, yet for our sake crowned with thorns and smitten with the reed; I salute Ye, most gracious Eyes of our Lord Jesus Christ, for our sake suffused with tears; I salute Ye, most noble Ears of our Lord Jesus Christ, for us wounded with revilings and reproach; I salute Thee, most sacred Mouth, most sweet Throat of our Lord Jesus Christ, for us made to drink gall and vinegar; I salute that most fair Countenance of our Lord Jesus Christ, most lovely to men and to Angels, for us spat upon and bruised with cruel buffetings; I salute Thee, lowly Neck of our Lord Jesus Christ, for our sake wounded with stripes, and that most holy Back, which was scourged; I salute Ye, reverend Hands and Arms of our Lord Jesus Christ, for us outstretched upon the Cross; I salute that most gentle Bosom of our Lord Jesus Christ, for us troubled in His Passion; I salute that most pure Heart of our Lord Jesus Christ, for our sakes pierced by the spear of the soldier, whence came forth Blood and Water for the redemption of our salvation; I salute Ye, venerable Knees of our Lord Jesus Christ, for us bent in prayer; I salute Ye, adorable Feet of our Lord Jesus

Chriſt, for our ſake on the Croſs of Suffering wounded, dead, and buried; I ſalute That moſt ſacred and precious Blood of our Lord Jeſus Chriſt, for us miſerable ſinners plenteouſly flowing from His Side, and from His whole Body; waſh away, we beſeech Thee, all our offences, and ſuffer us not to periſh, for whoſe redemption Thou waſt ſhed. O good Jeſus! by theſe Thy moſt ſacred Members, and Thy moſt kind Paſſion, grant me help in tribulation, comfort in perſecution, and at all times ſtrength againſt temptation. Give me, I beſeech Thee, pardon for the paſt, amendment of the preſent, and vouchſafe to beſtow upon me Thy protection in future, Who liveſt and reigneſt with God The Father in The Unity of The Holy Ghoſt God world without end. Amen.

Oriſon.

O Lord Jesus! I a miſerable ſinner intreat and admoniſh Thee, for that Thy noble Humanity which died upon the Croſs, and for the honour of that joy which Thou didſt feel when Thou perceivedſt that Thou hadſt overcome Thy ſtraitneſs, and hadſt redeemed all mankind, I beſeech Thee that by Thy Death in the hour of my death Thou wouldeſt deliver me from all mine enemies. Amen.

O Lord Jesu Christ! Saviour and Redeemer of the whole world! I beſeech and admoniſh Thee, by that joy which Thy beloved friends had within the priſon of Hell, who beheld that they were redeemed by the power of Thy Divinity, that Thou wouldeſt blot out in me every carnal pleaſure, and grant me to love Thee above all creatures. Amen.

O Lord Jesus Christ! I beſeech and admoniſh Thee, by that joy which Thy beloved Mother had, when Thou didſt appear to her in that moſt holy Paſchal night, and by that joy which Thou hadſt when Thou didſt behold Thyſelf glorified by the Power of Thy Divinity in Thy Clarity, enlighten me fully with The Seven Gifts of Thy Holy Spirit, that I may be enabled to fulfil Thy will all the days of my life! Amen.

ℭ *OF THE SACRED COUNTENANCE OF OUR LORD JESUS CHRIST.*

All hail! my kind Redeemer's confecrated Face,
Whence ftream divineft rays of Glory and of Grace;
Once on a Handkerchief of glittering white impreft,
And on Veronica beftowed, love's token bleft.
All hail! Thou Honour of the worlds! Thou Mirror of the Saints!
Whofe Vifion to enjoy each Heavenly Spirit faints;
O do Thou purge us free from every finful ftain,
And join us to the choirs on high, in endlefs joy to reign!
Hail! my Lord's Countenance! O blifsful Image, hail!
Bright with Deific radiance, which never fhall grow pale.
Richly into our hearts Thy peerlefs fplendours pour;
The darkling veils which blind our fenfe caft off for evermore.
Hail! mighty Rock! which doth our Chriftian Faith fuftain,
And crufheft heretics of minds elate and vain;
Increafe our merits who believe with fureft faith in Thee,
Image of Him Who here of bread our King is made to be!
All hail! our Joy and Crown in this life's dreary way,
So frail and fleeting, and fo foon to pafs away;
O guide us, lovely Portraiture! unto Thine own bleft place,
Unto th' entrancing Vifion of Chrift's own unclouded Face.
Hail! nobleft Gem! true Pearl ferene! how luftrous and how pure,
Decked with celeftial gifts in faultlefs ornature!
By mortal hands depicted not, nor wrought by human fkill,
That knoweth He, the Chief of Priefts, Who formed Thee by His will.
That Heavenly beauty wherein gliftening Thou'rt arrayed
Changelefs abideth, nor for evermore fhall fade.
From age to age enduring, its brilliance ne'er fhall pale;
The King of Glory made Thee! Whofe works can never fail.
Thou ne'er fhalt know decay, Thou corruptlefs fhalt abide,
Chrift's likenefs by Himfelf unto His worfhippers fupplied!
Thou turneft into gladnefs our mourning and our woe;
Of Thy fweet Vifion on our hearts the healthful fruit beftow!
Be Thou to us Thy faithful ones a rampart and a fhield,
All kindly confolation and fweet refrefhment yield;
So freed from ghoftly foes, and every conflict o'er,
Shall we find reft in Heaven with Thee for evermore. Amen.

Orifon.

Hail! That moft illuftrious Countenance, which for us upon the Altar of the Crofs became pale with anxiety and was darkened, was watered with a bloody Sweat, covered with a Handkerchief, whereon

Thy form is ſaid to have been imprinted, The form of Thy Paſſion, evident to all men. Be this impreſſed upon my heart by Thee, O Jeſu! nor ceaſe to inflame me with the inextinguiſhable torch of Thy Love, ſo that after this life with the bleſſed I may be able in felicity to contemplate the Countenance of Thy Divinity in everlaſting Glory. Amen.

Grant me a token for good, that they who hate me may ſee it and be aſhamed, for Thou, Lord, haſt holpen me and comforted me. The Light of Thy Countenance hath ſhined forth upon us, O Lord! Thou haſt given joy unto my heart. Save Thy ſervant, O my God! who putteth his truſt in Thee. Save me, O Lord! in Thy mercy; I ſhall never be confounded, for I have put my truſt in Thee. Make the Light of Thy Countenance to ſhine forth upon Thy ſervant, and teach me Thy Statutes. O Lord God of Hoſts! convert us, and ſhew us Thy Countenance, and we ſhall be ſaved. O Lord! hear my prayer; and let my crying come unto Thee.

Let us pray.

O God! Who hath ſhewn forth the Light of Thy Countenance upon us, by Thy Croſs and Paſſion, grant that as now upon earth we view Thee as in a glaſs, darkly, ſo hereafter we may be enabled to worſhip, adore, and honour Thine Own Self; and that when Thou ſhalt come, face to face, to be our Judge, we may with joy behold Thee, our Lord Jeſus Chriſt, Who with The Father and The Holy Ghoſt liveſt and reigneſt God for evermore. Amen.

¶ TO THE HOLY TRINITY. In adversity.

Holy Trinity! One God! Have mercy upon us.

O Bleſſed and Glorious Trinity! Have mercy upon us.

O Sacred, and Supreme, and Everlaſting Trinity! Have mercy upon us.

O True, and Glorious, and ineffable Trinity, and One Deity! Supreme and immutable Goodneſs! Eternal and moſt ſweet Clarity! Three in Perſon! undivided in Majeſty! O Good Father! O kind Son!

O Spirit Paraclete! O Light indefectible! One God! Whose work is life, Whose Love is Grace, Whose Contemplation is The Glory of All Saints! O Lord! I invoke Thee! I adore Thee! I bless Thee with all the affection of my heart, both now and for evermore. Alpha and Omega! Holy Immanuel! Holy God! Holy Mighty! Holy and Immortal! Have mercy upon us. Remember me, O my God! for my good, and mercifully forgive me, that the work of Thy hands perish not. Thou art my Creator, Thou art my Hope, Thou art my Salvation, O Lord! from Whom are all things, through Whom are all things, in Whom are all things; to Him be Honour and Glory for ever and ever. Amen.

Orison.

O God! Who resistest the proud and givest Grace to the humble, do Thou succour me in this tribulation and distress; for I believe that if Thou dost determine, there is none that can resist Thy will. Save us, we beseech Thee, and speedily deliver us. Through our Lord Jesus Christ. Amen.

Orison.

O God! Who didst deliver Susannah from false accusation, Daniel from the den of lions, and the Three Children from the burning fiery furnace; Who didst stretch forth Thy Right Hand to Peter when sinking in the sea, do Thou vouchsafe to deliver me from this and every tribulation and distress, and from the power of all mine enemies, and from all who conspire with them; for I know not whither to fly except unto Thee, my God; for there is none else that can help me but Thou God only, Who in perfect Trinity livest and reignest God world without end. Amen.

O Lord Jesu Christ! Who hast created and redeemed me, and didst preordain me to be what I am, Thou knowest what Thou shouldest do with me; do unto me in mercy according to Thy will. O Lord Jesu Christ! Who alone art Wisdom, Thou knowest what befitteth me a sinner. As it pleaseth Thee, and as it seemeth good in the eyes of Thy Majesty, so in mercy be it unto me. Amen.

OUR FATHER.

¶ *This Prayer is for any that falleth into slander, reproof, or any manner of tribulation, as the blessed Elder Thobias and Sarah, Raguel's daughter, were delivered graciously through God at his prayer.*

The Orison of Thobias the Elder and Sarah, daughter of Raguel.

Thou art Just, O Lord! and all Thy judgements are just, and all Thy ways are mercy, and truth, and judgement. Blessed be Thy Name, O God of our Fathers! Who when Thou art angry doest mercy, and in time of tribulation forgivest the sins of them that call upon Thee. Therefore unto Thee, O Lord! I turn my countenance; unto Thee I turn mine eyes. I beseech Thee, O Lord! that Thou wouldest absolve me from the chain of this reproach, or at least deliver me upon earth, for Thy counsel is not in the power of men; and of this every one who worshippeth Thee is assured, that his life, if it endure probation, shall be crowned, and if it be in tribulation shall be delivered; and although it be in corruption shall be permitted to attain Thy mercy; since Thou art not delighted with our destruction, but after the storm makest a calm, and after tearfulness and weeping pourest gladness upon us. Now, O Lord! be mindful of us, and take not vengeance on my sins, nor remember my faults, nor the faults of my forefathers; for we have not obeyed Thy precepts, and we have been rooted up to dispersion, and captivity, and death, a byword and reproach among all nations into which Thou hast scattered us! And now, O Lord! great are Thy judgements, for we have not done after Thy precepts, not walked in sincerity before Thee. Now, O Lord! do with me according to Thy will, and receive my spirit in peace; for it is better for me to die than to live, and I hope in Thee, because in Thy great mercy Thou wilt remember me, and wilt raise up my life from corruption to praise and glorify Thee for ever and ever. Amen.

¶ *This Prayer is for them that have sickness or adversity, to thank God and to pray all the days of their life to make satisfaction for their sins.*

The prayer of holy Job in the time of his probation.

Spare me, O Lord! for

my days are nothing. How long dost Thou not spare me? I have sinned. What shall I do unto Thee, O Keeper of men? Why dost Thou not take away my sin? And why dost not Thou remove mine iniquity? Behold! now I sleep in the dust; O my God! condemn me not! Remember, I beseech Thee, that Thou hast made me as the clay, and dost Thou bring me down to dust again? and as Thou hast granted me life and mercy, so Thy Visitation hath preserved my spirit. And what great iniquities and sins I have committed, mine offences and my faults shew unto me. Wherefore hidest Thou Thy face and esteemest me Thine enemy? Against a leaf which is carried away by the wind dost Thou shew Thy power, and wilt Thou pursue a dry straw? for Thou writest bitter things against me, and willest to consume me with the sins of my youth. Deliver me, O Lord! and set me nigh Thee, and let not the hand of any man fight against me. Let me go that I may bewail for a little time my sorrow, before I go to the land of darkness and covered with the shadow of death. For though Thou shalt slay me, yet will I trust in Thee, and until I fail away I will not depart from Thee, and Thy way which I have purposed to keep I will not forsake. And now stretch forth Thy Right Hand unto the work of Thy Hands, and spare Thou my sins.

¶ *This Prayer is for them that be in disease, or have their friends diseased, or imprisoned, or fall into some great sin, to pray God to deliver them, as the good Nehemiah prayed for them that were in the Captivity of Babylon, who were delivered.*

The Prayer of Nehemiah.

I INTREAT Thee, O Lord God of Heaven! mighty, great, and terrible, Who keepest covenant and mercy with them that love Thee and keep Thy commandments, let now Thine ears be intent and Thine eyes open to hear the prayer of Thy servant, which I put up before Thee this day and by night and by day for Thy servants. And I now confess before Thee their sins wherein they have sinned against Thee. I know, O Lord! that I and the house of my father have sinned greatly. We have been led astray by vanity, and have not kept Thy commandments and Thy judgements. Remember Thy commandment which Thou didſt command to Moſes, Thy ſervant, ſaying, When ye ſhall have tranſgreſſed I will ſcatter you among the people; But if ye return unto Me, both keeping My commandments and doing them, even if ye ſhall have been led away unto the uttermoſt part of the Heathen, from thence I will gather you, and I will bring you back into the place which I have choſen for My Name to dwell there. And we, even Thy ſervants, and the people whom Thou haſt redeemed with Thy great might, are turned back to Thee with all our heart. Wherefore, I beſeech Thee, O Lord! that Thine ear may be intent to the prayer of Thy ſervants, who deſire to fear Thy Name; and remember me, O Lord! ever for my good, and direct me in Thy way, that I may find favour, O Lord! in Thine eyes, and may pleaſe Thee in the light of the living. Amen.

Againſt luſt and concupiſcence.

¶ *Oriſon of Jeſus, the Son of Syrak.*

O Lord! Father and Ruler of my life! caſt me not out of Thy remembrance, and ſuffer me not to fall into the counſels of mine enemies, nor into any ſlander. O Lord! let not my ignorances increaſe, let not my ſins be multiplied, nor my offences abound; let me not fall before mine adverſaries, ſo that mine enemies may rejoice at it. But Thou, O Lord! Father and God of my life! forſake me not! Take away from me all haughtineſs of eye, and all depraved deſires; remove from me the luſt of gluttony, and may the ſin of fornication never overtake me. Give me not up to an irreverent and unbridled ſpirit. Beſtow on me neither poverty nor riches, leſt being filled to the full, or compelled by neceſſity, I blaſpheme the Name of my God, to Whom be Honour and Thankſgiving for ever and ever. Amen.

This Prayer is for them that be falſely accuſed, yet truſt in God.

Oriſon of Suſannah.

Eternal God! the Diſcoverer of Secrets! Who knoweſt all things before they happen, Thou knoweſt what falſe witneſs they have borne againſt me. Behold, Lord! I die; yet none of thoſe things have I done which they ſo maliciouſly have invented againſt me. But now do Thou, O Lord! help me in this hour; and I will bleſs Thee, The living God, Who ſaveſt them that truſt in Thee. And now I beſeech Thee, if Thou takeſt not away this ſlander and this ſtrait, take away my life from me; for it is better for me to die than live if it pleaſe Thee, O my God! Amen.

ℂ *To the Holy Trinity.*

O Lord God! Almighty Father, Son, and Holy Ghoſt! grant to me Thy ſervant victory over all the temptations of the Devil, and over all them that would harm me, that they may not hurt me nor vanquiſh me but that all their power and counſel may be guided for my good. And do Thou, O Almighty God! be my might and my refuge, the ſhield of my defence, an unquenchable flame, and an impregnable tower of ſtrength for my protection; ſo that all my foes and enemies may be ſcattered. God of Abraham! God of Iſaac! God of Jacob! God of all who live righteouſly! deliver me Thy ſervant from all my ſins, ſtraits, and tribulations, neceſſities and dangers, and grant me ſtrength, fortitude, and perſeverance in good, and a right and pleaſant ſpeech in my mouth, that all my words, my countenance, and my works may be pleaſing to all who ſee and hear me, ſo that I may receive Grace and help in anſwer to my requeſts. The Prophet crieth, the Apoſtles ſaith, Chriſt ſaveth all that truſt in Him. Chriſt ✠ conquereth, Chriſt ✠ reigneth; Chriſt ✠ vouchſafe to will that I ſhall be triumphant over all my adverſaries, and I will not fear what man can do unto me. O God! for Thy Name's ſake ſave me, and deliver me from all my foes, viſible and inviſible; and grant me ſpace for true penitence, and that for Thy Name's ſake I may attain to ſome proſperity in this earthly life. O Lord Jeſu Chriſt! Son of The living God! Who didſt will to be hanged on the Croſs, and didſt permit Thy Side to be pierced with a ſpear, and haſt redeemed me with Thy precious Blood, and didſt deliver the Three Children, Shadrach, Meſhach, and

Abednego, from the fiery furnace, and didst preserve Susannah from false slander, and didst deliver Daniel from the den of lions, so for the sake of these my prayers deliver me Thy servant from all adversity of body and soul, and from all evil works, present and future. In The Name of The Father, and Son, and Holy Ghost. Amen.

PSALM liii.

Deus in nomine Salvum me fac.

Save me, O GOD! for Thy Name's sake (*ante, p.* 81).

Orison of the First Lawgiver.

EXOD. xxxiii.

O LORD GOD, our Ruler! merciful and gracious, patient and of much pity, and true; Who keepest mercy for thousands, and takest away iniquity and wickedness and sin, although there is none who of himself is innocent before Thee; now O Lord! if I have found favour in Thy sight I intreat Thee that Thou wouldest go with us, for I know that this people is stiff-necked. Do Thou nevertheless take away their iniquities and their sins, and prosper us. For wherein shall we be able to know that I and Thy people have found favour in Thy sight, unless Thou shalt walk with us, that we may be glorified by all the people who dwell upon the earth. For Thou hast said to Thy servant Moses that Thou wouldest perform this word unto them. Wherefore then, O Lord! is Thine anger kindled against Thy people which Thou hast brought forth out of the land of Egypt with great might and a strong arm? lest the Egyptians say, He hath led them out craftily, that He might kill them in the mountains and blot them from the earth. Let Thine anger be assuaged and be appeased for the iniquity of Thy people. Remember Abraham, Isaac, and Jacob, to whom Thou hast sworn to give a land flowing with milk and honey; and if I have found favour in Thine eyes, pass not over Thy servant but hear my prayer; and I intreat Thee turn not away from Thy servant, but abide with me and forsake me not, and whom when lost

Thou didſt reſtore to Thy worſhip. Thou, O Lord! haſt ſaid Return to thy land and to thy birth place, and I will do thee good. I acknowledge before Thee this day that I am unworthy of all Thy pityfulneſs and of Thy truth which Thou haſt performed to Thy ſervant. Now therefore I intreat Thee, O Lord! deliver me from the hand of mine enemies, for I fear them greatly; leſt haply ſuddenly they ruſh in upon me, and aſſail me, and deſtroy me from the land of the living. I beſeech Thee, O my Lord! that Thy ſervant may find grace in Thy ſight, and magnify Thy mercy toward me, that I may glorify Thy Name now and for evermore. Amen.

This Prayer following is to thank God of His gracious gifts ſent to us, and to aſk mercy and grace to keep them continually.

Oriſon of Moſes and the People.

EXOD. XV.

THE LORD is my might and my praiſe, and is become my ſalvation. He is my God, and I will glorify Him. The God of my Father, and I will exalt Him. Who is like unto Thee in ſtrength, O Lord? Who is like unto Thee, glorious in holineſs, fearful, and to be praiſed, and doing wonders? Thou waſt a leader to Thy people, whom in Thy mercy Thou haſt redeemed.

Of Eleazar.

GEN. XXIV.

O BLESSED LORD GOD! Who haſt not taken away Thy mercy and truth from me, and haſt led me in the right way; Bleſſed Lord! Who haſt delivered me from the hand of mine enemies. Now have I known truly that I have found favour in Thine eyes, and that Thou, O Lord! art great above all gods.

Benediction.

NUMBERS VI.

Now therefore bleſs me and keep me. Shew me, O Lord! Thy Countenance, and have mercy upon me. O Lord! turn Thy Face unto me, and give me peace!

This Prayer is for them that have labour in temptation, or have any other diſeaſe with governance of the people.

Oriſon of Joſhua, the Leader of the People.

O MOST MIGHTY GOD! the

Spirit of all flesh, wherefore by reason of my sin hath Thine anger raged against all men? Ah! Lord God! why hast Thou willed to deliver this Thy people from many troubles and dangers, and now wouldest deliver them into the hands of their enemies to destroy them? O Lord God! what shall I say unto Thee, beholding Thy people turning their backs upon their enemies? They will see it, and all their other adversaries assembling together will surround them, and will destroy our name from the earth. And what wilt Thou do with Thy Great Name? We know, O Lord! that we have sinned and forsaken Thee our God. We have sinned; requite unto us whatsoever pleaseth Thee, only now deliver us, O Lord! and may our enemies be scattered, and may they who hate Thee fly from before Thy face. Remember us, O Lord! and return unto the multitude of our armies. Why, O Lord! hast Thou afflicted Thy servant? Wherefore have I not found favour before Thee? Wherefore hast Thou laid the burthen of all this people upon me? Whether have I conceived all this multitude and brought it forth, that Thou shouldest say unto me, Carry them in thy bosom as a nurse useth to carry a little infant, and bring them unto the land of which Thou didst swear unto their fathers. Whence, O Lord! have I such strength for such a multitude? Wherefore, O Lord God! hear my cry and the prayer of this people, and open unto them the measure of Thy mercy, Thy grace, the fountain of living water; and put into the hand of Thy servant this great might and grace, that he may be enabled to lead Thy people in Thy way even unto Thee. O Lord God! Who art our leader, do Thou Thyself fight for us as Thou didst for all who beheld Thee in the desert. Unless Thou O Lord! help us, Lo! we die in a strait and we fall in Thy sight into the hands of our enemies. But Thou O Lord God of our Fathers! do unto us according to Thy mercy, and add unto this number of Thy people many thousands, and bless us as Thou hast said. Amen.

¶ *This Prayer is to thank God for deliverance out of tribulation or straits, reproof, or other disease, and to be brought by God's help to much comfort, grace, and peace, as the elder Thobias was.*

TOBIT xiii.

The Orison of Thobias the Elder, giving thanks unto God.

THOU, O LORD! art great and everlasting, and for evermore is Thy Kingdom; for Thou dost scourge and dost make whole, and Thou bringest down to hell and bringest back again, and there is none that can escape Thy Hand. Give thanks unto The Lord all ye sons of God, and praise Him in the sight of the Gentiles, for He hath led us into tribulation that His wonderful works might be set forth by us, that even we might know that there is none other Almighty God beside Him. He hath chastised us because of our iniquities, and He will save us because of His great mercy. Behold therefore what He hath done unto us, and with fear and trembling give thanks unto Him. Exalt ye the King of the worlds in your doings. And I in the land of my captivity will give thanks unto Him, Who sheweth forth His power upon a sinful nation. Be converted therefore, ye sinners, and do righteousness before God, believing that He will do unto us according to His mercy; and I also and my soul will be joyful in Him. Bless ye The Lord, all ye His Elect. Celebrate a day of gladness, and give thanks unto Him. I will give thanks unto The Lord for His goodness, and I will bless The God of all worlds, that He may build up again His tabernacle within me, and I may rejoice for ever and ever. Blessed be all they that love me, and that rejoice at my peace. O my soul, bless The Lord for evermore, for He hath delivered my soul from all its tribulations. Amen.

¶ *This Prayer is for them that will praise God both for His goodness and also for His righteousness, and to ask time for repentance.*

Orison of King Solomon.

O HOW good and how sweet, O Lord! is Thy Spirit within us. Have mercy upon all, for Thou canst do all things, Thou Who dost pass over the sins of men, upon their penitence; for Thou lovest all things that be, and hatest nothing that Thou hast made, but ſpareſt all; for they are Thine, O Lord! Who loveſt our ſouls. That which proceedeth from the body, and wherein it ſinneth, Thou doſt chide and admoniſh, that they, forſaking evil, may believe and abide in Thee, O Lord! Thou hateſt and doſt abhor the ſtubborn, but ſpareſt the penitent amongſt men. Thou doſt judge on our behalf, and giveſt place for repentance, not forgetting the infirmity of our fleſh. If we have ſinned, we are Thine, acknowledging Thy greatneſs; and if we have not ſinned, we know that with Thee is our reckoning. But Thou, O Lord our God! art kind and true, patient and merciful, diſpoſing all things, becauſe Thou art God of all. Thou makeſt all things obey Thee. Thou takeſt care of all of us. Shew the power of Thy greatneſs upon us, Thou Who, as we believe, haſt no end of Thy might; Thou Who haſt the power of life and death, and bringeſt down to the gates of death, and bringeſt back. Thou art The Lord of Virtues! Who in quietneſs doſt judge, Who doſt diſpoſe of us in a fearful and awful manner. For it reſteth with Thee whether Thou willeſt to make us Thy children. Even Thou Who art our Judge, grant us a place of penitence; and thus ſhalt Thou ſhew to our enemies that Thou art He that doſt deliver us, and magnifieſt Thy people, and haſt honoured and not deſpiſed us; but wilt in all times and in all places be their help. Amen.

ℭ FOR THE SICK AND DYING.

ℭ *Theſe Prayers following ſhall be ſaid in the agony and laſt end of men and women labouring againſt death, and every man and woman may ſay theſe Prayers for themſelves or for another.*

ℭ *In the firſt place, ſay—*

Lord! Have mercy.
Chriſt! Have mercy.
Lord! Have mercy.
OUR FATHER.
Hail, Mary!

O Saviour of the world! ſave us; Who by Thy Croſs and Blood haſt redeemed us! Help us, we beſeech Thee, O Lord our God!

Oriſon.

O LORD JESU CHRIST! by Thine Agony and by that Thy moſt holy prayer which Thou didſt offer up for us in the Mount, when Thy Sweat became as it were drops of blood falling down upon the ground, I beseech Thee that all that the multitude of Thy bloody Sweat which for fear and anguish Thou didst so plenteously pour forth, Thou wouldest vouchsafe to offer to God The Father Almighty against the multitude of my sins; and deliver me in the hour of my death from all pains and anguish which for these my offences I fear that I have deserved! Who with God The Father and The Holy Ghost livest and reignest One God world without end. Amen.

In the second place, say—

Lord! Have mercy.
Christ! Have mercy.
Lord! Have mercy.
OUR FATHER.
Hail, Mary!

O Lord! have mercy upon us. Sanctify us, O Lord! with the Sign of Thy Holy Cross, that it may be unto us a defence against all the fierce assaults of all mine enemies. Defend us, O Lord! by that Thy Holy Tree, and with the ransom of Thy righteous Blood wherewith Thou hast redeemed us!

Let us pray.

O LORD JESU CHRIST! Who for our sake didst vouchsafe to die upon the Cross, I beseech Thee that Thou wouldest vouchsafe to offer all the bitterness of all Thy Sufferings which for us sinners Thou didst endure upon the Cross when Thy most Holy Soul departed from Thy most sacred Body to God The Father Almighty, for this sick soul of mine; and deliver me in the hour of my departure from all pain and suffering, Who livest and reignest with The Father and The Holy Ghost God world without end. Amen.

In the third place, say—

Lord! Have mercy.
Christ! Have mercy.
Lord! Have mercy.
OUR FATHER.
Hail, Mary!

O Lord! Have mercy upon us.

O Lord! protect and save, bless and sanctify all Thy people, and by Thy Cross avert from me Thy servant all disease of mind and of body; and against this Thy Sign may no danger be able to prevail, Who livest and reignest.

Let us pray.

O LORD JESU CHRIST! Who by the mouth of Thy Prophet

hast said, "With an everlasting lovingkindness have I loved Thee, and therefore have I drawn thee unto Me, and have had compassion upon thee," I beseech Thee that the same lovingkindness which drew Thee from Heaven to earth to the endurance of all Thy Sufferings Thou wouldest now vouchsafe to offer and to shew forth to God The Father Almighty against all the pains and sufferings which for my sins I fear that I have deserved. Save my soul in the hour of my departure; open unto it the gate of life, and make me to rejoice with Thy Saints in gladness, Who livest and reignest.

O Lord Jesu Christ! Who hast redeemed us with Thy precious Blood, write with that Thy precious Blood Thy Wounds in my soul; that I may learn in them to read Thy Sorrow and Thy Love. Sorrow, against all the sorrows, anguish, and pain which for my sins I fear that I have deserved; Love, that I may live to Thee with that inviolable love through which I may never forevermore be separated from Thee and Thine Elect. Make me, O Lord! a partaker of Thy Most Holy Incarnation, Passion, Resurrection, and Ascension. Make me to share all the prayers and benefits which are in Thy Holy Church. Make me a partaker of all the blessings, graces, merits, and joys of all Thine Elect, who have pleased Thee from the beginning of the world; and grant unto me that I may rejoice with them all in Thy presence for evermore, Who with God The Father and The Holy Ghost livest and reignest God world without end. Amen.

¶ OF HOLY ANGELS.

¶ *A good Orison to say daily, suggested by a divine revelation to a Monk of Bynham, about the year* 1465.

God be merciful to me a sinner, and be my keeper all the days of my life! God of Abraham! God of Isaac! God of Jacob! have mercy upon me, and send to my help Holy Michael Thy Archangel to guard, protect, and defend me from all mine enemies visible and invisible. O Holy Archangel Michael! stand up for me in the battle, that I may not be found a sinner in that tremendous Judgement. O Archangel of Christ! by that grace which Thou hast merited I intreat thee, through our Only-begotten Lord Jesus Christ, to deliver me this day and at all times from all deadly danger. Holy Michael! Holy Gabriel! Holy Raphael! all ye Holy Angels and Archangels of God, succour me! I intreat you all ye Heavenly Virtues, that through the might of God Supreme ye would give me aid; that no enemy may condemn me nor vex me neither at home nor abroad, neither sleeping nor waking. Behold the ✠ of The Lord. Begone ye adversaries; the Lion of the tribe of Judah hath conquered, the Root of David, the Stem of Jesse! Saviour of the world! save me; Who by Thy Cross and Thy Blood hast redeemed me; help me, O my God! Holy, Holy, Holy! Cross of Christ! protect me. Cross of Christ! save me. Cross of Christ! defend me, and deliver me from all evil. Amen.

℣. Pray for us, Holy Archangel Michael

℟. That we may be made worthy of the promises of Christ.

Orison.

God! Who dost ordain the ministrations of Angels and of men in a wonderful order, mercifully grant, that by them who alway do Thee service in Heaven, by the same our life may ever be defended here upon earth, through Our Lord Jesus Christ Thy Son, Who with Thee. Amen.

Our Father.

Hail, Mary!

¶ *Orison to Holy Gabriel.*

And I intreat thee, O illustrious Prince Gabriel! most mighty in battle! arise to help me against the wicked. Stand with me against my adversaries and against all who work iniquity. Bring to light my crafty foes, and tread down the violent; that all my adversaries through thy help may be conquered and put to flight by the favour of Our Lord Jesus Christ, Who with The

Father and The Holy Ghost liveth. Amen.

¶ *Orison to Holy Raphael.*

Be thou also my helper, I beseech Thee, O noble Prince Raphael! thou excellent physician of soul and body, who by thy presence and healing aid didst enlighten the bodily eyes of Thobias; illumine also my spiritual as well as carnal sight, and take away all the darkness of my heart and body. Thou who art in Heaven forsake me not who am praying unto thee on earth.

Our Father.

To all the Choirs of Angels.

Orison.

O ye fiery Seraphim! e'er burning with devout affection:
O ye resplendent Cherubim! beaming with knowledge and perfection:
O ye Supernal Thrones! in God's own judgement seat abiding:
O ye Illustrious Princedoms! Heaven's vicegerents over worlds presiding:
O ye wondrous Powers! with Christ your Chief infernal hosts repelling:
O ye noble Virtues! the faithful to confirm in miracles excelling:
O ye Holy Archangels! unto noble beings nobler things declaring:
O ye Good Angels! for mankind with ceaseless forethought caring:

Be ever intent upon your ministry for our guardianship; directing our endeavours, our words, our actions, into the way of salvation and prosperity; so that we, being willing observers of God's commands, may through the bounties of Divine mercy be enabled happily to replenish the ranks of your orders which were diminished by the fall of Lucifer.

℣. Bless ye The Lord, all ye His Angels.

℟. Ye Virtues, Powers who perform His commands.

Orison.

O God! Who in the beginning didst create divers orders of blessed Spirits to know Thine everlasting Divinity, and after the fall of Satan didst by Thy Son wonderfully redeem mankind, whom he had deceived, in order to make good their loss; grant unto us so to be fulfilled with the gifts of Thy Grace by the Spirit of Thy Mouth, that going on from strength to strength we may be enabled to attain to the happy society of the Choirs of Thy blessed Angels, Through Christ our Lord. Amen.

Orison to The Holy Angels.

All ye Holy orders of the

Bleſſed! pray for us. O ye happy dwellers in the celeſtial Country! Immortal Spirits! Morning Stars! Rulers of the world! Lovers of mankind! and chiefeſt miniſters of the Divine Will; who triumphant in might over the peſtilent Dragon, ſince his ruin abide in the glory of perpetual felicity! you, I ſay, I intreat, that moſt kindly defending me your fellow-ſervant with your might from the aſſaults of the enemy, ye would vouchſafe to be preſent as comforters of me miſerable when I am dying; leſt the hoſt of the malignant ſpirits with violence deſtroy my ſoul when I am in that great ſtrait; ſo that, relying on your guardianſhip, it may be delivered from all harm, and finally attain to reſt in God our Salvation, to Whom be Honour and Glory and Dominion for ever and ever. Amen.

Hymn.

(From the Ancient Hereford Breviary.)

Exultet Cœlum gaudiis.

Let Heaven reſound with joyful lays, [praiſe
Each heart in tones of rapturous
Extol the Angels' might and love
In God's eternal Courts above.

We would on earth that ſtrain prolong
Of Heavenly and ſeraphic ſong
"Thrice Holy!"; myſtic Anthem meet
The princely Hierarchy to greet.

And all the warrior hoſts on high,
The noble chieftains of the ſky,
Thoſe names adorned with Heavenly fame,
Demand our hymns of glad acclaim.

Michael, the Godlike Prince, we laud; [God;
Gabriel, the mighty Strength of
Raphael, who healing gifts doth bear,
As they Emmanuel's praiſe declare.

Before them trembles earth, and all
The lures of ſenſe defeated fall;
With wondrous and excelling might
They turn the infernal hoſts to flight.

To Nature's Lord of boundleſs ſway
The Courts celeſtial homage pay,
And Angels bow; whoſe love and peace,
And joy and glory, ne'er ſhall ceaſe.
Amen.

Hymn.

Excelſorum civium inclita gaudia.

The glorious hoſt on high,
Their joys beyond compare,
The proweſs of their deeds,
Ye friends, let us declare!
My ſoul deſires to greet,
With praiſe devout and meet,
Heaven's Princes excellent and fair!

Theſe are the chieftains bright,
Viceroys of God's domain,
Unwearied in their might
The demons to reſtrain;

All valiant in the fight,
The infernal foe to quell,
Giants of race celestial!

Great captains in the war,
And stalwart champions, they
The spirits chasten sore,
Undaunted in the fray.
Right fast their legions pour,
The upright soul to free,
And give him a glad victory!

What voice can e'er relate,
What writing can make known,
The gifts and glorious state
Which holy Angels crown?
Who in the warfare wait,
Their allies to protect,
And in right paths to Heaven direct!

O Deity Supreme!
Devoutly Thee we pray,
From sin our souls redeem,
And chase our woes away.
So, bright with Glory's beam,
Shall we Thy Name adore,
With holy Angels evermore.
Amen.

¶ FOR THE FAITHFUL DEPARTED.

May the Gracious Offspring of the Virgin Mary ever bless us! May the world's kind Saviour be evermore our helper. Amen.

And may the souls of all the faithful departed through the mercy of God rest in peace! Amen.

Grant repose, O God! to all who are buried here or elsewhere, that evermore they may rest through the Five dear Wounds of Thy Passion. Amen.

Praise be to God! Peace to the living! Repose to the departed. Amen.

I Believe in God.

Hail! all ye faithful souls whose bodies here and elsewhere rest in the dust! Our Lord Jesus Christ, Who redeemed you and us with His most precious Blood, vouchsafe to deliver you from pain, to place you among the Choirs of His Saints and Angels, and there remembering us, suppliantly beseech Him that we may be made fellows with you, and with you may be crowned in the Heavens.

℣. Enter not into judgement with the souls of Thy servants, O Lord!

℟. For in Thy sight shall no man living be justified.

Let us pray.

O Lord Jesu Christ! the Salvation and deliverance of faithful souls, Who camest not to destroy but to save them, and to give Thy Soul for the redemption of many; we humbly implore Thy boundless clemency and ineffable mercy that Thou wouldest vouchsafe mercifully to regard the souls of all the faithful with Thy most benign pity. May Thy mercy succour them whom by Thy precious Blood Thou hast redeemed; and for the sake of the blessed and glorious Virgin Mary and of All Thy Saints, vouchsafe to deliver them from the torments of Hell, and to place them among the ranks of Thy Saints; and command them to be clothed with the garment of immortality, and to be comforted by the pleasures of Paradise; Who with The Father and The Holy Ghost livest and reignest God, world without end. Amen.

Devout Orisons for the Departed.

Have mercy, O Lord! upon the souls which have no especial intercessors with Thee, nor any hope except that they are created after Thine image and likeness; who from age, or poverty, or negligence, or forgetfulness of their friends, or Thy servants, are forsaken; and whose day of remembrance is never observed. Spare them, O Lord! and defend Thy creatures; deliver them from all agony and torment; stretch forth Thy Right Hand unto them, and bring them into a place of refreshment, light, and peace, through Him Who shall come to judge the living and the dead with fire. Amen.

When ye enter into the Churchyard, say this Prayer.

Save you, all ye faithful souls whose bodies here and elsewhere rest in the dust! May our Lord Jesus Christ, Who hath redeemed you and us with His most precious Blood, vouchsafe to deliver you from pain, to add you to the company of the Angels; and there remembering us suppliantly on our behalf entreat Him that we may be joined to your society, and with you be crowned in the Heavens. Amen.

When ye go out of the Churchyard, say this Prayer.

Farewell, all ye faithful souls who lie in the bosom of the earth! Far and wide may The Sun of Righteousness bless you, and make you to enjoy the clearness of His Light for evermore. Amen.

Let us pray.

Regard, we beseech Thee, Almighty God! the souls of

Thy servants and handmaidens, and of all the faithful departed, and of all Christians, for whose salvation Thou, naked and with hands outstretched, didst hang upon the Cross, and suffer Thy Five Wounds, and didst will to endure the bitterness of death! Who livest and reignest God world without end. Amen.

❡ *Here beginneth* THE ROSARY *of the* BLESSED VIRGIN MARY.

Virgin! This Golden Rosary
To thee I make oblation;
Which decked with Jesu's life shall be,
Rehearsed in brief narration.

Hail, Mary! full of Grace. The Lord is with Thee! Blessed art thou among women, and blessed is the Fruit of thy womb, Jesus Christ!

Whom of The Holy Spirit, thou
A virgin pure conceivedst,
When Gabriel's word, with meekest bow
Assenting, thou believedst.

Hail Mary, &c.

Thou great with Him, forthwith didst haste
To give thy cousin greeting;
He the unborn John inspired and blest
At that most hallowed meeting.

In Bethleem Whom, a Holy Seed,
Thou didst bring forth with gladness;
In that thy wondrous labour freed
From human pangs and sadness.

Scion of Royal David's line,
New-born thou didst adore Him;
Whose nurturing breast with love benign
A wailing Infant bore Him.

Whom in the manger thou didst lay,
With swathing bands enfolding,
And Him to cherish, day by day,
No pains or care withholding.

Whom brightest Angels at His birth,
With laud and carol hailing,
Praised God; announcing Peace on earth,
Good will and love unfailing.

Whom wondering shepherds as of all
The Shepherd Prince declaring,
Yet found, a stable mean and small
With ass and oxen sharing.

Who, as for human kind was meet,
Enduring Circumcision,
Was called Jesus; Name most sweet!
In token of His mission.

Who was by Eastern kings adored,
As homage due they proffered;
When Him confessing for their Lord,
Their noblest gifts they offered.

Whom thou upon the fortieth day
In His own House presenting,
Didst freewill offerings duly pay,
To Moses' law consenting.

Whom safe to Egypt thou didst bear
Whilst Herod's rage was swelling;
But bring back with maternal care,
To Nazareth thy dwelling.

Whom once as lost thou didst deplore,
When from the Feast returning;
But in the Temple find once more,
'Midst doctors Him discerning.

Whom thou didst bring up at thy side,
Due care and toil expending;
And for His food and needs provide,
His holy childhood tending.

Whom, when baptized in Jordan's flood,
John, His forerunner, blesseth;
And pointing out The Son of God,
His Glorious Name confesseth.

Whom Satan laboured to delude,
With threefold guile assailing;
But He the Tempter vile withstood;
In wisdom all prevailing.

Who erst the water changed to wine,
Thou for that boon beseeching;
So, by a miracle divine,
His weak disciples teaching.

Who many souls from sin released,
With saving power restoreth;
And health upon the poor diseased,
Ofttimes in mercy poureth.

Who Lazarus and the widow's son
With mighty word did quicken;
And back to life and parents won
A maid with sickness stricken.

Who oft on earth to eat and live
With guilty men consented;
Pleased all their errors to forgive,
If truly they repented.

Whose feet the sinning woman laved
With tears in deep contrition;
Whom He in gracious pity saved
From her forlorn condition.

Transfigured Who, on Thabor's height,
Himself with light arrayeth;
And clad in robes of glistening white,
His Majesty displayeth.

Whom Jews in pomp, with palms escort
Into the Holy City;
Yet that same evening set at nought,
Reviling without pity.

Who washed His own disciples' feet,
At that last Supper seated;
Then unto them that noblest meat,
His Blood and Body meted.

With anxious soul, He many an hour
Within the garden spendeth;
His sweat for sorrow, like a shower
Of Blood, to earth descendeth.

See! wicked foes at that great Feast,
With staves and swords assail Him;
And unto Annas, the High Priest,
In bonds a prisoner hale Him.

With shame and spitting, ruffian bands
His countenance disgracing,
His beauty with relentless hands,
And cruel blows defacing.

Whom unto Pilate's judgment seat
They hurry, there to try Him;
And with false witness and deceit
Most guilefully belie Him.

Whom Pilate, brought forth to the Jews,
To Herod's rule commendeth;
Who Him doth scornfully refuse,
And back to Pilate sendeth.

Now to the gory pillar bound,
In purple robe they dress Him;
With thorns His noble brow is crown'd,
With scourges they distress Him.

Whom soldiers, galled with wounds, deride
With ribald jests and noises;
And Jews all "Crucify Him," cried,
With loud and savage voices.

Whom Pilate, by his stern decree,
Guilty of death declareth:
Lo! on His shoulders, He, the Tree,
The Cross, for sinners beareth.

Him of His garments they denude;
To Calvary they hale Him;
And there, unto the Holy Rood,
By hands and feet they nail Him.

Where for His torturers He prayed,
So vile, with kind compassion;
E'en when in agony He laid
Thereon in saddest fashion.

Who put all his offence away
From that good thief believing,
Him into Paradise that day
To promised rest receiving.

Who unto John the Apostle, thee
Commended for a mother;
And him for thine own son to be
Appointed as a brother.

Whom, when in agony He prayed,
And all His friends were failing,
His enemies with taunts upbraid,
Blaspheme and wound with railing.

Then as full mournfully He cried,
"I thirst," with vigour wasted,
Unto His lips by guards applied,
Vinegar and gall He tasted.

So, by His Passion and His Cross,
The Prophecies fulfilling;
And, for our first forefathers' loss
To pay the ransom willing.

Now to His Father's hands on high
His spirit He restoreth;
And "Eli," His last doleful cry,
With mournful voice outpoureth.

So thus He slept at last in peace,
This death of woe enduring,
And entered Hell's domains, release
For His elect procuring.

And now behold! His sacred Side
The soldier's spear is rending;
Whence gusheth forth a plenteous tide
Of Blood with water blending.

Whose sacred Body, stark and dead,
Down from the Cross they hurry,
And in a sepulchre's hard bed,
New-made and clean, they bury.

Who in the morning from the tomb,
By His own power arising
Roused His disciples from their gloom,
Thee, too, with joy surprising.

Who o'er the stars full mightily
To Heaven in state ascended,
At God's Right Hand sits gloriously,
Through ages never ended.

Who on the Day of Pentecost
Sent down from highest Heaven
The promise of The Holy Ghost
Upon the great Eleven.

Who now for thee to glory raised,
A blessed rest provideth,
At His Right Hand in honour placed,
Where He in bliss abideth.

Who of the sins of earth shalt come
Once more the Judge unbending
Each work shalt try, and fitting doom
Assign for years unending.

Who wicked men to endless woe
Shalt hurl in flames infernal;
But on His own elect bestow
Rewards and joys eternal.

Thy Mother's Rosary of Gold,
Sweet Jesus! we repeat Thee;
So may Thy Father us behold
With favour, we intreat Thee.
Amen.

APPENDIX I.

HYMNS FOR DAYS AND SEASONS.

For Sunday.

Ad templa nos rurſus vocat.

NCE more the beams of orient light
Thy flock unto Thy Courts invite;
For all the gifts of this Thy Day,
Their thankful oriſons to pay;

When Chriſt, on wings of victory borne,
Roſe glorious, and eclipſed the morn;
And we His members fain would raiſe
To Him triumphant ſongs of praiſe.

Lo! in the cradle of His Birth
Revealed unto the aſtonied earth,
He came, Fair Child! arrayed in light;
O wondrous deed of ſaving might!

And when, by traitorous rebels ſlain
For guilty mortals life to gain,
Him raiſed to life The Father's care;
O what ſurpaſſing love was there!

When firſt the world, divinely planned,
And framed by God's parental Hand,
Complete in priſtine beauty ſtood,
He ſaw, and then pronounced it good.

But decked in fairer robes of white,
It met the approving Father's ſight,
When dyed in that pellucid flood,
Th' Eternal Lamb's atoning Blood.

With golden brilliance ſhines the morn;
Bright hues the awakening world adorn,
And lift our quickened hearts and eyes
To fairer ſcenes beyond the ſkies.

So, Brightneſs of His Father's Face,
Chriſt, Light of lights and Fount of Grace,
Bids us, beneath His Manhood, learn
God in His Glory to diſcern.

Bleſt Trinity! a Beacon Light
Thy Law, within our hearts indite;
To help us ſhun the paths of ill,
And all Thy bleſt commands fulfil.
Amen.

On Sunday Evenings.

O God! enſhrined in Heavenly light
Beyond the ken of mortal ſight;
Where, awed, e'en ſaints before Thee quail,
And Angel hoſts their faces veil;

While theſe nocturnal glooms profound
Thy ſervants here on earth ſurround,
May beams from Thine Eternal Day
Chaſe all our worldly night away.

Day, with celeſtial ſplendours fair,
Which now for us Thou doſt prepare;
And faintly ſhadoweth here below
The flaming Sun's meridian glow.

Thou lingereſt! Ah! thou golden dawn!
Thou lingereſt! long-expected Morn!
When, quit of this encumbering clay,
Shall we behold that wiſhed-for Day?

Then, clogged by fleſhly bonds no more,
The ſoul, O God! to Thee ſhall ſoar;
Before Thy bliſsful Viſion bend,
And love and ſerve Thee without end.

Great Trinity! Thou Source of Grace!
O fit us for that happy place!
This brief and miſty twilight clear,
And make Thine endleſs Day appear!
Amen.

Chriſtmas-tide.

Jam deſinant ſuſpiria.

Calmed be our griefs, huſhed every ſigh,
For God hath heard our vows on high;
Heaven's gates expand, and, man to cheer,
Behold, our promiſed Peace appear!

Far echoing through the vault of night,
Celeſtial choirs their ſongs unite;
Right joyous are their feſtal ſtrains,
A God is born! On earth He reigns!

E'en now, as to His hallowed bed
Their path the wakeful ſhepherds tread,
Speed we with ſalutation meet,
His chaſte Nativity to greet.

And Lo! Behold what marvel lies
Diſplayed before our raviſhed eyes;
The Straw, the Crib, the Mother mild,
The ſwathing bands, the Infant Child!

Art Thou The Chriſt? The Mighty Son?
The Brightneſs of The Eternal One?
Who earth's expanſe of Sea and Land
Bears in the hollow of His Hand?

'Tis thus; for Faith can pierce the cloud
Wherewith Thou doſt Thy preſence ſhroud;
Proſtrate, with Angels evermore
I gaze, I tremble and adore!

What precepts from that lowly chair
Thou, ſilent Teacher! doſt declare:
The world's allurements to refuſe,
And all that fleſh rejects, to chooſe.

Implant Thy love in every breaſt;
Calm all our paſſions into reſt;
O Child Divine! this Holy Morn
Now in our very hearts be born.
Amen.

For the Epiphany.

Linquunt tecta Magi.

Lo! the pilgrim Magi
Leave their royal halls,
And with love devouteſt
Bethlehem's lowly walls
Seek with eager footſteps;
While firm Faith, which reſts,
Built on Hope unſwerving,
Triumphs in their breaſts.

Oh! what joys extatic
Thrilled each heart from far
When, to guide their footſteps,
Gleamed that Beacon Star
O'er that Home ſo holy,
Pouring down its ray,
In His Mother's boſom,
Where The Infant lay.

There no ivory gliſtens,
Glows no regal gold,
Nor doth gorgeous purple
Thoſe fair limbs enfold;
But His Court He keepeth
In a ſtable bare,
His throne is a manger,
Rags His purple are.

Coftly pomps and pageants
Earthly kings array;
He, a mightier Monarch,
Hath a nobler fway.
Straw though be His pallet,
Mean His garb may be,
Yet, with power tranfcendent,
He all hearts can free.

At His crib they worfhip,
Proftrate on the floor;
And a God there prefent
In that Babe adore.
Let us to that Infant,
We, their offspring true,
Hearts with faith o'erflowing
Give, our tribute due.

Holieft love prefenting,
As gold to our King,
To the Man pure bodies,
Myrrh-like, chaftely bring;
Unto Him, as Incenfe,
Vow and prayer addrefs;
So, with offerings meeteft,
This our God confefs.

Glory to The Father,
Fount of Light alone;
Who unto the Gentiles
Made His Glory known.
Equal Praife and Merit,
Bleffed Son, to Thee,
And to Thee, Sweet Spirit,
Evermore fhall be. Amen.

In Lent.

Audi, benigne Conditor.

O MERCIFUL Creator! hear!
Regard our mingled fighs and prayer,
Heavenward to Thee devoutly fent,
In this our Holy Faft of Lent.

Heart-fearcher kind! well known to Thee
Is all our foul's infirmity;
Repentant now we feek Thy Face,
Impart Thy bleffed pardoning Grace.

Much we have finned in Thy fight,
Spare all who own their guilt aright;
In honour of Thy Name, once more
To Health our ailing fouls reftore.

Grant that the body's outward fenfe
Be chaftened by fit abftinence;
That fo the fafting fpirit be
From every guilty blemifh free.

Beftow our prayer, bleft Trinity!
Grant, Undivided Unity!
That all the gifts Thy Faft imparts
May profit our repentant hearts.
Amen.

For Paffion-tide.

Vexilla Regis prodeunt.

THE Royal Banner forward goes,
The Myftic Crofs refulgent glows,
Where He in flefh, our flefh Who made,
Upon the Tree of pain is laid.

Behold! the nails with anguifh fierce
His outftretched Hands and Vitals pierce;
Here our redemption to obtain,
The Mighty Sacrifice is flain!

Here the fell fpear His wounded Side
With ruthlefs onfet opened wide;
To wafh us in that cleanfing flood,
Thence mingled Water flowed, and Blood.

Fulfilled is all that David told
In true prophetic Song of old;
Unto the nations "Lo," faith he,
"Our God hath reigned from the Tree."

O Tree! in radiant beauty bright,
With regal purple meetly dight!
Thou chofen Stem, divinely graced,
Which hath Thofe Holy Limbs embraced;

How bleſt thine arms, beyond compare,
Which earth's eternal Ranſom bare!
That Balance where His Body laid
The ſpoil of vanquiſhed Hell outweighed!

Hail! wondrous Altar! Victim, hail!
Thy glorious Paſſion ſhall avail,
Where death Life's very Self endured,
Yet life by that ſame Death ſecured.

Thee, Mighty Trinity! One God!
Let every living creature laud,
Whom by The Croſs Thou doſt deliver;
O guide and govern now and ever.
Amen.

For Eaſter-tide.

Chorus novæ Jeruſalem.

Ye Choirs of New Jeruſalem
Begin a new and ſweeter theme,
And let the Paſchal Feaſt employ
Your tongues with melodies of joy.

When Chriſt, the Dragon Fiend o'ercome,
Roſe, Lion Victor, from the tomb;
Far round His quickening voice is ſpread,
And unto life awakes the dead.

Hell vanquiſhed, from her ravenous jaws
Diſgorged, her ancient prey reſtores;
Her captives freed in glad array
Their Jeſus follow in the way.

In glorious triumph o'er His foes,
Auguſt in majeſty He goes;
And far as Heaven and Earth extends,
All in one commonwealth He blends.

Meekly let us in ſuppliant lay,
His liegemen, to our Monarch pray;
Within His palace bright and vaſt
May He array us at the laſt!

Through ages without end, to Thee,
Almighty Father! Glory be;
And Honour meet unto The Son,
And Spirit Paraclete, be done.
Amen.

For Penteco/t.

Veni Creator Spiritus.

Creator Spirit! Power Divine!
Come, viſit all the ſouls of Thine!
With Heaven-deſcending Grace pervade
The breaſts which Thou Thyſelf haſt made.

Thou! Who art named The Paraclete,
Rich gift from God's own mercy Seat;
O Fount of Life! and Fire of Love!
Soul quickening Unction from above!

Thou in Thy Sevenfold Glories bright!
Thou Finger of God's Hand of Might!
Who doſt o'er lips the timely ſtore
Of God The Father's promiſe pour;

Thy Light to every ſenſe impart,
Diffuſe Thy Love through every heart;
The weakneſs of our mortal fleſh
With Thine unfailing ſtrength refreſh;

Drive far away the aſſailing foe,
And all Thy holy peace beſtow;
If Thou be our preventing Guide,
No miſchief can our ſteps betide.

Through Thee may we The Father learn,
And know The ever bleſſed Son,
Sweet Spirit! and of Both receive
Thee, as we evermore believe.

Praiſe to The Father, as is meet,
The Son, and Holy Paraclete!
O may The Son to every heart
The Holy Spirit's gifts impart!
Amen.

For the Ascension.

Hymnum canamus gloriæ.

Sing we triumphant hymns of Praise,
New hymns to Heaven exulting raise;
Christ, by a new and wondrous road,
Ascends unto the Throne of God.

In regal pomp He sweepeth by
The lofty zenith of the sky,
Who late, o'er Death a Victor, died,
By mortals scorned and crucified.

Behold! The Apostolic Band
Upon the Mount of Olives stand,
And, with His Virgin Mother, see
Their Jesu's Glorious Majesty.

Lo! how with glad and wondering sight
They gaze upon His Heavenward flight,
With hearts rejoicing onward bear
The King of Nature through the air.

To whom the shining Angels cry,
"Why gaze ye on yon azure sky?
'Tis Jesus, on this Holy Morn,
Aloft in pomp triumphal borne;"

"Once more to earth shall come," they say,
"As ye have seen Him on this Day,
This Jesus, Who His bright ascent
Speeds o'er the glittering firmament."

"He hastes to mount His Heavenly Throne;
He takes the Kingdom for His own;
And thence again, at time's last end,
To judge the nations shall descend."

Oh! In that hour of dread we pray,
Jesu! Redeemer! be our stay;
With Thine, who meet Thee in the air,
Unite us by Thy kindly care.

May we, that Kingdom to possess,
With fond devotion onward press,
Where Thou, at Thy Great Father's side,
Dost in Thy Royal Court abide.

Then to our hearts, with joy elate,
With Thy sweet Spirit satiate,
Shew us The Father; to our eyes
That Only Vision shall suffice.
Amen.

On the Day of an Apostle.

Exultet cœlum laudibus.

Ye Heavens! exult with joyful Praise;
Earth! echo back the thankful lays;
This Festal-tide, in sweet accord,
The Apostles' glorious deeds we laud.

O righteous Judges of the Earth!
True Lights which o'er the world shone forth!
We praise you all with hearts sincere,
As suppliants now we worship here.

To your prevailing word 'twas given,
To close and ope the doors of Heaven;
And from their guilt, by your decree,
To set repentant sinners free.

To your instructions were assigned
The health and welfare of mankind;
May ye our sinful lives once more
To life and holiness restore;

That Christ, the avenging Judge of doom,
When He at Time's last end shall come,
May grant us, for His mercy's sake,
Of Joys eternal to partake! Amen.

On the Day of an Apostle Martyr.

Rex Jesu potentissime.

O King supreme of boundless might!
Who orderest Nature's laws aright,
And dost Thy truths, divinely bright,
Within believing bosoms write;

To Thee we pour our suppliant vows,
Our dull and slothful hearts arouse;
So fitly may our souls embrace
The gifts of Thy supernal Grace.

With these, as precious gems elect,
A diadem of beauty, decked,
We would, with praises glad and meet,
Thy Saint, the Holy Andrew,* greet;

Who,† on the Cross of suffering slain,
Hath won a rest in Christ's domain,
Nigh God's imperial Throne to reign,
A fellow with the saintly train.

So may we, in Thy Light Divine,
With soul illuming virtues shine;
Our hearts devout and sober be,
Our flesh from all pollution free.

Now unto us with Him be given
To climb the bright ascent of Heaven,
There, with enraptured eyes, to gaze
For evermore on Jesu's face.

Laud, Honour, Virtue, Glory be
To God The Father; Son, to Thee;
And to The Holy Paraclete,
Now and through ages infinite!
Amen.

On the Day of a Confessor or Evangelist.

O Christe splendor gloriæ.

O Sun of Glory! Christ, our King!
To Thee our meed of praise we bring,
Who with Thy miracles of love
Dost crown the sainted choirs above.

They, when the Church had rest from care,
As blooming lilies sweet and fair,
Preached to the world their Maker's will
Once more His Paradise to fill.

Against the infernal foe, to war
A sacred panoply they bore;
Of Faith the broad and Heavenly shield,
The Spirit's two-edged sword they wield;

Their mouths proclaim The Name of God,
And in their hearts is Christ's abode;
Within their minds His Love abides,
And Truth and Righteousness resides.

Raised from the dust, a noble band,
Shall they in faultless garments stand;
And, like to Angels made, possess
The joys of light and holiness.

Now in the tomb their limbs repose,
And still their Saviour's glory grows;
The wonders of His power are shewn.
For us they pray before the Throne!

With them Thy flock, O Lord of Grace!
Safe in Thy sheltering arms embrace;
From every ill our steps defend,
And grant us life that hath no end!

O King of Mercy! Christ! to Thee,
With God The Father, Glory be;
Like Glory, Holy Ghost! is Thine,
Thou Stay! Thou Comforter Divine!
Amen.

For the Day of a Martyr.

O beata beatorum.

Blessed Feasts of Blessed Martyrs,
Saintly days of saintly men!
With affection's recollection
Greet we your return again.

Noble acts they wrought, and wonders,
While the garb of flesh they wore;
We with meetest praise, and sweetest,
Honour them for evermore.

* Or St. Peter, St. Thomas, St Stephen, St. Laurence, &c.; or St. Paul, St. James, St. Jude, Thy Holy Martyr, Bartholomew, Thy Martyr, &c.

† Or "by the sword or rage of tyrants."

Faith unblenching, Hope unquenching,
Love of Chrift, and fingle heart,
Taught them. glorious and victorious,
To endure the Martyr's part.

Blood in flaughter, fhed like water,
Torments long, and heavy chain,
Flame, and axe, and fcourge, and torture,
They endured, and conquered pain.

They were mocked, diftreffed, afflicted,
Till in death they fank to reft;
Earth's rejected were elected
To have portion with the bleft.

So, defpifing worldly pleafures,
And by deeds of valour done,
They attained the land of Angels,
And with them are knit in one.

Crowned and made co-heirs of glory,
There they reign with Chrift on high;
Oh that, as He heard their weeping,
He may alfo hear our cry!

Till, this weary life completed,
And its toils and forrows paft,
He fhall call us to be feated
In our Father's home at laft.
Amen.

For Michaelmas.

Tibi Chrifte! Splendor Patris!

Christ! Mirror of Thy Father's Brightnefs!
Life and Strength of fouls Thou art;
And to Thee, before the Angels,
Sing we laud with voice and heart,
In alternate modulation
Bearing each our tuneful part.

Praife we with meet veneration
All the Warriors of the fky;
Before all, the Princely Chieftain
Of the Heavenly Chivalry,
Michael, Who, in battle victor,
Hurled Abaddon from on high.

By his prowefs all excelling,
Chrift! Thou King of boundlefs Grace!
All the Foe's affaults repelling,
Pure in heart, before Thy Face,
Us in Paradife, Thy Dwelling,
Of Thine only mercy, place.

Glory to The Father giving,
Him with anthems let us greet,
Glory unto Chrift afcribing,
Glory to The Paraclete,
Triune, yet One God, exifting
Throughout ages infinite. Amen.

APPENDIX II.

¶ COLLECTS THROUGHOUT THE YEAR.

The First Sunday in Advent.

AISE up, we pray Thee, O Lord! Thy Power, and come; that from the perils of our ſins, which threaten us, we through Thy protection may be reſcued, by Thy deliverance may be ſaved, Who liveſt and reigneſt with God The Father, in The Unity of The Holy Ghoſt, God world without end. Amen.

In the Second Sunday.

Stir up, we beſeech Thee, O Lord! our hearts to make ready the ways of Thine Only-begotten; ſo that by His Coming we may be enabled to ſerve Thee with pure minds, Who with Thee liveth and reigneth in The Unity. Amen.

In the Third Sunday.

O Lord! we beſeech Thee, incline Thine Ears to our prayers, and enlighten the darkneſs of our minds by the Grace of Thy Viſitation, Who liveſt and reigneſt.

On Wedneſday in the Third Week.

Grant, we beſeech Thee, Almighty God! that the approaching Solemnity of our Redemption may afford us ſuccour in this preſent life, and may procure for us the rewards of eternal bleſſedneſs. Through our Lord Jeſus Chriſt, Thy Son, Who with Thee.

On Friday in the Third Week.

Raise up, we beſeech Thee, O Lord! Thy Power, and come; that we who truſt in Thy compaſſion may ſpeedily be delivered from all adverſity, Who liveſt.

On Saturday.

O Lord! Who ſeeſt that we are afflicted by reaſon of our great ſinfulneſs, mercifully grant that we may be comforted by Thy Viſitation, Who liveſt.

Grant, we beſeech Thee, Almighty God! that we who are oppreſſed by the yoke of the ancient bondage may by the coming Nativity of Thine Only-begotten Son be delivered, Who with Thee.

God! Who to the Three Children didſt mitigate the flames of the fiery furnace, mercifully grant that the flames of our ſins may never conſume us Thy ſervants. Through our Lord.

On the Fourth Sunday.

Raise up, we beſeech Thee, O Lord! Thy Power, and come, and with great might ſuccour us; that through the help of Thy Grace that which our ſins hinder, the favour of Thy Lovingkindneſs may aſſiſt. Through our Lord.

The Vigil of the Nativity.

O God! Who makeſt us year by year to rejoice in the celebration of our Redemption; grant that Thine Only-begotten Whom we joyfully receive as our Redeemer, we may alſo without fear behold coming as our Judge, our Lord Jeſus Chriſt, Thy Son, Who.

In the Day of the Nativity.

At Cock-crowing.

God! Who didſt illumine this Moſt Holy Night with the glory of The True Light; grant, we beſeech Thee, that we who have known the myſteries of His Light on earth may alſo be partakers of His joys in Heaven. Through The Same.

Grant to us, we beſeech Thee, O Lord our God! that we who rejoice in celebrating the Nativity of our Lord Jeſus Chriſt, may by our holy converſation be found worthy of attaining to fellowſhip with Him. Through The Same.

In the Morning.

Grant, we beſeech Thee, Almighty God! that we, upon whom is poured forth the new Light of Thine Incarnate Word, may make that ſame Light, which through faith illumines our ſouls, to ſhine forth alſo in our actions. Through The Same.

Grant, we beſeech Thee, Almighty God! that the New Birth of Thine Only-begotten through the Fleſh may deliver us from our ancient bondage, and from the yoke of ſin, Who with Thee.

Grant, we beſeech Thee, Almighty God! that The Saviour of the world Who was this day born may, as He is the author unto us of a divine regeneration, be alſo the beſtower of immortality. Through The Same.

St. Stephen.

Grant to us, O Lord! we beſeech Thee, that we may imitate what we reverence, and learn to love our perſecutors by the example of him whoſe natal day we celebrate, who prayed even for his murderers to our Lord Jeſus Chriſt, Thy Son, Who with Thee.

St. John.

Merciful Lord! we beſeech Thee to caſt the beams of Thy Light upon Thy Church, that It being enlightened by the doctrine of Thy Holy Apoſtle and Evangeliſt St. John, may at length obtain Thine everlaſting rewards. Through Chriſt our Lord. Amen.

Holy Innocents.

God! Whoſe glory as on this day Thy Martyred Innocents proclaimed not with their tongues, but by their deaths, mortify all evils and vices in us; ſo that the Faith which we declare with our mouths, may be ſhewn forth alſo in our lives and behaviour. Through Chriſt our Lord. Amen.

On the Sixth Day.

Almighty and everlaſting God! direct all our actions according to Thy good will; ſo that through The Name of Thy beloved Son we may be enabled to abound in good works, Who with Thee.

The Day of the Circumciſion.

God! Who permitteſt us to celebrate the Eighth Day from the Birth of The Saviour Who was born for us; cauſe us, we beſeech Thee, to be ſtrengthened by His everlaſting Divinity, by Whoſe converſe with fleſh we were made whole, Who with Thee.

The Vigil of the Epiphany.

O Lord! we beſeech Thee, let the brightneſs of the coming Feſtival enlighten our hearts; ſo that we may be enabled to be quit of the darkneſs of this world, and may attain to the land of eternal brightneſs. Through our Lord.

On the Day of the Epiphany.

God! Who as on this Day by the leading of a Star didst manifest Thine Only-begotten Son to the Gentiles, mercifully grant that we who know Thee now by Faith may at length attain even to behold the fair beauty of Thy Majesty. Through The Same our Lord Jesus Christ, Thy Son, Who.

On the Sunday within the Octave, and the Octave.

God! Whose Only-begotten hath appeared in the substance of our Flesh; grant, we beseech Thee, that by Him Whom we confess to have been like unto us outwardly, we may desire to be reformed inwardly. Through The Same.

Grant, O merciful God! we beseech Thee, that we may be helped by the continual intercession of her from whose unspotted virginity we have received The Author of our Salvation, our Lord Jesus Christ, Thy Son, Who with Thee.

The First Sunday after the Octave of the Epiphany.

O Lord! we beseech Thee, of Thy heavenly pity regard the supplications of Thy people who call upon Thee; so that they may perceive what things they ought to do, and also may have power faithfully to fulfil the same. Through Christ our Lord. Amen.

The Second Sunday.

Almighty and everlasting God! Who dost govern all things both in Heaven and Earth, mercifully hear the supplications of Thy people, and grant us Thy peace in our time. Through Christ our Lord.

The Third Sunday.

Almighty and everlasting God! mercifully regard our infirmities, and evermore hereafter stretch forth the Right Hand of Thy Majesty to defend us. Through Christ our Lord.

The Fourth Sunday.

God! Who knowest us to be set in the midst of so many and great dangers, that by reason of the frailty of human nature we cannot stand upright; grant to us such health both of mind and of body, that those things which for our sins we suffer, by Thy help we may overcome. Through Christ our Lord.

The Fifth Sunday.

O Lord! we beseech Thee to keep Thy Household Thy Church, in continual godliness; that It, which doth rest only on the hope of Thy Heavenly Grace, may evermore be defended by Thy protection. Through.

Sunday in Septuagesima.

O Lord! we beseech Thee, favourably to hear the prayers of Thy people; that we who are justly punished for our offences may be mercifully delivered by Thy goodness, for the Glory of Thy Name. Through our Lord.

Sunday in Sexagesima.

O Lord! Who seest that we put not our trust in anything that we do; mercifully grant that by the power of Him Who is the Instructor of the Gentiles, we may be defended against all adversity. Through our Lord.

Sunday in Quinquagesima.

O Lord! we beseech Thee, graciously hearken unto our prayers, and releasing us from the chains of our sins, keep us from all adversity. Through our Lord.

On Ash-Wednesday, and for the rest of the Week.

Grant, we beseech Thee, O Lord! to Thy faithful people that they may undertake with suitable piety the reverend solemnities of the Fast, and perform them in peace and devotion. Through Christ our Lord. Amen.

O God! Who art offended by guilt, but appeased by penitence, graciously regard the prayers of us Thy suppliant people; and avert from us the scourges of Thy wrath which for our sins we have deserved. Through Christ our Lord.

O Lord! we beseech Thee, mercifully hearken unto our prayers, and spare all those who confess their sins unto Thee; that they whose consciences by sin are accused by Thy compassionate pardon may be absolved. Through Christ our Lord.

O Lord! we beseech Thee, may the inspiration of Thy saving Grace be present with Thy servants to soften their hearts, and in such wise to render them contrite, that they may appease Thy wrath by suitable penance. Through Christ our Lord.

Be present, O Lord! with our supplications, nor let the pitifulness of Thy Compassion be absent from us Thy servants; heal our wounds, pardon our transgressions, that separated from Thee by no iniquity, we may ever be enabled to adhere closely unto Thee, our God. Through our Lord.

O Lord! we beseech Thee, prevent the fasts which we have begun with Thy continual favour; that what we observe in the body we may be enabled also to practise sincerely in the soul. Through our Lord.

Be present, O Lord! with our supplications, and grant that this solemn Fast which Thou didst institute for the saving discipline of our souls and bodies we may celebrate with a devout spirit and service. Through our Lord.

The First Sunday in Lent, and in the Ember Week.

O God! Who purifiest Thy Church by the yearly observance of Lent; grant unto us Thy family that what we strive to obtain from Thee by abstinence, the same we may practise in good works. Through our Lord.

Convert us, O God! our Salvation; and that our Lenten Fast may profit us, do Thou instruct our minds in Thy Heavenly discipline. Through our Lord. Amen.

Absolve us, we beseech Thee, O Lord! from all the chains of our sins; and all the punishments that on their account we have deserved do Thou mercifully turn away from us. Through our Lord.

Regard, we beseech Thee, O Lord! this Thy family; and grant that as we chasten the flesh so our souls may glow with desire for Thee. Through our Lord.

O Lord! we beseech Thee, mercifully hearken unto our prayers, and stretch forth the Right Hand of Thy Majesty to be our defence against all our adversaries. Through.

O Lord! we intreat Thee, favourably regard the devotions of Thy people; and while we are chastened by abstinence in the body, may we be refreshed by the fruit of good works in the soul. Through.

O Lord! we beseech Thee, enlighten our hearts with the splendour of Thy Brightness; so that we may be enabled bo' to perceive what things we ought to do, and alſo may have grace and power faithfully to perform the ſame. Through.

Almighty and everlaſting God! Who haſt ordained faſting and almſgiving as remedies for our ſinfulneſs; grant that we may ever be devoted unto Thee both in body and ſoul. Through.

O God! Who through things temporal leadeſt us unto things eternal, extend Thy mercy unto us who reſt upon Thy Heavenly promiſes; and ſince it is of Thee that we believe in Thee, may we ever live in all things unto Thee. Through.

Regard us, O Lord! our Defender; that we who are oppreſſed by the burthen of our ſins, having obtained Thy mercy, may ſerve Thee with free minds. Through.

Be preſent, O Lord! with our ſupplications; that we may be enabled to deſerve Thy bounties, and in proſperity to be humble, in adverſity to be unſhaken. Through.

O Lord! we beſeech Thee, prevent our actions with Thy inſpiration, and further them with Thy help; that all our works may ever begin with Thee, and may be ended by Thee. Through.

O God! Who to the Three Children didſt mitigate the flames of fire, graciouſly grant that the flames of ſin may never conſume us Thy ſervants. Through.

O Lord! may Thy bleſſing which we earneſtly deſire ever ſtrengthen Thy faithful people; and both cauſe them never to tranſgreſs Thy holy will, and evermore to rejoice in the indulgence of Thy kind favour. Through.

Second Sunday in Lent, and in the Week.

Remember, O Lord! Thy compaſſions and Thy mercies, which are ever of old; and that our enemies may never have dominion over us, deliver us, Thou God of Iſrael, in all our neceſſities. Through.

O God! Who ſeeſt that we are deſtitute of all ſtrength, keep us both inwardly and outwardly; that we may be defended from all adverſities which may happen to the body, and may be cleanſed from all evil thoughts in the ſoul. Through.

Grant, we beſeech Thee,

Almighty God! that we Thy family who chasten their flesh by abstinence, may by following after righteousness fast from all sin. Through.

O Almighty God! assist our supplications; and upon us whom Thou dost comfort with trust in Thy hoped-for compassions, do Thou graciously bestow the effects of Thy wonted mercy. Through.

O Lord! we beseech Thee, graciously perfect in us the help of this Thy discipline; that as we acknowledge Thee to be its author, so we may fulfil it by Thine aid. Through.

Be favourable, O Lord! to our supplications, and heal the diseases of our souls; so that having obtained pardon, we may ever rejoice in Thy blessing. Through.

O Lord! we beseech Thee, mercifully look upon Thy people; and grant that we, whom Thou commandest to abstain from carnal feasts, may also be rid of all hurtful vices. Through.

O God! the restorer and lover of innocence, direct unto Thyself the hearts of Thy servants; that kindled with the fervour of Thy Spirit, they may be found both steadfast in faith and also fruitful in good works. Through.

O Lord! we beseech Thee, grant us the help of Thy Grace; that being dutifully intent upon fasting and prayer, we may be delivered from the enemies of our souls and bodies. Through.

Be present, O Lord! with Thy servants, and bestow Thy continual lovingkindness upon all who pray for the same; that we who glory in Thee our Creator and Governor, may by Thee be restored and preserved. Through.

Grant, we beseech Thee, Almighty God! that we, purified by this holy Fast, may with pure minds attain to those Holy Things which are to come hereafter. Through.

O Lord! we beseech Thee, grant unto Thy people health both of mind and body; that occupied in good works, they may be worthy of being defended by the protection of Thy mighty power. Through.

O Lord! we beseech Thee, bestow salutary effect upon our fasts; that the chastening of the flesh which we endure may be effectual to the renewing of our ſouls. Through.

O Lord! we beſeech Thee to keep Thy Houſehold with Thy continual pity, that we, who reſt only on the hope of Thy mercy, may alſo be defended by Thy Heavenly protection. Through.

The Third Sunday in Lent, and in the Week.

O Lord! we beſeech Thee, regard the vows of Thy humble ſervants, and ſtretch forth the Right Hand of Thy Majeſty to be our defence. Through.

O Lord! we beſeech Thee, of Thy goodneſs pour Thy Grace into our hearts; that whilſt we abſtain from bodily pleaſures, we may alſo withdraw our ſenſes from all hurtful indulgences. Through.

O Lord! we beſeech Thee, ſuccour us with Thy kind mercy; that from the perils of our ſins which threaten us we by Thy protection may be reſcued, by Thy deliverance may be ſaved. Through.

O Almighty and Merciful God! hearken unto us, and graciouſly beſtow upon us the healthful gift of continence. Through.

Grant, O Lord! we beſeech Thee, that diſciplined by this ſalutary Faſt, we may abſtain from hurtful offences, and the more eaſily obtain Thy propitiation. Through.

Grant, we beſeech Thee, Almighty God! that we who ſeek for the favour of Thy protection may be delivered from all evil, and ſerve Thee with quiet minds. Through.

Grant we beſeech Thee, Almighty God! that the holy devotions of our Faſt may procure for us purification, and alſo render us acceptable to Thy Divine Majeſty. Through.

O Lord! we beſeech Thee may Thy Heavenly propitiation enlarge Thy people who are ſubject unto Thee, and ever cauſe them to obey Thy Commandments. Through.

O Lord! we beſeech Thee acccompany us ever with Thy kind favour; that whilſt we abſtain from feaſting in the body we may likewiſe faſt from ſin in the ſoul. Through.

Grant we intreat Thee, Almighty God! that we who truſt in Thy protection may by Thy help vanquiſh all our enemies. Through.

Stretch forth, O Lord! unto Thy faithful people the Right Arm of Thy Heavenly help; that they who ſeek for Thee with their whole hearts may be enabled to obtain that for which they rightly aſk. Through.

Mid-Lent Sunday, and in the Week.

Grant, we beſeech Thee, Almighty God! that we who are afflicted for the evil deſerts of our actions may by the comfort of Thy Grace be relieved. Through.

Grant, we beſeech Thee, Almighty God! that we who year by year worſhip Thee in theſe holy obſervances, may pleaſe Thee both in body and ſoul. Through.

O **Lord**! we pray Thee of Thy kindneſs hearken unto our ſupplications; and beſtowing on us the effect of our intreaties, grant us alſo the help of Thy defence. Through.

O **Lord**! we beſeech Thee, ſanctify unto us the obſervance of this Faſt; that it may procure for us an increaſe in holy converſation, and the continual help of Thy protection. Through.

Lord! we pray Thee have pity on Thy people; and grant that they who do labour under continual tribulation may by Thy favour be relieved. Through.

God! Who beſtoweſt on the righteous the reward of their well-doing, and doſt pardon ſinners for their prayer and faſting, have pity upon us Thy ſuppliants; that we who confeſs our guilt, may be enabled to obtain the forgiveneſs of our ſins. Through.

Grant, we beſeech Thee, Almighty God! that we whom prayer and faſting doth chaſten, may be ſo made glad with holy devotion, that all earthly deſires being aſſuaged, we may the more eaſily attain to things which are Heavenly. Through.

Let Thy merciful ears, O Lord! be open to the prayers of Thy ſuppliants; and that they may obtain their petitions make them to aſk ſuch things as are pleaſing unto Thee. Through.

O **God**! The Inſtructor and Ruler of Thy people, purge away the ſins wherewith they are aſſailed; that being ever well-pleaſing unto Thee, they may alway remain in ſafety under Thy protection. Through.

God! Who doſt renew the world with the unſpeakable grace of Thy Sacraments; grant, we beſeech Thee, that Thy Church may profit by Thine everlaſting ſtatutes, and never be deprived of Thy help in this life. Through.

Grant, we beſeech Thee, Almighty God! that we who are conſcious of our infirmities, and truſt in Thy pity, may ever rejoice under Thy protection. Through.

O Lord! we beſeech Thee, may our devout affections become fruitful by the help of Thy Grace; and may the faſts which we obſerve, ſo far as they are agreeable to Thy goodneſs, be profitable unto us. Through.

God! Who art more ready to pity than to be wrath with them that hope in Thee; grant unto us ſo worthily to weep for the ſins we have committed; that we may be enabled to obtain the grace of Thy conſolation. Through.

Sunday in The Paſſion, and in the Week.

We beſeech Thee, Almighty God! favourably regard this Thy family; that by Thy goodneſs it may be governed in body, and by Thy care may be preſerved in ſoul. Through.

O Lord! we beſeech Thee, grant unto Thy people the Spirit of Truth and Peace; that they may know Thee with their whole minds, and with pious devotion practiſe thoſe things which are pleaſing unto Thee. Through our Lord. In The Unity of The Same.

O Lord! we beſeech Thee, grant unto Thy Houſehold perſeverance in Thy will; ſo that in our days the people who ſerve Thee may increaſe both in holineſs of life and in number. Through.

O God! in Thy pity enlighten the hearts of Thy faithful ones by ſanctifying this Faſt; and as Thou doſt inſpire them with devout affections, ſo of Thy goodneſs graciouſly hearken to their ſupplications. Through.

O Lord! we beſeech Thee, let Thy long deſired mercy viſit Thy ſuppliants, and be beſtowed upon them with Heavenly abundance; ſo that they may aſk thoſe things for which they ought to pray, and may obtain the fruit of their petitions. Through.

Grant, we beſeech Thee, Almighty God! that the dignity of our human nature, which was depraved by immoderate indulgence, may by the ſalutary practice of abſtinence again be reſtored. Through.

O Lord! we pray Thee be gracious unto Thy people; that rejecting all things that are diſpleaſing unto Thee, they may be rather fulfilled with delight in Thy commandments. Through.

O Lord! we beſeech Thee, of Thy goodneſs pour into our hearts the help of Thy Grace; ſo that ſubduing our ſins by voluntary chaſtiſement, we may chooſe to be afflicted for a time rather than given over to eternal puniſhment. Through.

O Lord! we pray Thee grant us pardon for our ſins, and increaſe of true religion; multiply in us Thy gracious gifts, and ever make us more ready to do Thy holy commandments. Through.

Grant, O Lord! we beſeech Thee, that Thy people who are ſanctified unto Thee may increaſe in the pious earneſtneſs of their devotions; ſo that inſtructed in the ways of holineſs, they may become more acceptable to Thy Majeſty, and may be the more enriched with Thy choiceſt gifts. Through.

O Lord! we pray Thee with Thy Right Hand to defend Thy people who cry unto Thee; and when cleanſed from their impurities worthily inſtruct them; ſo that they may be ſtrengthened by Thy comfort here, and go forward to eternal bleſſedneſs. Through.

Palm Sunday, and in the Week.

Almighty and eternal God! Who didſt cauſe our Saviour to take upon Him our fleſh, and to endure the Croſs, that all mankind might follow the example of His humility; mercifully grant that we may be enabled to imitate His patience, and alſo to obtain fellowſhip in His Reſurrection. Through The Same.

Grant, we beſeech Thee, Almighty God! that we who in our afflictions fall away through our many infirmities, may by The Paſſion and interceſſion of Thy Only-begotten Son be relieved. Through The Same.

Help us, O God our Salvation! and grant that with joy we may come to thank Thee for the benefits wherewith Thou hast vouchsafed to restore us. Through.

Almighty and everlasting God! grant unto us so to pass through the holy time of this our Lord's Passion, that we may be enabled to obtain Thy pardon. Through.

Let Thy mercy, O Lord God! purge away from us all remnants of the old Adam, and make us capable of Thy holy renewing. Through.

Grant, we beseech Thee, Almighty God! that we who for our many transgressions are continually afflicted, may by The Passion of Thine Only-begotten Son be delivered. Who with Thee.

God! Who for our sakes didst will Thy Son to undergo the suffering of the Cross, that Thou mightest expel from us the power of the enemy; grant to us Thy servants that we may obtain the grace of His Resurrection. Through The Same.

Regard, we beseech Thee, O Lord! this Thy Family, for which our Lord Jesus Christ was contented to be betrayed into the hands of wicked men, and to endure the pains of the Cross. Who with Thee.

Holy Thursday.

God! from Whom the traitor Judas received the punishment of his crime, and the thief the reward of his confession; grant unto us, we beseech Thee, the effect of Thy propitiation; that like as in His Passion Jesus Christ our Lord to both of them awarded the due recompence of their deeds, so taking away our old sins He may bestow on us the grace of His Resurrection. Who with Thee.

O Lord! we beseech Thee, that refreshed by the Food of life, what we long for in this mortal life we may by Thy gift obtain hereafter with Thee in immortality. Through Christ our Lord.

On Good Friday.

Almighty and everlasting God! Who hast revealed Thy Glory to all nations, in our Lord Christ; keep, we beseech Thee, in safety the works of Thy mercy; that so Thy

Church being ſpread throughout all nations, may continue ſtable in Faith, and in the confeſſion of Thy Name. Through The Same.

Almighty and everlaſting God! in Whoſe pleaſure all things conſiſt, mercifully regard our prayers, and preſerve by Thy goodneſs our Archbiſhops and Biſhops; that Thy Chriſtian people who are governed by Thee their Creator may, under theſe Thy Paſtors, increaſe in Faith and good works. Through.

Almighty and everlaſting God! by Whoſe Spirit the whole Body of the Church is governed and ſanctified, hear us, we beſeech Thee, who ſupplicate Thee for all orders and degrees of the ſame; that by the gift of Thy Grace they in their ſeveral ſtations may faithfully ſerve Thee. Through our Lord. In The Unity of The Same.

Almighty and everlaſting God! in Whoſe Hand is all the Power and the Laws of all nations, regard the Sovereigns of all Chriſtian kingdoms; that the Gentiles who truſt in their own ſtrength may be repelled by the might of Thine arm. Through.

Almighty and everlaſting God! Who ever ſuppflieſt Thy Church with new offspring, increaſe faith and underſtanding in our catechumens; that born again in the Fountain of Baptiſm, they may be numbered among Thine adopted children. Through.

Almighty and everlaſting God! the Conſolation of the ſorrowful, the Strength of the afflicted, let the prayers of all that cry unto Thee in any tribulation enter into Thine ears; that in all their neceſſities they may rejoice in the help of Thy mercy. Through.

Almighty and everlaſting God! Who ſaveſt all men, and wouldeſt that none ſhould periſh, regard the ſouls of them that are led aſtray by the arts of the Devil; that laying aſide all heretical wickedneſs, the hearts of the wanderers may be reclaimed, and return to The Unity of Thy Truth. Through.

Almighty and everlaſting God! Who doſt not reject even perfidious Jews from Thy mercy, hear our prayers which we offer unto Thee for the blindneſs of that people; that acknowledging the Light of Thy Truth, which is Chriſt, they may be delivered from their darkneſs. Through The Same.

Almighty and everlaſting God! Who wouldeſt not the death of a ſinner, but ever ſeekeſt for him that he may live, mercifully receive our ſupplications; and deliver all heathen nations from the worſhip of idols, and gather them into Thy Holy Church. To the praiſe and glory of Thy Name. Through.

The Vigil of Eaſter.

God! Who didſt wonderfully create mankind, and more wonderfully redeem him, grant to us, we beſeech Thee, with firm purpoſe of mind to reſiſt the allurements of ſin; that by the help of Thy Grace we may attain to joys everlaſting. Through.

God! Whoſe miracles of old we perceive to ſhine forth even in our days; grant, we beſeech Thee, that what the might of Thy Right Hand beſtowed upon Thine ancient people by delivering them from Egyptian bondage, the ſame Thou wouldeſt perform for the ſalvation of the nations by the waters of regeneration; ſo that the fulneſs of the whole earth may become the children of Abraham, and attain to the privileges of the true Iſrael. Through.

God! Who both in the pages of the Old and of the New Teſtament haſt taught us Thy Paſchal Sacraments; cauſe us, we beſeech Thee, to underſtand Thy mercies; that ſo whilſt we thankfully receive theſe Thy preſent gifts, we may look forward with firm hope to thoſe which are to come hereafter. Through.

Grant, we beſeech Thee, Almighty God! that we who celebrate Thy Paſchal Feaſt kindled with Heavenly deſires, may ever thirſt for The Fountain of Life, Jeſus Chriſt, Thy Son, our Lord. Who.

Almighty and everlaſting God! mercifully regard the devotions of Thy people, who thirſt for Thee as doth the hart for the ſtreams of water; and grant that the thirſt of faith may ſanctify the bodies and ſouls of all them that are born again to Thee in the Myſtery of Baptiſm. Through.

God! Who didst enlighten this most Holy Night with the Glory of The Lord's Resurrection, preserve in the society of this Thy family the Spirit of adoption which Thou hast given unto them; so that refreshed both in body and soul, they may perform unto Thee a pure service. Through.

Pour into our hearts, O Lord! the Spirit of Thy Charity; so that us whom Thou dost satiate with Thy Paschal Sacraments, Thou mayest also keep in concord by Thy goodness. Through.

On Easter Sunday, and in the Week, and on the Octave.

O God! Who hast willed Thy Son for our sakes to undergo the suffering of the Cross, that Thou mightest expel from us the power of the enemy; grant to us Thy servants that we may ever live in the joys of His Resurrection. Through The Same.

God! Who as on this day through Thine Only-begotten Son hast overcome death, and opened unto us the gate of everlasting life; do Thou with Thy continual help make effectual the prayers which by Thy preventing Grace Thou dost inspire. Through The Same.

Grant, we beseech Thee, Almighty God! that we who celebrate the Solemnities of The Lord's Resurrection, by the renewing of Thy Holy Spirit may rise again from the death of the Soul. Through The Same.

O Lord! we beseech Thee, pour Thy Grace into our hearts; that we who have known the Incarnation of Christ Thy Son by the message of an Angel, by His Passion and Cross, may be guided to the Glory of His Resurrection. Through The Same.

God! Who in the Solemnity of Easter-tide didst bestow health upon the world, accompany Thy people, O Lord! we pray Thee, with Thy Heavenly gifts; that they may be enabled to attain perfect freedom, and go forward to everlasting life. Through.

Grant, we beseech Thee, Almighty God! that we who are oppressed by the weight of our sins may by Thy Paschal Feast be delivered from all the dangers which threaten us. Through.

Grant, we beseech Thee, Almighty God! that we who celebrate this Paschal Feast, may in our lives hold fast that which we worship and venerate. Through.

God! Who ever multipliest Thy Church with new offspring; grant unto Thy servants that in their lives they may ever hold fast that Sacrament which by faith they have received. Through.

Grant, we beseech Thee, Almighty God! that we who celebrate these Paschal Feasts may ever devoutly live in Thy praise and sanctification. Through.

God! Who dost make us rejoice in the yearly Solemnity of The Lord's Resurrection; mercifully grant that through the temporal feasts which we celebrate we may be enabled to attain to eternal joys. Through The Same.

Grant, we beseech Thee, Almighty God! that the marvellous Sacrament of this Paschal Feast may afford us temporal tranquillity, and also everlasting life. Through.

Grant, we beseech Thee, Almighty God! that we who celebrate this Paschal Feast kindled with celestial desires, may ever thirst for Thee, the Fountain of Life. Through.

God! Who hast united together divers nations in the confession of Thy Name; grant unto all that are born again in the Fount of Baptism, one faith in their minds, and piety in their actions. Through.

God! Who hast given unto us with enlarged minds to celebrate Thy Paschal Feast, teach us to fear what displeases Thee, and to love that which Thou dost command; that so Thy Church may ever be strengthened in its members, and rejoice in continual fruitfulness. Through.

Almighty and everlasting God! Who hast ordained Thy Paschal Sacraments to reconcile mankind by covenant unto Thyself; grant unto our souls that what we celebrate in profession we may also effectually follow in reality and effect. Through.

God! through Whose mercy both Redemption cometh and adoption is bestowed upon us, look down upon the works of Thy mercy; so that we who are born again in Christ may attain unto true freedom and an eternal inheritance. Through.

O LORD! we beſeech Thee, be preſent with this Thy Family; and in Thy condeſcenſion grant that they on whom Thou haſt beſtowed the grace of faith may by Thy bounty obtain an everlaſting Crown of Glory. Through.

GRANT, we beſeech Thee, Almighty God! that we who have completed Thy Paſchal Solemnities may by Thine aid ever hold them faſt in our lives and behaviour. Through.

POUR into our hearts, O Lord! the Spirit of Thy Charity; ſo that us whom Thou haſt ſatiated with Thy Paſchal Sacraments Thou mayeſt alſo keep in concord by Thy goodneſs. Through.

The Second Sunday after Eaſter.

GOD! Who by the humiliation of Thy Son didſt raiſe up the proſtrate world, grant unto Thy faithful ones perpetual gladneſs; and thoſe whom Thou haſt delivered from the danger of everlaſting death do Thou make partakers of eternal joys. Through The Same.

The Third Sunday.

GOD! Who ſheweſt to them that be in error the Light of Thy Truth, to the intent that they may return into the way of righteouſneſs; grant to all them that are reckoned of the Chriſtian profeſſion, both to eſchew thoſe things that are contrary to this name, and to follow all ſuch things as are agreeable to the ſame. Through.

The Fourth Sunday.

GOD! Who doſt cauſe the minds of the faithful to be of one accord, grant unto Thy people to love that which Thou doſt command, and to deſire that which Thou doſt promiſe; that ſo among the changes of this world our hearts may ſurely there be fixed, where true joys are to be found. Through.

The Fifth Sunday.

GOD! from Whom all good things do proceed, grant to us Thy ſuppliants, that by Thy holy inſpiration we may think thoſe things that be right, and by Thy merciful guiding may perform the ſame. Through.

On Rogation Monday.

GRANT, we beſeech Thee, Almighty God! that we w

in our afflictions trust in Thy pity may by Thy protection be ever defended against all adversities. Through.

The Vigil of the Ascension.

GRANT, we beseech Thee, Almighty God! that the desires of our souls may be ever intent upon that blessed place where Thine Only-begotten Son, our Lord, the glorious Author of the approaching Solemnity, hath entered in; so that in our conversation we may attain to that country whither we hasten by faith. Through.

On Ascension Day.

GRANT, we beseech Thee, Almighty God! that like as we do believe Thine Only-begotten Son, our Lord Jesus Christ, as on this day to have ascended into the Heavens, so we may also in heart and mind ever dwell with Him in the celestial mansions. Through The Same.

On the Sunday within the Octave.

ALMIGHTY and everlasting God! cause us always to have our wills devoted unto Thee, and ever to serve Thy Majesty with sincere hearts. Through.

Saturday, the Vigil of Pentecost.

GOD! Who art the glory of the faithful, the life of the righteous, Who through Moses Thy servant didst instruct us also by his holy writings; bestow the gifts of Thy mercy upon all nations; grant them Thy blessing, and take away all fear; so that what was pronounced as a punishment may be changed into an eternal benefit. Through.

GOD! Who by the mouths of Thy Prophets hast commanded us to relinquish things which are temporal, and to go forward to those which are eternal; grant unto Thy servants that what we know to have been ordained by Thee, the same we may be enabled by Thy Heavenly inspiration fully to perform. Through.

GRANT, we beseech Thee, Almighty God! that we who celebrate the Anniversary of the Gift of Thy Holy Spirit, kindled with celestial desires may ever thirst for the Fountain of Life, our Lord Jesus Christ, Thy Son, Who with Thee liveth and reigneth in The Unity of The Same Spirit God world without end. Amen.

Almighty and everlasting God! Who hast willed Thy Paschal Sacraments to be comprehended in a mystery of fifty days; grant, we beseech Thee, that the dispersion of the Gentiles which was caused by the confusion of tongues, may by Thy heavenly gift be gathered together again into one confession of Thy Name. Through. In The Unity of The Same.

Grant, we beseech Thee, Almighty God! that the splendour of Thy Brightness may shine forth upon us; so that the beams of Thy Light through the illumination of Thy Holy Spirit may confirm our hearts, and renew them by Thy Grace. Through. In The Unity of The Same.

On Whitsunday, and in the Week.

God! Who as on this day didst teach the hearts of Thy faithful people by the enlightening of Thy Holy Spirit, grant to us by The Same Spirit to have a right judgement in all things, and ever to rejoice in His holy Consolation. Through. In The Unity of The Same.

O God! Who didst give Thine Holy Spirit to Thine Apostles, grant unto Thy people the performance of their petitions; so that on us to whom Thou hast given Faith Thou mayest also bestow Peace. Through. In The Unity.

O Lord! we beseech Thee, let the virtue of Thy Holy Spirit ever be with us mercifully to cleanse our hearts, and also to defend us against all adversities. Through. In The Unity.

Grant, we beseech Thee, Almighty God! that Thy Holy Spirit may remove all carnal affections from our minds, and mightily pour into us all spiritual gifts. Through. In The Unity.

O Lord! we beseech Thee, let The Holy Ghost The Comforter, Who proceedeth from Thee, enlighten our minds, and lead us as Thy Son hath promised into all Truth, Who with Thee. In The Unity.

Grant, we beseech Thee, Almighty and Merciful God! that Thy Holy Spirit may come and dwell within us, and perfect us to be a worthy temple of His Glory. Through. In The Unity.

O Merciful God! grant unto Thy Church, we beseech Thee, that united together by Thy Holy Spirit it may never be disturbed by any assaults of the enemy. Through. In The Unity.

O Lord! we beseech Thee, mercifully pour Thy Holy Ghost into our hearts; so that we may be grounded on His Wisdom, and ever guided by His Providence. Through. In The Unity.

O Lord! we beseech Thee, may the Fire of Thy Holy Spirit which our Lord Jesus Christ sent down upon earth inflame our souls, and according to His will be vehemently kindled within them. Through. In The Unity.

O Lord! Who to the Three Children didst mitigate the flames of the fiery furnace, mercifully grant that through The Coming of The Holy Ghost the flames of our sins may never consume us. Through. In The Unity.

In the Day of the Holy Trinity.

Almighty and everlasting God! Who hast given unto us Thy servants in the confession of a true Faith to acknowledge the Glory of The Eternal Trinity, and in the power of The Divine Majesty to worship The Unity; we beseech Thee that by our steadfastness in the same Faith we may evermore be defended against all adversities, Who livest and reignest God world without end. Amen.

In the Feast of Corpus Christi.

O God! Who unto us in this wonderful Sacrament hast left a Memorial of Thy Passion; grant to us, we beseech Thee, so to venerate the Sacred Mysteries of Thy Body and Blood that we may evermore perceive in ourselves the fruit of Thy Redemption, Who livest and reignest with God The Father, in The Unity of The Holy Ghost, God world without end. Amen.

Of the Holy Cross.

God! Who wast pleased to sanctify the standard of the life-giving Cross by the precious Blood of Thine Only-begotten Son, our Lord Jesus Christ; grant, we beseech Thee, that all who rejoice in honouring Thy Holy Cross may also in all places be joyful under Thy Protection. Through The Same.

In Commemorations of the Blessed Virgin Mary.

O Merciful God! grant, we beseech Thee, Thy succour to our frailty; that we who celebrate the memory of the Holy Mother of God and ever Virgin Mary, may by the help of her intercessions rise again from our iniquities. Through The Same, our Lord Jesus Christ.

The First Sunday after Trinity.

O God! The Strength of all them that put their trust in Thee, graciously assist our supplications; and because the weakness of our mortal nature can without Thee do nothing, grant us the help of Thy Grace, that in fulfilling Thy commandments we may please Thee both in will and deed. Through.

In the Second Sunday.

O Lord! make us to have a perpetual fear as well as love of Thy Holy Name; and never deprive us of Thy governance whom Thou dost nurture in the steadfastness of Thy Love. Through.

In the Third Sunday.

O Lord! we beseech Thee, favourably hearken to our supplications; and grant that we to whom Thou hast given a hearty desire to pray may ever be defended by Thy help. Through.

In the Fourth Sunday.

O God! The Protector of all that trust in Thee, without Whom nothing is strong, nothing is holy; multiply upon us Thy mercy; that Thou being our Ruler, Thou our Guide, we may so pass through good things temporal as not to lose those which are eternal. Through.

In the Fifth Sunday.

Grant to us, O Lord! we beseech Thee, that the course of this world may be so peaceably ordered for us by Thy governance, that Thy Church may ever rejoice in tranquil devotion. Through.

In the Sixth Sunday.

O God! Who hast prepared for them that love Thee such good things as pass man's understanding, pour into our hearts the Affection of Thy Love; that we loving Thee in all things and above all things, may obtain Thy Promiſes, which exceed all that we can deſire. Through.

In the Seventh Sunday.

Lord of all power and might! of Whom are all things that are excellent; graft in our hearts the love of Thy Name, increaſe in us true religion; nouriſh all goodneſs in us; and by the care of Thy loving-kindneſs keep us in the ſame. Through.

In the Eighth Sunday.

God! Whoſe Providence infallibly diſpoſeth all things; we humbly beſeech Thee to put away from us all hurtful things, and to grant us thoſe things which be profitable for us. Through.

In the Ninth Sunday.

Grant to us, O Lord! we beſeech Thee, of Thy goodneſs the ſpirit to think and to do ſuch things as be rightful; that we who cannot exiſt without Thee, may be enabled to live according to Thy will. Through.

In the Tenth Sunday.

Let the ears of Thy mercy, O Lord! be open to the prayers of Thy ſupplicants; and that Thou mayeſt grant what they deſire to their petitions, make them to aſk ſuch things as are pleaſing unto Thee. Through.

In the Eleventh Sunday.

God! Who declareſt Thine Almighty Power moſt chiefly in ſparing and ſhewing mercy, multiply upon us Thy Grace; that ſo running after Thy promiſes Thou mayeſt make us partakers of Thy Heavenly Treaſures. Through.

In the Twelfth Sunday.

Almighty and everlaſting God! Who in the abundance of Thy goodneſs doſt exceed the deſerts as well as the deſires of Thy ſupplicants, pour down upon us the abundance of Thy mercy; forgiving us thoſe things whereof our conſcience is afraid, and adding unto us thoſe things which our prayer preſumeth not to aſk. Through.

The Thirteenth Sunday.

Almighty and Merciful God! of Whoſe gift it cometh that Thy faithful people do unto Thee worthy and laudable ſervice; grant to us, we beſeech Thee, to run onward without ſtumbling to the obtaining of Thy Promiſes. Through.

The Fourteenth Sunday.

ALMIGHTY and everlaſting God! give unto us an increaſe of Faith, Hope, and Charity; and that we may be enabled to obtain that which Thou doſt promiſe, make us to love that which Thou doſt command. Through.

The Fifteenth Sunday.

KEEP, we beſeech Thee, O Lord! Thy Church with Thy perpetual Mercy; and becauſe the mortal nature of man without Thee cannot but fall, may it ever by Thy help be delivered from all things hurtful, and guided to all things profitable to Salvation. Through.

The Sixteenth Sunday.

O LORD! we beſeech Thee, let Thy continual Pity cleanſe and defend Thy Church; and becauſe it cannot continue in ſafety without Thee, may it ever be governed by Thy help. Through.

The Seventeenth Sunday.

LORD! we pray Thee that Thy Grace may ever prevent and follow us; and make us continually to be given to all good works. Through.

The Eighteenth Sunday.

LORD! we beſeech Thee, grant that Thy people may avoid the temptations of the devil, and with pure minds follow Thee The Only God. Through.

The Nineteenth Sunday.

O LORD! foraſmuch as without Thee we are not able to pleaſe Thee; grant, we beſeech Thee, that Thy merciful operations may ever direct and rule our hearts. Through.

The Twentieth Sunday.

ALMIGHTY and Merciful God! of Thy goodneſs keep off from us all things that may hurt us; that we being ready both in ſoul and body, may with cheerful minds accompliſh thoſe things which pertain unto Thee. Through.

The Twenty-firſt Sunday.

O LORD! we beſeech Thee, of Thy good favour beſtow upon Thy faithful people both pardon and peace; that they may be cleanſed from all their offences, and ſerve Thee with quiet minds. Through.

The Twenty-second Sunday.

O Lord! we beseech Thee to keep Thy Household in continual godliness; that through Thy protection it may be free from all adversity, and devoted to good works, for The Glory of Thy Name. Through.

The Twenty-third Sunday.

O God! our Refuge and Strength, Thyself the Author of all godliness; be present with the devout prayers of Thy Church; that what we ask faithfully we may obtain effectually. Through.

The Twenty-fourth Sunday.

O Lord! we beseech Thee, absolve Thy people from their offences; that by Thy goodness we may be delivered from the bands of those sins which through our frailty we have committed. Through.

The Twenty-fifth Sunday.

Stir up, we beseech Thee, O Lord! the wills of Thy faithful people; that they more zealously accomplishing the fruit of good works, may of Thy goodness receive greater remedies for their sins. Through.

In the Purification of the Blessed Virgin, Feb. 2.

Almighty and everlasting God! Who didst send into the world Thine Only Son, begotten before all worlds of Thee, but in this our time incarnate of the Virgin Mary, The True and indefectible Light, to dispel the darkness of mankind, and to kindle the brilliance of Faith and Truth; mercifully grant that as we are enlightened outwardly by corporeal light, so we may be illumined inwardly by that which is spiritual. Through The Same.

Almighty and everlasting God! we humbly intreat Thy Majesty that as Thine Only-begotten Son was as on this Day presented in the Temple in the substance of our flesh, so we with pure minds may be presented unto Thee. Through The Same.

The Annunciation, March 25.

We beseech Thee, O Lord! pour Thy Grace into our hearts; that as we have known the Incarnation of Christ Thy Son by the Message of an Angel, so by His Passion and Cross we may be guided to

The Glory of His Refurrection. Through The Same.

God! Who for our fakes didft will Thy Word to take upon Him our flefh in the Womb of the Bleffed Virgin Mary; grant to us Thy fupplicants, that we who truly believe her to be the Mother of God may with Thee be ever affifted by her interceffions. Through The Same.

The Transfiguration, Auguft 6.

God! Who permitteft us this day with devout praife to celebrate Thy Holy Transfiguration, grant, we befeech Thee, that we may attain to the contemplation of Thy Divinity, Who didft vouchfafe to become partaker of our humanity, Who liveft.

God! Who as on this day didft reveal from Heaven Thine Only-begotten Son, wonderfully transfigured, to the Fathers of both Teftaments; grant to us, we befeech Thee, that doing what is well pleafing unto Thee, we may attain to behold Him in His Glory, in Whom Thou, O Father! didft declare Thou waft well pleafed. Through The Same.

The Name of Jefus, Auguft 7.

God! Who haft caufed Jefus, The moft Glorious Name of Chrift, Thine Only-begotten Son, to be loved with the greateft fervour of affection by Thy faithful ones, but to be terrible and tremendous to evil fpirits; gracioufly grant, that all who devoutly reverence this Name of Jefus upon earth, may receive the fweetnefs of His confolation in this prefent life, and may obtain joy and gladnefs and never-ending felicity in that which is to come. Through The Same.

The Day of All Souls, Nov. 2.

O Merciful God! Who haft again called the firft man to eternal Glory; O Good Shepherd! Who haft carried back unto the fold the loft fheep upon Thy kind fhoulders; O Thou juft Judge! when Thou fhalt come to judgement, deliver from death the fouls of thofe whom Thou haft redeemed; give not up the fpirits of them that confefs Thee to the wild beafts, nor forfake them for ever!

Eternal reft grant them, O Lord!

And may perpetual light ſhine upon them.

O God! The Creator and Redeemer of all Thy faithful people, grant remiſſion of all their ſins to the ſouls of all the faithful departed; and that pardon which they have ever deſired, by the fervour of our ſupplications may they obtain. Through our Lord Jeſus Chriſt, Thy Son, Who with Thee liveth and reigneth, in The Unity of The Holy Ghoſt, God world without end. Amen.

Milton Keynes UK
Ingram Content Group UK Ltd.
UKHW021104040424
440454UK00022B/78